"My" Official Georgia Geechee Cookbook

"My" Official Georgia Geechee Cookbook

Geechees, Low Country Cooking and History Facts

Georgia's Sea Islands
Located
In the
Atlantic Ocean

Tybee Island	Isle of Hope	Skidaway Island
Thunderbolt	Little Tybee Island	St. Simons Island
Oatland	IslandWassaw Island	Jekyll Island
Dutch Island	Ossabaw Island	Sea Island
Burnside Island	St. Catherine Island	Cumberland Island
Blackbeard Island	Hampton Island	Hampton Island
Cockspur Island	Little Cumberland Island	Wilmington Island
Butler Island	Wolf Island	Sapelo Island

Sharon Kaye Hunt, RD

To order additional copies of this book, contact:
Xlibris
1-888-795-4274
www.Xlibris.com
Orders@Xlibris.com
627080

Contents

THE GEECHEE COOKBOOK

"My" Official Geechee Cookbook highlights Geechee low-country cooking and food preparations that were popularized on the Georgia's barrier sea islands from the early 1700s until up to the end-of-the Civil War. A special effort has been made to include the similarities of possible African culture and slaves' tradition on each island. Recorded history has been included about each area. Although much of the history has been lost, the slaves made do with what they were able to simulate from their culture. The efforts in this cookbook have been dedicated to the impact of the "Geechee" contributions to the state of Georgia.

Some people in Georgia call themselves "Gullah". However, my grandmother was a "Geechee".

The research honors her heritage. "Gullahs" are popular in the low country areas of the Carolinas.

"My" Official Geechee Cookbook is a result of my research with certain people who said they were Geechee and collected recipes from these people. The cookbook is not comprehensive of all Geeches' recipes. Historical influences surrounding the Geechees' survival on the Georgia sea coastline from slavery until present day have been examined.

DEDICATION

The cookbook is dedicated to my grandmother, Ida Frazier Hunt, who was my father's mother.

My father said that my grandmother was a Geechee, who had molly-glassy hair. The type of hair meant straight cold black hair in color. According to my father, my grandmother could speak Arabic and she had a Hebrew Bible. I am convinced that my grandmother Hunt was a relative of Garrison Frazier.

My father shared with me her beliefs, wisdom and cooking procedures. Through my father I learned a lot about the history of Savannah and the Georgia Sea Islands. I dedicate this cookbook to all of the Geechees/Gullahs who came from Africa with nothing but their knowledge of food and seasonings help to set the good tastes for America's and the World's Food Table.

Above all, I always dedicate my work to Jesus Christ, who is my Lord and Savior.

ACKNOWLEDGEMENTS

I wish to thank my grandmother, Ida B. Frazier Hunt, who was a wonderful mother to my father and his siblings and taught them how to carry on the traditions of learning the importance of their Geechee/Gullah culture. My father tried to teach his children about our heritage and how to appreciate it.

Even though the Geechee/Gullah people did not realize it, they were able to influence generations of cooks and their customers with affluent taste with simple methods of cooking. Because of their cooking skills, the Geechees were able to travel with their masters up north to Philadelphia, New York and throughout the world. Everywhere Geechees cooked all cultures of people have enjoyed the "Geechees' low country" food preparations.

Possible Ida Frazier Hunt Connection:

Garrison Fraizer, 67, a slave until he was 59 and a possible relative of my grandmother's, convinced Major- General William Tecumseh Sherman to issue the Special Field Order No. 15, which handed over abandoned rice plantations and the sea islands of South Carolina, Georgia and northern Florida to freedmen. Major -General Sherman completed his March to the Sea in Georgia on January, 1865.

The Special Field Order No. 15 was said to give each family a land parcel of not more than 40 acres to cultivate and excess Army mules to freedmen. Therefore, each freedman was given forty acres and a mule.

After President Lincoln's death, President Andrew Johnson stopped the order and in October 1865, a U.S. Army General Oliver O. Howard gave most of the land back to the white owners. Some of the Geechee families held on to their land. Other Geechee families had to endure reconstruction, sharecropping and survival.

Disclaimer: The making of this cookbook is about the author's research and none other. The research is not to offend. The work is to shine a light on an important people who came to America under unwillingly, however, their contributions have not been properly displayed or talked about.

Bible Citation

Scripture quotations marked are from the Holy Bible, King James Version (Authorized Version). First published in 1611. Quoted from the KJV Classic Reference Bible, Copyright © 1983 by The Zondervan Corporation.

ABOUT THE AUTHOR

Sharon Hunt is a freelance writer. She is a registered dietitian. Ms. Hunt is a granddaughter of a "Geechee", Ida Frazier Hunt.

She writes cookbooks about African-American heritage and plantation cooking. Ms. Hunt has written eight cookbooks. She sold many of her cookbooks -Bread from Heaven -three times on the QVC Home Shopping Network. In 1997, she was selected as an Artist-in-Residence at the Georgia National Fair in Perry, Georgia. For the Peach Festival held in Fort Valley, Georgia, she created the original recipe for the World Largest Peach Cobbler.

At the 1996 Summer Olympics, she demonstrated and showcased her "World Famous Sweet Potato Pie" on stage at the "Georgia on my Plate" celebrity showcase held in Macon, Georgia. Also, she showcased

"World Famous Sweet Potato Pie" at a festival held in St. Simons, Georgia held at famous Lutheran Church.

For more than thirty years, Ms. Hunt taught food preparation and recipe analysis methods classes at two Historically Black College and Universities(HBCU) in Georgia and Oklahoma. She has studied the food preparation methods and menus for all occasions that were popular on plantations and foods eaten by slaves.

Ms. Hunt was the charter president of the Warner Robins Alumnae Chapter of Delta Sigma Theta Sorority, Inc. Currently, she is a Diamond Life Member of Delta Sigma Theta Sorority, Inc.

Chapter 1

Introduction

The Georgia's Geechees culture began in the Georgia's Barrier Sea islands with slave traders and plantation owners who purchased slaves and bought the slave to the islands to cultivate the islands and to build a prosperous life.

The culture included all slaves and slavery on the plantation along the coastline from Savannah and Brunswick to St. Mary's. To understand, the Geechees cooking and food ways, it is important to get a background of where some of the slaves came from in Africa.

Even though some of the slaves worked in the house and others worked in the fields, they had blended and similar food patterns. The slaves who lived in the islands had similar food traditions as slaves throughout Georgia. This was due to slave trade done within the state of Georgia.

The Geechees have a strong religious belief. In the early days of Georgia, the Geechees mixed with many other cultural groups-Native Americans, especially, the Creeks and Seminoles, Irish, and Jewish.

Some Geechees practiced the some of the Jewish traditions, such as Passover.

About Georgia -Georgia Facts

History: Georgia was discovered by James Edward Oglethorpe in 1732.

Georgia was the last of the 13th colonies

Georgia was named for King George II of England

Georgia bought the first slaves in 1750s

Georgia became the fourth state to ratify the constitution in January 7, 1788

Eli Whitney invented the cotton gin in 1783.

John Pemberton invented Coca Cola in 1886,

Summer Olympic Games held in Atlanta in 1996.

James Earl Carter became 39th president in 1976

STATE FACTS:

State Song: "Georgia on my Mind"

State Motto: "Wisdom, Justice and Moderation"

State Capital City: Atlanta

Georgia Population: Over 9 million (9th most populous state of U.S.)

States that Border Georgia: Florida, Alabama, Tennessee, South Carolina, North Carolina

State Nickname: "The Peach State" –"Empire State of the South"

Oldest City of Georgia: Savannah(1733)

Georgia has 159 counties (youngest county Peach, 1924)

State Symbols:

State Flower: Cherokee Rose

Wild Flower: Azalea

Tree: Live Oak

Bird: Brown Thrasher

Fish: Large Mouth Bass

Crop: Peanut

Dish: Grits

AFRICAN-AMERICAN GEORGIA FACTS:

OLDEST BLACK BAPTIST CHURCH LOCATED IN SAVANNAH

(Andrew Bryan, a slave from a plantation, Brampton Plantation, founded the first Negro Baptist church in the United States in the plantation's barn on January 20, 1788.

There were sixty-seven members and a descendent of the Brampton services obtained the oldest parcel of black-owned real estate in the country. Purchased in 1793, the lot was located at 575 West Bryan Street)

OLDEST HISTORICALLY BLACK COLLEGE AND UNIVERSITY IN GEORGIA: SAVANNAH STATE UNIVERSITY

FIRST AFRICAN –AMERICAN TO WIN NOBEL PEACE PRICE IN GEORGIA: MARTIN LUTHER KING JR

FIRST GEORGIA SUPREME COURT JUDGE: CLARENCE THOMAS

THE FIRST BLACK MAJOR OF ATLANTA: MAYNARD JACKSON, JR

ONLY BLACK MALE COLLEGE IN GEORGE IN GEORGE: MOREHOUSE COLLEGE

ONLY ALL-FEMALE COLLEGE IN GEORGIA: SPELMAN COLLEGE

FIRST BLACK MAN TO PLAY PROFESSIONAL BASEBALL: JACKIE ROBINSON

Counties

The Sea Islands cooking is known as low country cooking. Even though many of the food products, were first prepared on the islands, the recipes and similar methods of preparation have been transported throughout the south and other parts of the United States. The Georgia Sea Islands stretch through Chatman, Liberty, Camden, Glynn and McIntosh counties.

For this research, highlighted are twelve islands from Chatman, five islands from Liberty, four islands from Camden, Four islands from Glynn and four islands from McIntosh.

Georgia's Barrier Sea Islands. The barrier islands off the coast of Georgia are known as the Georgia Sea Islands. The barrier islands are formed as the first defense against the Atlantic Ocean. Even though the sea islands are homes to many types of wild life, sea urchins, animals and hundreds of species of plants, Georgia sea islands were first to be used in processing the slaves who were transported in the Middle Passage. Some of the islands were used as quarantine islands for the slaves.

The sea islands were home to some of the Native Americans before the 13th colony of Georgia was discovered by James Edward Oglethorpe.

From the 1700s until the emancipation of the slaves, plantation owners grew large crops of rice, indigo, cotton and other crops on some of the islands. The islands served as providers of live oak wood for the northern ship builders.

The Georgia Sea Islands stretched from Savannah to Brunswick to St. Mary's. All of the plantation owners used slave labor to develop and cultivate every aspect of the islands from conservation to producing food to serving food. The last group of slaves were brought to Jekyll Island in 1848 on a ship known as the Wanderer.

(African servants (slaves) assist in setting up Georgia as shown in letter)

LETTER WRITTEN BY JAMES OGLETHORPE TO THE TRUSTEES OF ENGLAND:

To The Trustees for Establishing the Colony of Georgia in America:

Gentlemen-I give you an Account in my last of our Arrival at Charles –Town. The Governor and Assembly have given us all possible Encouragement. Our people around at Beaufort on the 20th of January where I lodged them in some new Barracks built for the Soldiers, which I went myself to view the Savannah River. I fix'd upon a healthy situation about ten miles from the sea. The River here forms a half-Moon, along the South-Side of which the Banks are about forty foot high, and the Top a Flat which they call a Bluff. The plain high Ground extends unto the Country five or six miles and along the River side about a Mile. Ships that draw twelve Foot water can ride where ten birds, in the water of this River Side, in the Center of this River is pretty wide the water fresh, and from the Key of the Town, you see its whole Course to the Sea, with the Island of Tybe; which forms the Mouth of the River; and the other way you see the River for almost six miles up into the River for about six miles up into the Country. The Whole People arrived here on the first of February. At night their Tents were got up. 'Til the seventh were taken upon unloading and making a Crane which I then could not get finished get finish'd, so took off the Hands, and set some to the Fortification and began to fell the woods. I mark'd out the Town and common. Half of the former is already cleared, and the first House was begun Yesterday in the Afternoon. Mr. Whittaker has given us one hundred Head of Cattle, Col Bull, M. Barlow, Mr. Julien and Mr. Woodward are come up to assist us with their own Servants

A little Indian nation, the only one within fifty Miles, is not only at Lands given them among us, and to breed their children at our Schools their Chief and the Beloved Man, who is the Second Man in the Nation, desire to be instructed in the Christian Religion.

I am. Gentlemen

Your most Obedient Humble Servant

James Oglethorpe
February 10, 1733(Old Style)

Civil War

During the Civil War (1861-1865), Major- General William Tecumseh Sherman created an independent nation state for the freed slaves consisting of all sea islands from Charleston, South Carolina south to the St Mary's River in Florida. The plantation owners left the islands and former slaves were given status for maintaining the islands. However, in the late 1890s the hurricanes and poverty caused the residents to move to the inlands. Following the Reconstruction, rich northerners came to the islands and set up paradises.

Slavery in Georgia

Georgia was discovered by James Edward Oglethorpe in 1733. Slavery was permitted in 1743. The first slaves in the Geechee/Gullah region was transported from Charleston, South Carolina. The slaves were brought from Africa in the mid1660s. Georgia increased its importation of slaves from West Africa and South Africa. The slaves were shipped through the Savannah River and the Sea Islands. Many of the slaves were imported to the banks of Dunbar Creek called Ebo Landing. Slavery was the main reason why the plantations were so successful in the sea islands. It has been said that the slaveholding plantation owners were responsible for starting the Civil War, with the first shot being fired from Sumter, South Carolina.

Slavery lasted in Georgia until March or April, 1865.

Words To Know

Africa-The first continent made by God, most of the first people were all black. Home of many different types of peoples and ancient artifacts, including Egyptian. The Pyramids, ancient Phoenicians, Seaport. The slaves were imported from rice producing areas of West Africa such as Sierra Leone, Nigeria, Ghana, Senegal. However, some of the slaves came from Angola and the Congo.

Antebellum   The term refers to before the Civil War or War Between the States -1861 -1865.

Antebellum Homes- Typical antebellum homes, sometimes, had four to six white columns on the exterior and the interior consisted of living room, master dining room with an art gallery ballroom for dancing, reception room or drawing room and four to six bedrooms. The kitchen was connected to the antebellum homes after 1800s. Before the 1800s, the kitchen was separated and set off to itself. Food had to be brought in and out of the house. House servants or slaves lived in slave quarter in the back of the 'Big House'.

Big House – The house where the plantation owners and his family lived on the plantation.

Lowcountry –The area nearest the coastal areas that had rich soils and many plantations with Geechee/Gullah slaves.

Broad wife- When a male slave married a woman from another plantation she was known as a broad wife".

Confederate - Georgia was the second state to secede from the Union and accept the Confederate Flag until after a long time.

Union – The United States of America and President Abraham Lincoln was trying to preserve the Union by winning the Civil War.

Lowcountry cooking -special food preparations of foods common to the Atlantic Ocean coastline.

Marsters-Name referred to by slaves as head of the plantation.

Mistress-Name referred to by slaves as wife to the owner of the plantation.

Plantation –A large acreage of land owned by planters before the Civil War.

Slaves – Slaves in America were purchased or stolen from various countries in Africa. Former Slaves describe Slave Sales

"SLAVE SALES IN GEORGIA"

There were two legal places for selling slaves in Augusta: the Lower market, at the corner of Fifth and Broad Street, and the Upper Market at the corner of Broad and Yarbury Streets. The old slave quarters are still standing in Hamburg S.C. directly across the Savannah River from the Lower Market in Augusta. Slaves who were to be put up for sale were kept there until the legal days of sales.

Advertisements in the newspapers of that day seem to point to the fact that most slave sales were the results of the death of the master, and the consequent settlement of estates, or a result of the foreclosure of mortgages.

In the Thirty-Seventh Section of the Ordinances of the City of Augusta August 10, 1820-July 8, 1829is the following concerning Vendue Masters:

"If any person acts as a Vendue Master within the limits of this City without license from the City Council, he shall be fined in a sum not exceeding $1,000.00. There shall not be more than four Vendue Masters for this city. They shall be appointed by ballot, and their license shall expire on the day proceeding the 1st Saturday in October of every year. No license shall be issued to a Vendue Master until he was given bond, with approved security to the Council for the faithful discharge of his duties in the sum of $5,000.00."

The newspaper of the time regularly carried advertisements concerning the sale of slaves. The following is a fair sample: "Fould sell slaves: With this farm will be sold about Thirty likely Negroes mostly country born, among them a very good bricklayer, and driver, and two sawyers, 17 of them are fit for field or boat work, and the rest fine, thriving children."

The following advertisement appeared in The Georgia Constitutionslist on January 17, 1769: "To be sold in Savannah on Thursday the 15th. Inst. A cargo of 140 Prime Slaves, chiefly men. Just arrived in the Scow Gambia Captain Nicholas Doyle after a passage of six weeks directly from the River Gambia". By Inglis and Hall.

Most of the advertisements gave descriptions of each slave with his age and the type of work he could do. They were generally advertised along with other property belonging to the slave owner.

The following appeared in the Chronicle and Sentinel of Augusta on December23rd, 1864: "Negro Sales.

At an auction in Columbus the annexed prices were obtained: a boy 16 years old, $3,625.

"At a late sale in Wilmington the annexed prices were obtained: a girl 14 years old $5, 400; a girl 22 years old $4,850; a girl 13 years $3,500; a negro boy, 22 years old $4,900.00".

Janie Satterwhite, who was born on a Carolina plantation, and was about thirteen years old when she was freed, remembered very distinctly when she was sold away from her parents.

"Yes'm my Mama died in slavery and I was sold when I was a little tot" she said, "I 'member when dey put me on de block"

"Were you separated from your family?" we asked

"Yes'm. We wuz scattered eberywhere. Some went to Florida and some to odder places. De Missus she die and we wus all sold at one time. Atter dat nobody could do nothin' on de ole plantation for a year—till all wus settled up. My brudder he wasn't happy den. He run away for five years."

"Where was he all that time?"

"Lawd know, honey. Hidin', I reckon, hidin in de swamp."

"Did you like your master?"

"Honey, I wus too little to have any sense. When dat man brought me—dat Dr. Henry, he put me in a buggy to take me off. I kin see it all right now, and I say to Mama and Papa, 'Good-bye, I'll be back in de mawnin'"

And dey all feel sorry for me and say, 'She don' know what happenin'."

"Did you ever see your family again?"

"Yes'm. Dey wusn't so far away. When Christmas come de Marster say I can stay wid Mama de whole week."

Georgia Slave Narratives

Cabins – Slaves lived in the one or two room cabins on plantations. Slave quarters living areas for the slaves.

Freedmen- Slaves that were freed through the Union soldiers winning the Civil War.

Emancipation Proclamation (1863)

The Emancipation Proclamation, drafted in 1862 and put into effect on January 1, 1863, freed the slaves in those states that had seceded from the Union. All other slaves —and were some 800,000 unaffected by the provisions of this act —were not yet free.

By the President of the United States of America:

A Proclamation

Whereas on the 22d day of September, A.D. 1862, a proclamation was issued by the President of the United States, containing, among other things, the following, to wit:

"That on the 1ˢᵗ day of January, A.D., 1863, all persons held as slaves within any State or designated part of a State the people whereof shall then be in rebellion against the United States shall be then, thenceforward, and forever free; and the executive government of the United States, including the military and the naval authority thereof, will recognize and such persons, or any of them, maintain the freedom of such persons and will do not act or acts to repress such persons, or any of them, in any efforts they may make for their actual freedom.

"That the executive will on the 1ˢᵗ day of January aforesaid, by proclamation, designate the States and parts of States, if any, in which people thereof, respectively, shall then be in rebellion against the United States, and the fact that any State or the people thereof shall on that day be in good faith represented in the Congress of the United States by members chosen thereto at elections wherein a majority of the qualified voters of such States shall have participated shall, in the absence of strong countervailing testimony, be deemed conclusive evidence that such State and the people thereof are not then in rebellion against the United States."

Now, therefore, I, Abraham Lincoln, President of the United States, by virtue of the power in me vested as Commander-in-Chief of the Army and Navy of the United States in time of actual, armed rebellion against the authority and government of the United States, and as a fit and necessary war measure for suppressing said rebellion, do, on this 1ˢᵗ day of January, A.D. 1863, and in accordance with my purpose so to do, publicly proclaimed for the full period of one hundred days from the first day above mentioned, order and designate as the States and parts of States wherein the people thereof, respectively, are this day in rebellion against the United States the following, to wit:

Arkansas, Texas, Louisiana(except the parishes of St. Bernard, Plaquemines, Jefferson, St. John, St. Charles, St. James, Ascension, Assumption, Terrebonne, Lafourche, St. Mary, St. Martin, and Orleans, including the city of New Orleans), Mississippi, Alabama, Florida, Georgia, South Carolina, North Carolina, and Virginia(except the forty-eight counties designated as West Virginia, and also the counties of Berkeley, Accomac, Northampton, Elizabeth City, York, Princess Anne, and Norfolk, including the cities of Norfolk and Portsmouth), and which excepted parts are for the present left precisely as if this proclamation were not issued.

And by virtue of the power and for the purpose aforesaid, I do order and declare that all persons held as slaves within said designated States and parts of States are, and henceforward shall be free, and that the Executive Government of the United States, including the military and naval authorities thereof, will recognize and maintain the freedom of said persons.

And I further enjoin upon the people so declared to be free to abstain from all violence, unless in necessary self defense; and I recommend to them that, in all cases when allowed, they labor faithfully for reasonable wages.

And I further declare and make known that such persons of suitable condition will be received into the armed service of the United States to garrison forts, positions, stations, and other places, and to man vessels of all sorts in said service.

And upon this act, sincerely believed to be an act of justice, warranted by the Constitution upon military necessity, I invoke the considerate judgment of mankind and the gracious favor of Almighty God.

Note: Before the Emancipation Proclamation was issued, many slaves escaped. One of the most noted story was the Underground Railroad Story.

Story of Harriet Tubman

"Sometimes between 1820 and 1822, Harriet Tubman was born Araminta Ross to slaves in Dorchester County, Md. She was nicknamed "Minty". Around 1844, she married John Tubman, a free man, and took her mother's name of Harriet. Fearing she would be sold from her family after the death of her owner, she escaped with her two brothers, some accounts say. The men got cold feet and wanted to turn back. With a strong determination, she escorted them home and set out alone, leaving her the only one to cross into freedom.

Tubman would put her life in jeopardy at least 19 times as she crossed back into the South to lead others away from bondage. On her first two trips back, she rescued her siblings. The third time, she went to retrieve her husband, only to find he had remarried and would not leave.

Tubman found other slaves seeking freedom and led the way across the Mason-Dixie line. In her documented Underground Railroad, Tubman led at least 300 others to the North via safe houses along the way. She helped countless others by sharing survival secrets, such as using sap to throw off blood hounds and following the North Star.

The Fugitive Slave Act of 1850 ordered the return of all escaped slaves to their Southern masters, which forced Tubman into Canada with her human cargo.

She carried the scars of whipping and suffered intense headaches and seizures most of her life due to a head injury. As a young teen, Tubman was nearly killed protecting another slave from an angry overseer. The man threw a 2-pound iron weight that hit her in the head knocking her unconscious. By 1856, there was a $40,000 bounty on her head.

The wanted poster stated she was illiterate so when Tubman overheard men reading it, she pretended to be reading a book and avoided capture.

She was modestly educated woman, who had brains. With all the people looking for her, she was able to keep everyone safe furious slave owners.

As a "conductor on the Underground Railroad" she never lost a passenger. She served as a nurse, scout and spy for the Union Army during the Civil War. She threatened to use her pistol on any slave who wanted to turn back and endanger others.

"You'll be free or die" she is quoted as saying."

On her Auburn, N.Y. property given to her by abolitionist Sen. William Seward, she built a home for women and the aged and cared for others until her death. She is buried in New York."

End of Slavery

On April 8, 1864, the United States Senate passed 38-6, the 13th Amendment to the U.S. Constitution abolishing slavery. (The House of Representatives in Jan. 1865; the amendment was ratified and adopted in Dec. 1865.)

April 9, 1866

Congress passes the Civil Rights Act guaranteeing African Americans' legal equality with whites.

The first important law to be enacted despite presidential veto, the Civil Rights Act forbid individual states from denying African Americans the rights of citizenship. It was enacted in response to Southern states' creation of Black Codes, which punished African -Americans for crimes such as being without a job and preaching without a license. The codes, which varied from state to state, also limited blacks' mobility by preventing them from renting land anywhere but in rural areas and requiring them to sign and fulfill year -long labor contracts.

Slave Narratives

The Georgia Slave Narratives were taken from the Federal Writer's Project. The ex-slaves described their life on the plantation. Using twenty questions, interviewers recorded answers from ex-slaves. The Project was a federal project funded from 1936-1938. Portions of the slave Narratives will be used in this cookbook. The slave sayings will be as stated in the Slave Narratives.

Possible Africa Connections:

Most African Americans do not know where in Africa their ancestors once lived. Even though recorded history showed that slaves came from West Africa, this author believes that the slaves came from all parts of the continent. The possible Africa Connections will be included for each island of Georgia's early slaves. Present day Africa countries and tribal connections will be used to assist in identifying the ethnic groups.

BIBLICAL CONNECTIONS:

Where did African-Americans come from in the Bible? (reference – Seminar manual –The Black Presence in The Bible-Black Light Fellowship: Fellowship Copyright 1989 RWAM)

Bible references to the Hamitic/Black Family Tree as based on Genesis 10. It is traced through the men presented in the passage. The Table of Nations and The Hamitic Black/African Family Tree

1- NOAH - Sons-SHEM –HAM AND JAPHATH
2- HAM- Sons- CUSH –MIZRAIM(Egypt)-Put – Caan

The Hamities had more contact with the Israelites (Semites) than did the Haphethities from whom white people are descended). Ham and his descendants settled (for the most part) in northern Africa and western Asia.

EXPLICIT BLACKS MENTIONED IN OLD AND NEW TESTAMENT PERSONS AND NATIONS

The Old Testament contains many more references to Black people than the New Testament, even though each of the Testaments demonstrate a great interest in the varied ethnological divisions of humanity. Following are a few of the Black persons mentioned in the New Testament:

1. Explicit Black Persons Mentioned in Both Testaments

    A. The Queen of the South, I Kings 10:1-10; Luke 11:3
    B. Rahab the Harlot, Joshua 2:1-21 and 6: 22-25;
        Hebrews 11:31; James 2:25
    C. Hagar, Genesis 16:1ff; Galatian 4:21 ff.
    D. Melchizedek, Psalm 110:4; Hebrews 5:5 ff.
    E. The Sons of Joseph, Genesis 48 and 47:31; Hebrews 11:21
    F. The Haven of Egypt, Exodus 4:2; Hosea 11:1; Matthew 2:13-23

2. Explicit Black Persons Mentioned in the New Testament

    A. The Wise Men, Matthew 2:1-2
    B. Simon of Cyrene, Mark 15.21
    C. Alexander and Rufus, Mark 15:21
    D. The Canaanite Woman, Matthew 7:21-28
    E. The Man of Ethiopia, Acts 8:26-40
    F. Candace, Queen of the Ethiopians, Acts 8:27
    G. Simeon called Niger, Acts 13:1-3
    H. Lucius of Cyrene Acts 13:1-3

RETURNED SLAVES FROM MACON, GEORGIA TO AFRICA:

After each section, a present day African country where a guess of where some of the slaves were from, will be included. Slaves probably came from all over Africa. It has been documented that on November 21, 1886 about 194 former slaves from Macon, Georgia and 406 ex-slaves from elsewhere boarded a clipper ship Coloanda sailed from Charleston for Liberia. They got money from the American Missionary Association.

The Gullah/Geechee Heritage Cultural Corridor

Even though, many people refer to Gullah and Geechee. In this cookbook, Geechee will be majorly highlighted in honor of my grandmother, Ida

Frazier Hunt, whom my dad said was a true Geechee. Geechees have a special place in Georgia history.

The Gullah/Geechee Heritage Cultural Corridor has been proposed to stretch from the Carolinas to Florida. The culture is known as Gullah in the Carolinas and Geechee in Georgia and Florida. The culture is designated to the culture of slaves descendants along the sea islands of the southeast. In Georgia, the Geechee/Gullah is along the U.S. Highway 17.

General William Tecumseh Sherman awarded the barrier islands from North Carolina, South Carolina, Georgia and Florida to the freed slaves by the Emancipation Proclamation. The planters purchased many slaves from Sierra Leone to work the rice plantation because the Planters believed that these slaves could endure muggy weather and conditions of the islands.

GULLAH/GEECHEE CULTURE

Common Gullah/Geechee Traditions:

    -basket making-woven baskets of sweet smelling pliable marsh grass
    or wood to hold vegetables, cotton, shellfish, clothing, fish and food
    -slave spiritual songs
    - shouts
    -work songs
    -old time blues and guitar playing
    -old-time choir singing
    - old time spirituals and gospels
    -old time blues and piano playing
    -banjo and buck dancing
    -old time fiddlers
    -jubilee singers off
    -song and games of African nature
    Traditional Crafts and Activities
    -story telling —Dr. Buzzard, Uncle Remus told stories about animals
    and riddles

-smoking mullet

-potash(lye) soap making

-quilting

-fish net knitting

-old fashioned barbequing

-weaving cast nets for catching shrimp and fish

-down fold trapping

- weaving rush baskets, including the fanner, from which rice was tossed into the air to allow the wind to carry off the chaff

-beating the rice

-painting window trim blue –to scare off evil spirits

-painting a room blue – to keep off evil spirits during child births. The evil spirits of childbirth are known as hags.

-fish net casting

-shrimp –boat net knitting

-grape vine craft

- Black smith
- Row boat building
- Cotton and flax spinning
- Tapping tar from pine trees

-Making Fox traps

-African dyeing

-whittling toys from wood

-traditional arrow carving

-whistling from sea shells

-crab-trap making

-medicine man who used what many people, call voodoo to heal the sick and jinx the enemy

-herbal remedies such as spider webs to stop bleeding and life everlasting tea for colds.

-Dancing –Tap dancing, Buzzard Lopes

-playing music-beating drums, blowing combs, playing guitar

-singing church songs and plantation songs

- rice cooking

-green and okra cooking from Africa

-Geechee/Gullah cooking of oysters, shrimp and fish

Food Traditions

-Sea foods
-shrimp and grits
-smoking mullet
-boiled crabs
-cooking hominy grits
-eating game birds
-eating wild turkey
-eating kumquats
-sesame seed wafers
-eating wild fruits, green fruits and drying fruits
-Rice
-Sweet Potatoes
-Yams
-Greens
-Polk Sallet greens
-alligator dishes
-Field Peas
-Corn
-Smoke Houses
-Sorghum
-Coffee
-Spices
-Pound cake
-cooking grits

ABOUT GEORGIA:

James Edward Oglethorpe, who discovered Georgia was the first leader of Georgia from 1733-1743.

However, the first governor was Adam Treutlen -1777-1778. Georgia was the 13th colony of the United States of America. Georgia became the fourth state of the United States in 1738.

The oldest county in Georgia is Chatman County. The youngest county is Peach County. Peach County became a county in 1924. Peach County is named in honor of the peach. There are 159 counties in Georgia.

DEFINITION OF GULLAH/GEECHEE:

1.   What does Gullah/Geechee mean?

Answer: According to some authors, Gullah/Geechee is the term given for the mixture of West African, English and sometimes French traditions and culture.

Because of isolation, poverty and a strange land, former slaves formed their traditions along the South Atlantic coast.

2.   What are the difference between Gullah and Geechee?

Answer: Some of the former slaves said that Gullahs are from the Carolinas' low country and the Geechees are from Georgia Sea Islands and northern Florida.

However, some people refer to Gullah as a language type.

3.   What do the names Gullah and Geechee come from? Where did the people come from?

Answer. Some former slaves believed that the names were derived from tribal groups in countries in West Africa. Gullah may have come from Angola or Gola countries in South Africa.

-The Gullah/Geechee were captured from the 'Rice Coast" of Africa from tribal group such as Mende, Djoles, Serer, Mandingo, Wolof, and Val.

Countries in Africa on the South Atlantic Coast that were known for the Gullah/Geechee slave trade – Senegal, Gambia, Guinea Bissau, Guinea, Sierra Leone, Liberia, Ivory Coast, Ghana, Togo, Benin, Nigeria, Cameroon, Gabon, Congo, and Angola.

-Geechee Kunda Culture/ Arts Center and Museum is located in Riceboro. The Geeche Kunda is a living museum with African art, textiles, painting, textiles and crafts used by the Gullah-Geeche from 1700s to the 1900s. It is located 622 Ways Temple Road.

Chapters Outline —Each of the chapters will be outlined as follows: 1. Name of the chapter, 2. Recipes, 3. County, city connections to Georgia's Barrier Sea Islands, slaves presence in the Georgia's Barrier Sea Islands, 4. Possible Africa Connection, 5. Former Georgia Slaves' Sayings, and 5. Selected bible verse or verse. Traditional and nontraditional recipes will be used for each section showing the diversity of the Geechees cooking.

The Georgia Slave Narratives will be used for to show what plantation life was like during slavery. During 1936-1938, the Works Progress Administration (WPA) asked 600 former Georgia slaves about 20 questions about their experiences on Georgia plantations. To give some inside of what happened on the plantations, several of the Former slaves; sayings will be given. The plantation life is about various situations surrounding all aspects of the plantation up to the end of the Civil War. In 1865, all slaves were freed. The sayings will be in the slaves language.

Bible Verse(s):

19 And lest thou lift up thine eyes unto heaven, and when thou seest the sun, and the moon, and the stars, even all the host of heaven, shouldest be driven to worship them, and serve them, which the Lord they God hath divided unto all nations under the whole heaven.

20 But the Lord hath taken you, and brought you forth out of the iron furnace, even out of Egypt to be unto him a people of inheritance, as ye are this day.

Deuteronomy 4: 19, 20

Chapter 2

Slave Ship Menu

Popular slave ship menus include split pea soup and boiled peanuts.

Split Pea soup and gruel

Number of Servings: 75 Amount of serving: 8 ounces per cup

Amount	Ingredients
40 pounds	Split Green English peas, dried
20 Pounds	shorts from whole wheat flour
5 pounds	sea salt
80 gallons	water

Directions

1. Combine all ingredients in a large 100 gallon steel drum barrel.
2. Make fire underneath large 100 gallon steel drum barrel and stir with long handle paddle.
3. Stir constantly until mixture thickens and then cook for 45 minutes.
4. Serve in cup size portions.

Boiled Peanuts

Number of Servings: 3000 Amount per servings: 10 peanuts once per day for 2 weeks for fifty slave passengers on a slave ship

Amount	Ingredients
500 pounds	goober peanuts
20 pounds	sea salt
50 gallons	water

Directions

1. Divide peanuts into 5-100 gallon capacity large steel drum barrels.
2. Add salt and water. Stir well. Bring to a boil and cover.
3. Boil for 45 minutes. Cool. Drain. Serve in buckets.

COUNTY, CITY, CONNECTION TO GEORGIA'S BARRIER ISLAND, SLAVES IN THE GEORGIA SEA ISLANDS:

Chatman County – 38 per cent of the population -African -Americans

Chatman County was established in 1777 and named in honor of William Lord Pitt, the Earl of Chatman. He was an English nobleman, entered Parliament 1735 and Secretary of State and leader of House of Commons in 1756.

The county seat is located in Savannah.

Incorporated Communities: Bloomingdale, Garden City, Pooler, Port Wentworth, Savannah, Thunderbolt, Tybee Island.

Unincorporated Communities: Abercon Heights, Alabama Junction, Ardsley Park, Avalon, Avon Park, Avondale, Bacon Park, Bakers Crossing, Battery Point, Beaulieu, Berkshire Woods, Bethesda,

Bon Bells, Buckhead, Burnside, Burnside Islands, Burroughs, Carver Village, Cedar Grove, Cedar Hammock, Central Junction, Chatman City, Chatman Village, Chippqwa Terrace,

Keller, Montgomery, Ogeecheton, Oglethorpe, Oglethorpe Park, Oleary, Paradise Park, Parkerburg, Packework, Pin Point, Rine Gardens, Port Wentworth, Junction, Reber, Richfield, Ridgewood, Rio Vista, Rivers End, Riverside, Rose Ohu, Rose Hill, Rossignol Hill, Sandfly, Sharon

Park, Shirley Park, Silk Hipe, Skyland Terrace, Somerset Park, Sunset Park, Tatumsiville, Telfair Junction, Vernonburg View, Victory Heights,

West Savannah, Wheat Hill, White Bluff, White Marsh Island, Williams, Windsor Forest,

There are sixteen barrier sea islands in Chatman County.

Savannah – The city is located 57 square miles on the Savannah River, 16 miles from the Atlantic Ocean. Founder James Oglethorpe named the city.

The city is the oldest city of Georgia is also known as the mother city of Georgia. General James Oglethorpe and 120 followers settled the last of the 13 original colonies here, site of the Revolutionary War battle and of General Sherman's Civil War's March to the Sea.

The city is on the mainland and it provides a connection to many of the barrier islands. The slave ship menus were very skimpy for the slaves. The slave trip took two weeks from Africa to the Georgia coast. The slaves were bounded and packed from head -to -feet and feet -to -head. The ships had as few as thirty slaves or more than one hundred.

Slaves were imported to lay out the city and to build all of the first buildings in the city. Savannah is a connecting city to many old slave historical point. Today it is known as the "port city".

After emancipation, many of the African-Americans formed their own communities in and around Savannah area. The original areas are:

1. Tin City –East of Savannah
2. Yamacraw –West of Savannah
3. Frogtown and Currytown –West of Savannah
4. Springfield –West of Savannah
5. Brownville – Southwest of Savannah
6. Tatemville –Southwest of Savannah
7. Pin Point – Nine miles southeast of Savanne of Supreme Court Justice –Clarence Thomas
8 White Bluff

9   Sandfly – 9 miles southeast of Savannah
10   Possum Point –near Savannah
11   Jewtown – in Savannah

(PASSOVER CELEBRATED BY THE JEWISH TRADITION)

Passover is a celebration of the ancient Hebrew deliverance from slavery in Egypt. The holiday is observed for eight days. The story of Passover starts in the Hebrew Bible in the book of Exodus. In the book of Exodus, the story of the Israelites, Moses and the Red Sea. The name "Pass Over" came from God passed over the children of Israel with plagues. Passover begins with a ceremonial feast called the Seder. Some traditional foods:

1. Hard-boiled egg- The hardness of the egg stands for the Jews strength.
2. Roasted lamb bone- Symbolizes the lamb that was sacrificed in ancient days before the Temple was destroyed.
3. Salt Water –Stands for tears shed by the slaves and for the salty Red Sea.
4. Matzos – Three pieces of the unleavened bread, each representing a group of slaves. When the Jews fled Egypt in haste, they took their bread dough without letting it rise and baked it quickly in the sun.
5. Bitter herbs – Horseradish roots recall the suffering of the slaves.
6. Harosct - Made with apples, nuts, cinnamon and wine. Its clay is reminiscent of the clay the slaves used to make bricks for the Pharoah's pyramids.
7. Wine –Drank from a goblet known as the "cup of Elijah". Elijah was one of the Jewish prophets.
8. Greens –Parsley and celery are dipped into salt water as a reminder of the parting of the Red Sea,)

Additional Historical Points-

1. First African Baptist Church/ First Bryan Baptist Church – Founded in 1788, oldest African-American Baptist Church on the North American continent. The studied the whole Bible, but follow the teachings of Jesus Christ.

The church split in 1832. The new church was named First Bryan Baptist Church.

One Solitary Life

Luke 2:1-20

And it came to pass in those days, that there went out a decree from Caesar Augustus that all the world should be taxed.

And this taxing was first made when Cyrenius was governor of Syria.

And all went to be taxed every one into his own city.

And Joseph also went up from Galilee, out of the city of Nazareth, into Judaea, unto the city of David, which is called Bethlehem;(because he was of the house and lineage of David:) To be taxed with Mary his espoused wife, being great with child.

And so it was, that, while they were accomplished that she should be delivered.

And she brought forth her firstborn son, and wrapped him in swaddling clothes, and laid him in a manger; because there was no room for them in the inn.

And there were in the same country shepherds abiding in the field, keeping watch over their flock by night.

And lo, the angel of the Lord came upon them, and the glory of the Lord shone round about them: and they were sore afraid.

And the angel said unto them, Fear not: for, behold, I bring you good things of great joy, which shall be to all people.

For unto you is born this day in the city of David, a Saviour which is Christ the Lord. And this shall be a sign unto you.

Ye shall find the babe wrapped in swaddling clothes, lying in a manger.

And suddenly there was with the angel a multitude of the heavenly host praising God, and saying Glory to God in the highest, and on earth peace, good will toward men.

And it came to pass, as the angels were gone away from them into heaven, the shepherds said one to another. Let us now go even unto Bethlehem and see this thing which is come to pass which the Lord hath made known unto us.

And they came with haste, and found Mary and Joseph, and the babe lying in a manger.

And when they had seen it, they made known abroad the saying which was told them concerning this child.

And all they had heard it wondered at those things which were told them by the shepherds. But Mary kept all these things, and pondered them in her heart.

And the shepherds returned, glorifying and praising God for all the things that they had heard and seen as it was told unto them.

Luke 2: 1-20

2. Beach Institute – Established in 1865 by the American Missionary Association to educate freed slaves.
3. Factors Walk -A nine block walk that celebrates that once saw the labors of slave stevedores as they unloaded the cargo vessels along the Savannah River dock. The same place marked the site of James Oglethorpe's first landing.

(Black laborers men and women in ante-bellum Savannah)

Men

1. Carpentry Women –laundress, servants, cooks and nurses
2. Blacksmithing
3. Cabinet making
4. House and ship carpenters
5. Caulkers
6. Butchers

7. Bricklayers
8. Tailors
9. Barbers
10. Bakers
11. Boat pilots
12. Fishermen
13. Brick layers
14. porters

4. Georgia Infirmary – Infirmary established in 1832 for relief and protection of aged and infirmed slaves.
5. Laurel Grove-South Cemetery Savannah's only cemetery that has historical African-Americans buried. The cemetery was set aside for the burial of free persons of color and slaves. The cemetery has 15 acres. The graves include Jane Deveaux, Andrew Marshall, Andrew Marshall, Andrew Bryan and Jams Simms. The cemetery is located on 37th street.

James Simms was a legislator from Savannah in 1870.

6. In March 1865, the 33rd, 54th and 102nd Massachusetts Negro regiments guarded Savannah.
7. In 1875, a group of Negro ministers in Savannah directed their attention to the elimination of segregation in Antioch Baptist Church on Augusta Road. The Church belonged to a white congregation that allowed Negroes to attend but assigned separate section in the back.
8. Practically all of the important Negro politician who served in the Georgia legislature lived in or near Savannah. Bishop Henry M. Turner, bishop in the African Methodist Episcopal Church, was pastor of a Savannah church.
9. In 1854, St. Stephens Episcopal Church was organized by free mulattoes. J.S. Atwell was the pastor. St. Augustine Church was for the darker blacks.
10. In Savannah at the Mulberry Grove Plantation in 1793, Eli Whitney a native of Massachusetts and a Yale law graduate was invited and came south to tutor children is said to have invented the cotton gin. Port Wentworth is home to Mulberry Grove Plantation, where Eli Whitney invented the cotton gin –located near downtown Savannah.

Civil War and U.S. Colored Troops – A Special Poem

There were several regiments of U.S. Colored Troops (U.S.C.T.) who fought near Savannah. Many of the USCT were captured and taken to Andersonville- Camp Sumter the Prison camp for Union troops. The anonymous poem was written entitled "53". The poem explains the prison exchange. There is a 'Providence Spring' that has been made into a special fountain at Andersonville. The argument was always did the U.S.C.T. dig the spring for the lightning to strike to cause the Providence water to come forth.

*"53"

In Andersonville on that scorching day,
Wounds and bleeding, friendless and sad,
He thought of loved ones far away,
Suffering with hunger and thirst was he,
With no one to pillow his aching head,
Nothing to comfort but one little book,
He begged them to comfort,
No shelter from storm or cold or rain,
No water to drink but from a spring
That flowed over bodies freshly slain.
While his garment were wet with the recent rain.
The sun beat down in its fiery bold,
They were sheltered by only one high wall.
With dead and dying on every side.
Horrors none living could describe.
Day after day in that horrible pen.
With foul bread thrown from wagon where.
Thy had handed dead bodies by the score,
Was thrown from over the high board wall.
To be scrambled and fought for by one and all.

Three thousand prisoners old and young
Huddled together in that horrible pen.
While armed guards sat upon the wall.
Forbidding water to one and all.

And many a soldier maddened with thirst,
Crawled to the spring and were shot down.
By the ruthless order of one named Wertz.
Who ordered the shot at the price of a drink.

An order came one cold winter day.
To exchange some soldiers over the way.
And what was left of the brave little hand.
March out free men on that frosty morn.

With bodies wasted by hunger and cold.
With tattered garments rotting and old
These men came forth from their prison pen.

Like skeletons waking from graves.

Please give me a pen one faint voice said.
And a piece of paper I ask no more.
Sweet heart tell mother I am still alive.
Meet me at Bremen was all it read.

She pressed those lines to her throbbing heart.
Come brother make ready your fleetest steed.
We will ride to Bremen over the way.
And break the news to that Mother gray."

Anonymous

*Taken from files at the National Park Service at Andersonville, Georgia

(In 1864, one of the largest Confederate military prison was at Americus, Georgia. The name of the prison was Camp Sumter. Nearly 13,000 Union soldiers were buried at the prison. During the Civil War, over 84 U.S. Colored Troops were prisoners at the Camp Sumter in 1864.) Today, the prison is known as Andersonville National Cemetery. The entire area is a tourist site.

POSSIBLE AFRICA CONNECTION:

Some reports showed that slaves were transported to Savannah from Nigeria and other parts of Africa. The tribes included Fula, Mandinka, Val, Kissi, Kpelle, Wolof, Temne, Limba and Susu

NIGERIA –Nigeria is located in West Africa. Major ethnic groups or tribes Hausa, Fulani Yorbua, Igbo(Ibo), Ijaw and many others.

Popular foods introduced to America include roast chicken in peanut sauce stews with meat pumpkins greens and red pepper. Popular beverages: Cocoa, Coffee, beer and special red tea.

Nuts and seeds-Palm nuts cashews, kola nuts watermelon seeds(egusi seeds), mango seeds

FORMER GEORGIA SLAVES' SAYING:

PLANTATION LIFE:

1. Food for the Slaves on the Plantation

"Now 'bout dat somepin t'eat. Sho dat! Us had plenty of dem good old collard, turnips and dem sort of oatments, and dar was allus a good chunk of meat to bile wid 'em.

Marse Ike, he kep' plenty of evvy sort of meat folks knowed about dem days. He had his own beef cattle, lots of sheep, and he killed more'n hunnert hogs evvy year. Dey tells me dat old bench dey used to lay de meat out on to cut it up is standin' dar yet.

"Possums? Lawd, dey was plentiful, and dat ain't all dere was on dat plantation. One time a slave man was 'possum huntin' and, as he was runnin' 'round in de bresh, he looked up and dar was a b'er standin' right up on his hind laigs grinnin' and ready to eat dat Nigger up. Oh, good gracious, how dat nigger did run! Dey fetched in 'possum in piles, and dere was lots of rabbits, fixas and coons. Dem coons, foxes and 'possum hounds sho knowed deir business. Lawsy, I kin jus' smell one of dem good old 'possum roastin' right now, atter all dese years. You parboiled de 'possum fust, and den roasted him in a heavy iron skillet what had a big old thick lid. Jus' 'fore de 'possum so as dey would soak up some of dat good old gravy, and would git good and brown. Is you ever et any good old askcakes? You wropped de raw hoecake in cabbage or collard leafs and roasted 'em in de ashes. When dey got done, you had somepin fit for a king to eat.

"De kitchen was sot' off a piece from de big house, and our white folkeses wouldn't eat their supper 'fore time to light de lamps to save your life' den I had to stan' 'ind Old Miss' cheer and fan her wid a turkey-feather fan to keep de flies off. Nomatter how rich folkeses was dem days dere wasn't no screens in de houses.

"I never eill forgit old Aunt Mary; she was our cook, and she had to be tapped evvy now and den 'cause she had de drapsy so bad. Aunt Mary's old man was Uncle Harris, and I 'members how he used to go fishing at night. . De udder slaves went fishin' too. Many's de time I'se seed my mammy come back from shoulders down to de ground. Me, I lakked milk more'n anything else. You jus' oughta seed dat place at milkin' time. Dere was a heap of cows a fightin', chillum hollerin's, and sich a bedlam as you can't think up/ Dat old platation was a good place for chillum, in summertime 'specially,'cause dere was so many branches and cricks close by what us chillum could hop in and cool off."

Former Slave Addie Vinson, pages 100-101

2.   Feeding Children on the Plantation

"The little slaves were fed pig-fashion in the kitchen, but they were given just so much food and no more."

Former Slave Emma Hurley, page 2

Bible Verse(s):

7.   In God is my salvation and my glory: the rock of my strength and my refuge, is in God.

Psalm 60:7

SHERMAN'S MARCH TO ATLANTA

On December 22, 1864 – General Sherman presented Savannah to President Abraham Lincoln as a Christmas gift. Savannah was the meeting place for the 22 ministers and General William Tecumseh Sherman.

"Sherman Meets The Colored Ministers In Savannah"

Minutes of an interview between the colored ministers and church officers at Savanah with the Secretary of War and Major-General Sherman.

HEADQUARTERS OF MAJOR-GENERAL SHERMAN
In the City of Savannah, Ga., Thursday evening.
January 12, 1865-8 p.m.

On the evening of Thursday, the 12th day of January, 1865, the following persons of African descent met, by appointment, to hold an interview with Edwin M. Stanton, Secretary of War, and Major-General Sherman, to have a conference upon matters relating to the freedmen of the State of Georgia, to wit:

1. William J. Campbell, aged fifty-one years, born in Savannah, slave until 1849, and then liberated by will of his mistress, Mrs. Mary Maxwell, for ten years pastor of the First Baptist Church of Savannah, numbering about 1800 members, average congregation.

1900, the church property, belonging to the congregation(trustees white), worth $18,000.

2. John Cox, aged fifty-eight years, born in Savannah, slave until 1849, when he bought his freedom for $1,100;

Pastor of the Second African Baptist Church; in the ministry fifteen years; congregation, 1,222 persons, church property, in the ministry about twenty years, worth $10,000, belonging to the congregation.

3. Ulysses I. Houston, aged forty-one years, born in Grahamville, S.C. slave "until the Union army entered Savannah,"

Owner by Moses Henderson, Savannah, and pastor of Andrew's Chapel, Methodist Episcopal Church,

Congregation numbering 400; church property, worth $5,000, belongs to congregation, in the ministry about eight years.

4. William Bentley, aged seventy-two years, born in Savannah, slave until twenty-five years of age When his master, John Waters, emancipated him by will, pastor of Andrew's Chapel Methodist Episcopal Church (only One of that denomination in Savannah), congregation numbering 360 members; church property worth about $20,000, And is owned by the congregation, been in the ministry about twenty years, a member of Georgia conference.

5. Charles Bradwell, aged forty years, born in Liberty County, Ga.; slave until 1851; emancipated by will of his master, J.L. Bradwell local preacher, in charge of the Methodist Episcopal congregation (Andrew's Chapel) in the absence of the minister; in the university ten years.

6. William Gaines, aged forty-one years, born in Willis County, Ga. Slave "until the Union army freed me", owned by Robert Toombs, formerly U.S. Senator, and his brother, Gabriel Toombs, local preacher of the Methodist Episcopal Church (Andrew's Chapel); in the ministry sixteen years.

7. James Hill, aged fifty-two years, born in Bryan County, Ga.; slave "up to the time the Union army come in" owned by H.F. Willings, of Savannah, in the ministry sixteen years.

8. Glasgow Taylor, aged seventy-two year, born in Wilkes County, Ga.; slave "until the Union army come" owned by A.P. Wetter; Is a local preacher of the Methodist Episcopal Church (Andrew's Chapel); in the ministry thirty-five years.

9. Garrison Frazier, aged sixty-seven years, born in Granville County, N.C. slave until eight years ago, when he bought himself and his wife, paying $1,000 in gold and silver, is an ordained minister in

the Baptist Church, but, his health failing, has now charge of no congregation, has been in the ministry thirty-five years.

10. James Mills, aged fifty-six years, born in Savannah; freeborn, and is a licensed preachers of the First Baptist Church; has been eight years in the ministry.

11. Abraham Burke, aged forty-eight years, born in Bryan County, Ga.; slave until twenty years ago, when he bought himself for $800; has been in the ministry about ten years.

12. Arthur Wardell, aged forty-four years, born in Liberty County, Ga; slave until "freed by the Union army," owned by A.A. Solomons, Savannah, and is a licensed minister in the Baptist Church; has been in the ministry six years.

13. Alexander Harris, aged forty-seven years, born in Savannah, freeborn, licensed minister of Third African Baptist Church, licensed about one month ago.

14. Andrew Neal, aged sixty-one years, born in Savannah; slave "until the Union army liberated me," owned by Mr. William Gibbons, and has been deacons in the Third Baptist Church for ten years.

15. James Porter, aged thirty —nine year, born in Charleston, S.C.; freeborn, his mother having purchased her freedom, is a lay reader and president of the board of wardens and vestry of Saint Stephen's Protestant Episcopal Colored Church in Savannah; has been in communion nine years, the congregation numbers about 200 persons, the church property is worth about $10,000, and is owned by the congregation.

16. Adolphus Delmonte, aged twenty-eight years, born in Savannah; freeborn, is a licensed minister of the Missionary Baptist Church of Milledgeville, congregation numbering about 300 or 400 persons, has been in the ministry about two years.

17. Jacob Godfrey, aged fifty-seven years, born in Marion, S.C.; slave "until the Union army freed me" owned by James E. Godfrey, Methodist preacher, now in the rebel army, is a class leader and steward of Andrew's Chapel since 1836.

18. John Johnson, aged fifty-one years, born in Bryan County, Ga.; slave "up to the time the Union army came here," owned by W.W. Lincoln, of Savannah, is a class leader and treasurer of Andrew's Chapel for sixteen years.

19. Robert N. Taylor, aged fifty-one years, born in Wilkes County, Ga.; slave "to the time of the Union army come," was owned by Augustus P. Wetter, Savannah, and is class leader in Andrew's Chapel for nine years.

20. James Lynch, aged twenty-six years, born in Baltimore, Md.; freeborn, is presiding elder of the Methodist Episcopal Church, and missionary to the Department of the South; has been seven years in the ministry and two years in the South.

Garrison Frazier, being chosen by the persons present to express their common sentiments upon the matters of inquiry, makes answers to inquiries as follows:

First. State what your understanding is in regard to the acts of Congress and President Lincoln's proclamation touching the condition of the colored people in the rebel States.

Answer. So far as I understand President Lincoln's proclamation to the rebellious States, it is, that if they would lay down their arm and submit to the laws of the United States before the 1st of January, 1863, all should be well, but if they did not. Then all the slaves in the rebel States should be free,

Henceforth and forever. That is what I understood.

Second. State what you understand by slavery, and the freedom that was to be given by the President's proclamation,

Answer. Slavery is receiving by irresistible power the work of another man, and not by his consent. The freedom, as I understand it, promised by the proclamation is taking us from under the yoke of bondage and placing us where we could reap the fruit of our own labor and take care of ourselves and assist the Government in maintaining our freedom.

Third. State in what manner you think you can take care of yourselves, and how can you best assist the Government in maintaining your freedom.

Answer. The way we can best take care of ourselves is to have land, and turn in and till it by our labor- that is, by the labor of the women, and children, and old men-and we can soon maintain ourselves and have something to spare, and to assist, the Government, and serve in such manner as they may be wanted. (The rebels told us that they piled them up and made batteries of them, and sold them to Cuba, but we don't believe that). We want to be placed on land until we are able to buy it and make it our own.

Fourth. State in what manner you rather live, whether scattered among the whites or in colonies by yourselves?

Answer. I would prefer to live by ourselves, for there is a prejudice against us in the South that will take years to get over, but I do not know that I can answer for my brethren. (Mr. Lynch says he thinks they should not be separated, but live together. All the other persons present being questioned, one by one, answer that they agree with "Brother Frazier".)

Fifth. Do you think that there is intelligence enough among the slaves of the South to maintain themselves under the Government of the United States, and the equal protection of is laws, and maintain good and peaceable relations among yourselves and with your neighbors?

Answer. I think there is sufficient among us to do so.

Sixth. State what is the feeling of the black population of the South toward the Government of the United States; what is the understanding in respect to the present war, its causes and object, and their disposition to aid either side. State fully your views.

Answer. I think you will find there is thousands that are willing to make any sacrifice to assist the Government of the United States, while there is also many that are not willing to take up arms. I do not suppose there is a dozen men that is opposed to the Government. I understand as to the war that the South is the aggressor. President Lincoln was elected

President by a majority of the United States, which guaranteed him the right of holding the office and exercising the right over the whole United States. The South, without knowing what he would do, rebelled. The war was commenced by the rebels before he came into the office. The object of the war was not, at first, to give the slaves their freedom, but the sole object of the war was, at first, to bring the rebellious States back into the Union and their loyalty to the laws of the United States.

Afterward, knowing the value that was set on the slaves by the rebels, the President thought that his proclamation would stimulate them to lay down their arms, reduce them to obedience, and help to bring back the rebel States, and their not doing so has now made the freedom of the slaves a part of the war. It is my opinion that the Is not a man in this city that could be started to help, the rebels one inch, for that would be suicide. There was two black men left with the rebels, because they had taken an active part for the rebels, and thought something might befall them if they stayed behind, but there is not another man. If the prayers that have gone up for the Union army could be read out you would not get through them these two weeks.

Seventh. State whether the sentiments you now express are those only of the colored people in the city, or do they extend to the colored population through the country, and what are your means of knowing the sentiments of those living in the country.

Answer. I think the sentiments are the same among the colored people of the State. My opinion is formed by personal communication in the course of my ministry, and also from thousands that followed the Union army, leaving their homes and undergoing suffering. I did not think there would be so many; the number surpassed my expectation.

Eighth. If the rebel leaders were to arm the slaves what would be its effect!

Answer. I think they would fight as long as they were before the bayonet, and just as soon as they could get away they would desert, in my opinion.

Ninth. What, in your opinion, is the feeling of the colored people about enlisting and serving as soldiers of the United States, and what kind of military service do they prefer?

Answer. A large number have gone as soldiers to Port Royal to be drilled and put in the service, and I think there is thousands of the young men that will enlist; there is something about them that, perhaps, is wrong; they have suffered so long from the rebels that they want to meet and have a chance with them in the field. Some of them want to shoulder the musket, others want to go into the quartermaster or the commissary's service.

Tenth. Do you understand the mode of enlistment of colored people in the rebel States, by State agents, under the act of Congress? If yea, state what your understanding is.

Answer. My understanding is that colored persons enlisted by State agents are enlisted as substitutes, and give credit to the States, and do not swell the army, because every black man enlisted by a State agents leaves a white man at home; and also that larger bounties are given or promised by the State agents than are given by the States. The great object should be to push through this rebellion the shortest way, and there seems to be something wanting in the enlistment by State agents, for it don' strengthen the army, but takes one away for every colored man enlisted.

Eleventh. State what, in your opinion, is the best way to enlist colored men for soldiers,

Answer. I think, sir, that all compulsory operations should be put a stop to. The ministers would talk to them, and the young men would enlist. It is my opinion that it would be far better for the State agents to stay at home, and the enlistments to be made for the United States under the direction of General Sherman.

In the absence of General Sherman the following question was asked:

Twelfth. State what is the feeling of the colored people in regard to General Sherman, and how far do they regard his sentiments and actions as friendly to their rights and interests, or otherwise.

Answer. We looked upon General Sherman, prior to his arrival, as a man, in the providence of God, specially set aside to accomplish this work, and we unanimously felt inexpressible gratitude to him, looking upon him as a man that should be honored for the faithful performance of his duty. Some of us called upon him immediately upon his arrival, and it is probable he did not meet the Secretary with more courtesy than he met us. His conduct and deportment toward us characterized him as a friend and a gentleman. We have confidence in General Sherman, and think that what concerns us could not be under better hands. This our opinion now from the short acquaintance and intercourse we have had.

(Mr. Lynch states that, with his limited acquaintance with General Sherman, he is unwilling to express an opinion. All others present declare their agreement with Mr. Frazier about General Sherman.)

Some conversation upon general subjects relating to General Sherman's march then ensued, of which no note was taken.

WAR DEPARTMENT, ADJUTANT-GENERAL'S OFFICE,
Washington, February 1, 1865.

I do hereby certify that the foregoing is a true and faithful report of the questions and answers made by the colored ministers and church members of Savannah in my presence and hearing at the chambers of Major-General Sherman, on the evening Thursday, the 12th day of January, 1865. The questions of General Sherman and the Secretary of War were reduced to writing and read to the persons present. The answers were made by the reverend Garrison Frazier, who was selected by the other ministers and church members to answer for them. The answers were written down in his exact words, and read over to the others, who, one by one, expressed his concurrence or dissent, as above set forth.

E.D. TOWNSEND,
Assistant Adjutant-General

Savannah History:

Savannah-Eugene Jacques Bullard, the first black pilot anywhere, from Macon Georgia left Savannah in 1906 and not yet a teenager ran away from home after listening to his father talk about a place called France where color didn't seem to matter;

-that in 1914 he joined the French Foreign Legion to fight in the First World War.

To sign up in the U.S. military would mean washing pots and cleaning latrines.

In 1917, Bullard earned his flying certificate. He was the first Black military pilot. Anywhere.

-that on September 8, 1917, he made his first combat flight in the skies over Verdun. He scored a "kill" that first day, and when he landed, they counted 78 bullet holes in his plane;

-that he continued to fight bravely for "our side" but in the French uniform and in French Spad aircraft. When the U.S. flyers under its flag, they had no place for Eugene Bullard. French doctors apparently hadn't noticed his flat feet and color blindness.

-that after the war he wanted to go home to Georgia where he might live and work with his brother, Hector, who had acquired some land in Peach County. He didn't learn until later that when Hector Bullard tried to move onto his land, he was lynched;

-painted on the fuselage of Gene Bullard's plane:

"All Blood Is Red"

FORMER GEORGIA SLAVES' SAYINGS:

PLANTATION LIFE:

1. Number of Slaves on One Plantation

"His master owned over a hundred grown slaves and the children were "thick as blackbirds". Some worked in the master's house

Some did the washing, others drove the horses, and others did the same kind of work for the overseer. The majority of them helped in the tobacco fields. George worked there when he was about fourteen years of age. His job was to pick the worms off the leaves and, if the overseer when inspecting would find a worm, he immediately called George and made him bite off his head. George said this was to make him more careful next time."

"At night, after their work was over, the slaves would meet out "in the sticks" and dance in some of the old houses. Forming into a circle they would march around singing, when suddenly an order was given and they would pair off and begin dancing. Banjos and guitars furnished the music. Christmas and the Fourth of July were great days for the slaves. Then, they were given passes and allowed to visit other plantations where great feasts were prepared for them. Sometimes the master furnished the feasts and they were allowed to invite their friends from the neighboring plantations."

"On Sundays, if the weather was warm and pleasant, there was a service held in the "bush arbors" for the white and colored. In the winter the master carried the slaves into town to church. He would give them a lecture on good behavior before leaving home so they knew what was expected of them. Their place was in the back of the church. Pass was absolutely necessary for a slave to have if he wanted to leave the plantation."

Former Slave George Caulton page 169,170

2.   Jobs for Some Slaves on the Plantation

"Uncle Nelson was also a carpenter. Uncle Joe Browning was a waggoner and attended to the stock on the plantation. The blacksmith shop on the plantation was operated by Uncle Bob Browning who was a skilled blacksmith. The tannery was operated by Uncle Ben Browning." Leather for everyone's shoes was made by "Uncle". Last but not least, father Cicero Browning was a shoe maker. Mr. Browning quote: "Many a night I have held the light for my father to see by to make shoes for us. He often give me a dime." On the plantation was every known convenience for the owner and his slaves. There was the cotton gin which saved them the trouble of having to go to town to get the cotton ginned; besides this there was a syrup mill which supplied the whole plantation with syrup. A broad smile crossed Mr. Browning's face as he remarked slowly, "We even had a still from which the whiskey could be made." After the juice from fruits had fermented the master would measure out to each family as much whiskey as was practical. It was not necessary for the master to buy anything they desired."

Former Slave George Washington Browning, page 113

3.   Death in the Neighborhood

"When dere was a death 'round our neighborhood, evvybody went and paid their 'spects to de fambly of de dead. Folkses set up all night wid de corpse and sung and prayed. Dat settin' up was mostly to keep cats offen de corpse. Cats sho is bad atter dead folks; I'se heared tell dat dey most et up some corpses what nobody warn't watchin'. When de time come to bury de dead, dey loaded de coffin on to a wagon, and most times de fambly rode to de graveyard in a wagon, and most times de fambly rode to de graveyard in a wagon too, but if it warn't no fur piece off, most of de other folkses walked. Dey started singin' when dey left de house and sung right on 'til dat corpse was put in de grave. When de preacher had done said a prayer, dey all sung: I'se Born to Die and Day Dis Body Down. Dat was 'bout all dere was to de buryin', but later on dey had de funeral sermon preached in church, maybe si months atter de burpin' De white folkses had all deir funeral sermons preached at the time of de buryin'.

Former Slave Paul Smith page 330

Possible Africa Connection:

Benin- Benin is West African country and west of Nigeria. Tribal groups include Fon, Adja, Yoruba, Bariba and many others. Foods introduced to America chickens, beans, pumpkins, kola nuts, black-eyed peas, watermelons, peanuts, corn and locusts (for eating).

Bible Verse(s):

5 Thou shall not bow down thyself to them, nor serve them: for I the Lord thy God am a jealous God, visiting the iniquity of the fathers upon the children unto the third and fourth generation of them that hate me;

6 And showing mercy unto thousands of them that love me, and keep my commandments.

Exodus 20:5,6

Chapter 3

Appetizers and Beverages

Appetizers

Appetizers included fresh fruits, vegetables, boiled peanuts, and sugar cane joints.

Steamed Popcorn Shrimp

Ingredients

    1 pound popcorn shrimp, cleaned and deveined
    1 quart water
    1 teaspoon salt

Directions

    1. Clean and devein shrimp
    2. Heat water and add salt.
    3. Bring to a boil add in shrimp.
    4. Cook until pink.
    5. Drain and cool down. Serve with dipping sauce.

Shrimp Dip

Ingredients

   1 pound jumbo shrimp, deveined, shelled and cooked
   1 -8 ounce package cream cheese
   ¼ cup mayonnaise
   ½ cup sour cream
   ¼ cup onion, minced
   2 tablespoons garlic, minced
   1 teaspoon salt
   1 teaspoon Tabasco sauce
   1 teaspoon Worcestershire sauce

Directions

   1. Cook shrimp as directed. Cool and drain. Chop. Set aside.
   2. In a large bowl, whip cream cheese, mayonnaise and sour cream together. Add remaining ingredients and stir well.
   3. Add chopped shrimp. Cover and chill for 1 hour before serving.

Sugar Cane Joints

Ingredients

   Long stalk of Sugar Cane

Directions
1 portion of cane per person

   1. Disjoint stalk of cane.
   2. Serve one section per person.

Spiced Peanuts

Ingredients

   1 teaspoon chili powder
   1 teaspoon garlic powder
   ½ teaspoon curry powder
   2 tablespoon brown sugar
   3 tablespoons soy sauce
   2 cups shelled raw peanuts

Directions

   1. In a medium mixing bowl, combine chili powder, garlic powder, curry powder, brown sugar and soy sauce.
   2. Add peanuts. Stir.
   3. Spread on a baking sheet and bake at 325 degrees F and stir until golden brown. Cool. Store in air tight container until ready-to-use,

Akara —Black-eyed Pea Balls

Ingredients

   1 cup fresh black eyed peas
   1 egg
   ½ of a small onion, finely chopped
   ½ teaspoon cayenne pepper
   1 teaspoon salt
   Peanut oil for frying

Directions

   1. Soak the peas in cool water for 10 20 minutes. Then remove the skins.
   2. Drain the peas and puree the peas with food processor and add water.
   3. Place peas in a bowl with egg, onions, pepper and salt.
   4. Beat for 2 to 3 minutes with a wooden spoon.
   5. Heat oil and drop mixture by tablespoons in hot peanut oil.

6. Fry to golden brown. Drain on paper towels.

Peanut Brittle

Ingredients

2 1/2 cups sugar
½ cup water
1 cup light corn syrup
3 cups raw peanuts
1 teaspoon salt
¼ cup butter
1 teaspoon vanilla
1 tablespoon baking soda

Directions

1. Butter a cookie sheet or bread pan.et aside for later.
2. Combine sugar, syrup and water in a heavy skillet. Cook stirring until all sugar is dissolved.
3. Add salt and peanuts. Cook stirring constantly for about ten minutes.
4. Add butter and vanilla. Stir well, then add soda. Stir well to make certain all soda is dissolved. Pour into a buttered surface. Spread thin. Cool and then break into pieces.

Pecan Pralines

Makes 12

Ingredients

2 cups granulated sugar
1 cup dark brown sugar
1 cup butter
1 cup evaporated milk
¼ cup dark corn syrup
4 cups pecan halves

Directions

1. Combine all the ingredients in saucepan except pecan halves.
2. Cook in a medium sauce pan for 20 minutes, stirring constantly after the syrup begins To boil.
3. Continue to boil for 15 minutes.
4. Stir in pecan halves.
5. Drop the mixture by tablespoonsful on wax paper one inch apart.
6. Cool. Serve.

Deviled Eggs

Ingredients

8 large eggs
½ cup mayonnaise
¼ cup mustard
1 teaspoon salt
1 teaspoon black pepper
½ cup sweet pickle relish
Paprika for garnish

Directions

1. Boil eggs. Cool. Peel. Cut into half. Put yolks in a bowl. Set whites aside.
2. Mash yolks; add to the yolks mayonnaise, salt, pepper, and sweet pickle relish.
3. Stir and stuff egg whites and garnish with paprika.

Fresh Fruits(unripen and ripen)

- Selected groups enjoy many fresh fruits before the fruits ripens- wild green plums, green apples, green pears and mayhaws.

Ripen fruits enjoyed include —mangoes, plums, apricots, peaches, watermelons, cantaloupes, muskmelons, cherries, strawberries, wild dew berries and blackberries.

Beverages

Geechees love sweet tea, lemonade, black coffee and cane juice punch.

Black Coffee

Ingredients

> 1 cup Coffee grounds (favorite coffee)
> 2 quarts water

Directions

1. Combine coffee and cold water in a pot or pan.
2. Cover and bring to a boil. Boil for 10 minutes.
3. Remove from heat strain and serve hot.

Egg Nog

Ingredients

> 6 eggs, separated
> 1 cup sugar
> 4 cups milk, scalded
> 2 cups heavy cream
> 2 teaspoons vanilla
> 1 cup bourbon
> 1 teaspoon cinnamon

Directions

1. Separate eggs. Beat egg yolks gradually adding in ½ of sugar. Add milk slowly, beating vigorously until all milk has been added. Beat egg whites.
2. Gradually add in all of the ingredients in the egg yolks. Stir well. Blend in egg fluffy whites.

Lemonade

Ingredients

- 3 lemons
- 2 cups sugar
- ½ gallon warm water
- 1 lemon for slices and serving with lemonade

Directions

1. Squeeze lemons to get ¾ cup of lemon juice.
2. Pour lemon juice in a pitches and stir in sugar.
3. Slowly stir in warm water,
4. Serve over ice with lemon slices.

Sweet Tea-Low country most popular and signature drink

Ingredients

- 2 large family size tea bags
- 1 gallon water
- 1 pinch baking soda (less than 1/8 teaspoon)
- 2 ½ cups sugar
- 1 quart water

Directions

1. Place large tea bags and one gallon of water in large pot. Cover.
2. Bring to a boil and boil for 10 minutes add pinch of baking soda.
3. Remove tea bags and stir in sugar. Pour in pitcher and gradually add 1 quart of water if needed.
4. Serve over ice.

Sugar Cane Juice Punch

Ingredients

8 cups cane juice
½ cup lemon juice
¼ cup lime juice
1 quart water, cold

Directions

1. Grind juice from stalks of cane.
2. Strain into a pitcher.
3. Stir in lemon juice, lime juice and cold water
4. Serve over ice.

Peach Brandy

Ingredients

8 to 10 pounds peaches, washed and crushed
10 pounds sugar

Directions

1. Place peaches and sugar together in a large container. Cover with a cheese cloth. Let stand 6-7 days. Do not add water. The peaches and sugar will form a juice. Place mixture in a dark, dry and cool place. Strain with cheese cloth. Then let stand 2 to 3 more days. Strain. Add 3 pounds more of sugar.
   Let stand for six days. Then strain; pour into jugs let set 3 to 4 weeks. Then strain.
   The brandy is ready to serve.

Honey Water

Ingredients

½ cup honey
½ cup lemon juice
½ cup sugar
1 gallon water

Directions

1. Combine all ingredients with half of the water. Stir well.
2. Add remaining water and stir well. Serve over ice.

Hot Toddy

Ingredients

2 cups hot tea
2 lemons
1 tablespoon honey
1 cup bourbon
Sugar to taste

Directions

1. Boil three cups of water and add two tea bags. Boil for 5 minutes.
2. Remove tea bags and add hot tea to a pitcher. Stir in remaining ingredients and serve.

Favorite Instant Coffee Mix

Ingredients

4 cups instant coffee granules
1 ½ cups sugar
2 cups dairy coffee creamer
1 ¼ cups hot cocoa mix
1 tablespoon cinnamon
½ teaspoon ginger

Directions

1. Combine all ingredients in the food processor.
2. Store in a tight container
3. To make a cup of coffee, use 2 teaspoons of mix to one cup of boiling water.

Gnamacoudji (African Drink from Ivory Coast)

Ingredients

14 ounces ginger root, peeled and cut into 2 –inch pieces
5 blades lemon grass, or 5 tablespoons dried, soaked for 30 minutes
¼ cup fresh mint leaves
4 cups water
12 cups pineapple juice
Approximately 1 ¼ cups confectioner's sugar
2 ½ teaspoons vanilla extract

Directions

1. In a food processor, grind ginger to a paste. Put into a cheese cloth bag add lemon grass and mint leaves. Place in 4 cups of water in a sauce pan and heat to boiling. Remove from heat and add cheese cloth bag. Steep for 30 minutes. Squeeze bag occasionally.
2. Discard bag. Strain juice into a large bowl. Stir in pineapple juice, sugar and vanilla flavor. Serve over ice.

Peach Chock

Ingredients

> 8 cups well ripened peaches, remove pits and slice peaches
> 6 cups sugar
> 3 cups water

Directions

1. In a large crock, lace all ingredients. Stir. Put lid on top of crock.
2. Place in dry, cool place and let ferment for 6 weeks.
3. Strain with cheese cloth into clean glass containers and place lid on tightly.
4. Refrigerate until use.

TALKING POINTS:

COUNTY, CITY, CONNECTIONS TO GEORGIA'S SEA ISLAND:

Entrance to the Barrier sea island

Sandfly – A small town located nine miles southeast of Savanah Georgia's Barrier Sea Island

Thunderbolt Island – The Island is a shrimping village along international water way off U.S. 80 route to beaches and islands.

POSSIBLE AFRICA CONNECTION:

Benin(second reference) -Benin is a West African Country. Tribal groups are Fon, Adja, Yoruba, Bariba and many others.

Foods brought to America includes black-eyed peas, watermelon, okra, greens and buttermilk.

FORMER GEORGIA SLAVES' SAYINGS:

PLANTATION LIFE:

1. Dishes and Cooking at the Big House

"All the dishes was flowered. I don't know as I ever saw a plain plate, except in the quarters. They had blue and yellow flowered plates, cups, and saucers flowered too; and, great big, long, covered dishes to match. There were great big goblet they used for everyday; they held about three cups, not like they ones they use now, shaped different. Mistis had a set of fine glass she hardly ever used 'cept for might special company; mighty special company had its come fore you could go in the sideboard and get 'em, 'cause they was easy broke. That big sideboard, used Mahogany, the finest thing! I ain't seen one like that, well I did too. I saw one one time since, like it in Atlanta.

"Our kitchen was off from the big house. The kitchen was bigger than this house; and that fireplace! I never saw such a big one. The sticks of wood for the fireplace was twelve feet long. There was hooks, two big hooks up in the chimney. I've seen 'em hang lambs' and calves' hind quarters up in the chimney to smoke. You know, they'd kill more than they could eat and didn't have ice like they do now to keep things from spoiling, so they hung 'em up in that chimney to smoke, how good! The sweetest stuff you ever et in your life!"

Former Slave Aunt Cicely Cawthon page 179

2. Slaves' Housing

"We stayed in a one room lawg cabin with a dirt flo'. A frame made outen pine poles was fastened to the wall, to hold up the mattresses. Our mattresses was made outen cotton baggin' stuffed with wheat straw. Our kivers was quilts made outen ole clothes. Slave 'omans too ole to wuk in the fiel's made the quilts."

"Maw, she went up to the big 'ouse wunst a week to git the 'lowance or vittuls. They 'lowanced us a week's rations at a time. Hit were genully hawg meat, cawn meal an' some times a little flour. Maw, she done our cookin' on the coals in the fire place at our cabin. We had plenny er 'possums, an' rabbits, an' fishes some times we had wile tukkeys an' partridges.

Slaves woan' spozen to go huntin' at night, an' evvybody know you kyan' ketch no 'possums 'ceppin at night. Jes/ the same, we had plenny 'possums, an' no buddy ax' how we cotch 'em/ Now 'bout them rabbits! Slaves woan' 'lowed to have no guns an' no dawgs to run down rabbits. All the dawgs on our plantation b'llonged to mah employer, Ah means, to mah marstr, an' he 'lowed us to use his dawgs to run down the rabbits. Nigger mens an' boys 'ud go in crowds, sometimes as many rias twelve at one time, an' a rabbit ain't got no chanct 'ginst a lot er niggers an' dawgs, when they light out fer to run 'im down. Whut wile critters we wanted to eat an' coulden' run down, we was right smart 'bout ketchin In traps. We cotch lots or wile turkeys an' partridges in traps an' nets. Long Crick runned thoo' our plantation an' the river woan' no fur pieces off. We sho' did ketch the fishes. Gawd only knows how long it has been since this ole

Nigger pulled a big shad outer the river. Ain't no shad been cotch in the river 'roun' hyar in so long Ah disremembahe when"

"We diden' have no gyardens er our own 'roun' our cabins, Mah employer, Ah means, mah marster, had one big gyarden fer our whole plantation, an' all his niggers had to wuk in it when some-ever he wannid 'em to, then he giv 'em all, plenny good gyarden jess for thryselves. They was collards, an' onions, an' cabbages, an' turnips, an' beets, an'

English peas, an' beans and was allus some gyarlic ailments.

Gyarlic was mostly to kyore wums. They roasted the gyarlic in the hot ashes an' squez the juice outen it, an' made the chilluns take it. Sometimes they made poultices outen gyarlic for the pneumony."

Former Slave James Bolton page 78

Bible Verse(s):

1. In the beginning, God created the heaven and the earth.

26. And God said, Let us make man in our image, after our likeness: and let them have dominion over the fish of the sea, over the fowl of the air, and over the cattle, and over all the earth, and over every creeping thing that creepeth upon the earth.

27. So God created man in his own image in the image of God created he him, male and female created he them.

GENESIS: 1, 26, 27

Chapter 4

Seasonings

The Geechees have herbs, spices and flavorings on their shelves. Popular herbs are sage, peppers, basil, oregano extracts —vanilla, lemon, and almond flavors.

Six basic seasonings were used. To customize or personalize the seasonings, each cook would add or delete some of the ingredients.

1. Meat Rubs

Ingredients

> 1 cup salt
> ½ cup cracked black pepper
> ½ cup dark brown sugar
> 2 tablespoons cayenne pepper
> 1 tablespoon garlic granules
> 1 tablespoon paprika
> 1 tablespoon seasoning salt
> 1 tablespoon thyme, ground

Directions

1. Measure and mix all ingredients in a large mixer. Mix well;
2. Place in large jar. Use as rub.

2. Collard Greens, Other Greens, Field Peas, Dried Beans and Peas Seasonings

Ingredients

> 1 cup salt
> 1/3 cup red pepper flakes
> ½ cup sugar
> 1 cup ham base seasoning
> 2 chicken bouillon granules

Directions

1. Mix all ingredients together in a large mixer.
2. Seal in large container until use.
3. Use one tablespoon or adjust seasoning for each use.

3. Sweet Potato and Pumpkin Pie Seasonings

Ingredients

> 3 tablespoons cinnamon
> ½ teaspoon nutmeg
> 1 teaspoon ginger
> 1 teaspoon salt

Directions

1. Mix together all ingredients in a mixer.
2. Store in jar until ready to use.

Fish Seasonings

Ingredients

1 cup black pepper
½ cup salt
½ cup seasoning salt
1 tablespoon cayenne pepper
1 tablespoon paprika
1 tablespoon garlic salt

Directions

1. In a mixer, mix all ingredients well.
2. Store in tightly fitted container until ready-to-use.
3. Use as intended.

Turkey or Chicken Dressing Seasonings

Ingredients

½ cup salt
1 cup black pepper
1 tablespoon rosemary, ground
1 teaspoon cayenne pepper
1 teaspoon garlic powder
¼ cup onion salt

Directions

1. Mix in a large mixer.
2. Store in a large jar.
3. Use one tablespoon at a time or as needed.

Sesame Seeds (Benne Seeds) Seasonings

Ingredients

1 cup Sesame seeds
1 tablespoon olive oil

Directions

1. Heat oil in a large skillet. Toast sesame seeds until golden brown.
2. Drain. Cool. Store as needed.

(The Benne seeds were brought from Africa by the slaves. The Benne seeds were planted at the end of the row of cotton, corn or row crops in the field. This method was known as the 'good luck' plant. From the sesame or benne seeds, such items as benne cakes, wafers and candies were made or the seeds were ground to make a shortening or oil that was used in the making of cakes, oyster stews and a butter substitute. Currently, the benne seeds or sesame seeds on hamburger buns and used in many recipes. Benne seeds or sesame seeds were first brought to Savannah by African slaves in the seventeenth century. The slaves called the seeds - Benne Seeds.)

Pepper Sauce

Ingredients

20 hot peppers
2 cups boiling vinegar

Directions

1. Wash jars and peppers.
2. Stuff pepper in jars.
3. Heat vinegar to boiling and pour over peppers. Seal tightly until ready to use.
4. Use as a condiment with cooked vegetables.

Barbecue Sauce

Ingredients

 1 cup vinegar
 1 cup molasses
 1 cup prepared mustard
 1 cup ketchup

Directions

 1. Mix all ingredients together in a medium sized pan.
 2. Bring to a boil. Cool. Place in a jar with a top until ready to use.

TALKING POINTS:

Georgia's Barrier Sea Islands

Chatman County has more sea islands than the other counties.

Possible Africa Connection:

Cameroon- Cameroon is located in Central Africa. Tribal groups include Bantu, Nigritic and many others. The food introduced to America from Cameroon include rice, fish, coffee, plantains and bananas.

PLANTATION LIFE:

An excerpt from a letter showing how bad slavery was in America written by a possible seventh generation grandson of ex-slave- Senator Hank Senator of Alabama –

 1. First, African people were snatched from their families, their villages, their tribes, their continent, their freedom, their people were made to walk hundreds of miles in chains. They were often beaten, poorly fed and abused in many ways. Women and girls were routinely raped. The whole continent was ravaged and still suffers in this day........

2. Second, African people were placed in "slave dungeons" for weeks and sometimes months until the slave ships came. They were often underfed, terribly beaten raped and stuffed together so tightly, raped and stuffed together so tightly they could hardly move. African people were packed so tightly in the holds of ships with little space to even move. They performs bodily functions where they lay an then lived in it. They were oftentimes beaten, raped and abused mentally, physically and emotionally. Many died from disease and broken spirits. Some were so terribly impacted that they jumped overboard and drowned when brought up to the deck of the ships. Millions They died during the Middle Passage from Africa to the Americas.........

3. Third, African people were broken like wild animals. They were stripped of every element of their identity. Their names were taken. Their language were taken. Their histories were taken. They were forbidden to have family. They had no rights to own anything. They were considered property. Their personalities were permanently altered. Their freedoms was taken. They became chattel sold from "slave blocks". This crushing of identity impacts us today, I call it the psychology of the oppressed.

4. African-American were worked from "kin to can't:" that is from "can see" in the morning to "can't see" at night. There was no pay for their long, hard labor. Many were poorly fed. Most felt the lash of the whip. All feltthe lash of the tongue. Many were epeately raped. Their children and loved ones were sold at will. Some mothers killed their baby girls so they id not have to do the ravages of slavery.

5. Fifth, AfricanAmericans had no right to defend themselves no matter what was done and how wrong it was. By law, they could not even testify against their abusers. As U.S. Supreme Court Chief Justice Roger B. Toney said in the 1857 Dred Scott case, "A Black man has no rights a White man is bound for respect."

This became the law of the land and its legacy bedevils us to this day.

6. Sixth, African Americans were perceived and treated as sub human. The only way enslavers could square this terrible treatment with their Christian beliefs was see us as less than human. Therefore, they could proudly place such beautiful words in the Declaration of Independence and the U.S. Constitution with impunity; i.e. −"We hold these truths to be self-evident that

all men are created equal; that they are endowed by their creator with certain inalienable rights; that among these are life, liberty and the pursuit of happiness." In them, African Americans were not human so these beautiful words did not apply. Even the U.S. Constitution designated us as 3/5 of a person. That's why White terrorists, in and out of uniforms, can kill us without punishment. The legacy of being less human lingers us today. Black lives are worth much less than White lives.........

7. Seventh, it required great violence to implement and maintain the worse form of human slavery known to human kind, It required unbridled violence by enslavers, slave catchers, local, state, federal governments and the entire society. Maintaining the institution of slavery created a very violent society that infests us to this day. That's why the United States has far more violence than any country in the world.......

8. Eighth, even after slavery formerly ended, we still had Jim Crow. These same imbedded attitudes generated state sanctioned terrorism for nearly another 100 years. The Ku Klux Klan and other terrorist groups hanged, mutilated, maimed and murdered without any punishment. It was state sanctioned terrorism because the "state" did not do anything to prevent it. That's why even during the Civil Rights Movement murders took many years before even a modicum of justice was forged. Just look at the deaths of Medgar Evers, James Chaney, the three little girls murdered by bombing of a Birmingham Church and so many others

The legacy of slavery is everywhere..........."

Written by Alabama State Senator Hank Sanders- January 2015. The Informer – Macon, Georgia page 27

Bible Verse(s):

31 And the people believed and when they heard that the Lord had visited the children of Israel, and that he had looked upon their affliction, then they bowed their heads and worshipped.

EXODUS 4:31

Chapter 5

Rice Cooking

All of the Sea Islands were known for rice growing during the plantation times. The slaves were brought to the Sea Islands as early as 1749 to run the rice plantations.

The slaves worked the plantations and rice fields from sun-up to sun down all year round. The slaves cleared the fields, constructed the levees and ditches, sowed the rice during March and April. After this time, the slaves continued to work the fields until harvest time. The rice was cut with a sickle or as a rice hook after the field were drained. To get the rice from its stalks and husk, the slaves would spread the grains on a sheet and beat the rice.

Geechee slaves were bought into the area because they knew how to cure the rice. To get the rice from its stalk and husks, the slaves would spread the grains on a sheet and beat the rice. If the wind did not blow, then the slaves would sing the "Flail song" to call up the wind. The nickname for the wind was "Tony". "Tony"

Would help separate the straw from the shaft. The "Flail Song" was song as:

"Blow, Tony, blow; O, blow, Tony; Blow, Tony; Blow, Tony, blow;
I whip dis rice as "I whip 'em so; Blow, Tony, blow!"
Blow, Tony, blow; O, blow, Tony; Blow, Tony; Blow.
Slave Song

The Geechee like long grain rice, wild rice and brown rice. Today they eat more converted rice than ever before. The Geechee eat rice as a starch, accompaniment and a dessert.

RICE AS A STARCH

Ingredients

Buttered Long Grain Rice
1 quart water
1 cup long grain rice
1 teaspoon salt
1 tablespoon butter

Directions

1. In a large sauce pan, add water, rice and salt. Stir well. Bring to a boil for 3 minutes. Cover.
2. Cook on low heat until done. Fluff up and add butter.

Steamed Brown Rice

Ingredients

1 tablespoon onions, minced
1 teaspoon celery, chopped
1 tablespoon olive oil
1 cup brown rice
1 cup beef stock
1 cup water

Directions

1. Prepare vegetables. Cook until soft in the skillet.
2. Add to a large saucepan with brown rice and remaining ingredients.
3. Stir and bring to a boil. Cover. Bring to a boil.
4. Cook for 20 minutes or until desired doneness.

Wild Rice

Ingredients

2 cups wild rice
1 teaspoon salt
1 tablespoon butter
11/2 quarts water
2 teaspoon thyme

Directions

1. In a large saucepan, place all ingredients. Stir, cover and bring to a boil for 5 minutes. Reduce heat and cook for 15 minutes.

ACCOMPANIENTS

Ingredients

Dirty Rice
1 ½ quarts water
1 pound chicken gizzards
1 pound chicken livers
1 pound chicken necks
2 cups rice
1 medium onion, chopped
½ cup celery, chopped
½ cup bell pepper, chopped
1 teaspoon red pepper flakes
1 teaspoon salt
1 teaspoon seasoned salt
1 teaspoon black pepper

Directions

1. Boil chicken gizzards, livers and necks in the water until done. Save broth, Debone necks and place with gizzards and livers in a large blender. Set aside.
2. Cook rice in broth (add enough water to make into 1 quart) with onions, celery, bell pepper, red pepper flakes, seasoned salt, salt and black pepper.
3. In a large making bowls stir together meats and cooked rice. Pour into buttered 13 X 9 X2 in casserole dish.
4. Bake for 10 to 15 minutes.

Rice and Oyster Dressing

Ingredients

1 cups cooked rice
2 cups oyster, cooked and chopped
2 tablespoon vegetable oil
1 cup onion, chopped
½ cup green bell pepper, chopped
1 cup celery, chopped
1 cup turkey livers cooked and chopped
1 cup gizzards, cooked and chopped
1(10 ¾ ounce) can condensed cream of mushroom soups
1 (10 ¾) can condensed cream of celery soup
2 cup turkey broth
1 teaspoon black pepper
1 teaspoon seasoned salt
1 teaspoon rosemary leaves

Directions

1. Cook rice as indicated.
2. In a skillet, heat vegetable oil and saute vegetables until tender.
3. In a large bowl, stir together all ingredients.
4. Bake in a large roasting pan for 30 minutes at 350 degrees F.

Broccoli, Rice and Cheese Casserole

Ingredients

   1 tablespoon butter
   1 package onion soup mix, dissolved in 1 cup water
   2 cups long grained rice, cooked
   2 cups chopped broccoli, cooked
   2 tablespoons onions, minced
   1 tablespoon flour
   1 cup milk
   ¼ cup shortening
   11/2 cups shredded extra-sharp cheddar cheese

Directions

1. Grease with butter a 13 x 9 x 2 inch casserole dish. In a large bow, mix together broccoli, rice, and soup mix. Set aside.
2. In a saucepan melt shortening and saute onions until tender, add flour, stir well. Gradually add milk.
3. Add ½ of cheese and pour mixture over broccoli-rice mixture. Stir well. Pour into casserole dish,
4. Sprinkle remainder of cheese on top. Bake at 350 degrees Fahrenheit for 10 minutes.

Savannah Red Rice

Ingredients

   ½ cup butter
   ¼ cup celery, chopped
   ¼ cup bell pepper, chopped
   ½ cup onions, chopped
   2 cups long grain rice, cooked
   1 pound smoked sausage, chopped
   2 cups tomato sauce
   1 cup tomato paste

Directions

1. Melt butter in a skillet, saute celery, bell pepper and onions in butter until tender.
2. Add smoked sausage and cooked rice. Add tomato sauce and tomato paste. Cook for 15 minutes, continue to stir until well done.

Mulatto Rice

Ingredients

1 pound smoked sausage, cut into-inch slices
½ pound bacon, cut into 1-inch pieces
1 cup onions, chopped
⅓ cup celery, chopped
½ cup bell pepper, chopped
1 teaspoon jalapeno pepper, minced
2 (16-ounce) cans tomatoes, chopped
2 cups water
2 cups uncooked long grained rice
1 teaspoon black pepper
½ teaspoons red pepper flakes
2 bay leaves, dried

Directions

1. In a large skillet, saute sausages and bacon.
2. Drain and discard fat. Return meat to pan and add onions, celery, bell pepper and jalapeno pepper.
3. Place in a large saucepan add saute meats and vegetables add tomatoes, water, rice, black pepper and red pepper flakes. Stir and cover.
4. Bring to a boil and cook for 10 minutes. Turn off heat, Pour into a large casserole dish and cover. Bakr a 350 degrees F for 30 minutes.

Stew Beef and Rice

Ingredients

¼ cup fat
1 pound stew beef
1 cup flour
1 teaspoon salt
1 tablespoon pepper
1 quart water
2 cups carrots, sliced
1 cup onions, chopped
1 cup bell pepper, chopped

Directions

1. Melt fat in skillet. Season stew beef and coat with flour; brown in melted fat.
2. In a large saucepan and add seasoned stew beef, carrots, onions and bell pepper. Add water and bring to a boil.
3. Simmer for 1 hour 30 minutes.

Country Fried Steaks and Rice

Ingredients

1 pound cubed steak
1 teaspoon salt
1 teaspoon black pepper
1 cup flour self rising
1 medium onion, slices
1 tablespoon flour
2 cups water
2 cups cooked rice

Directions

1. Season steak with salt and black pepper. Dredge in self-rising flour. Pan fry and drain. Put 1 tablespoon fat in skillet add 1 tablespoon of flour.
2. Brown flour and gradually add water. Add onions. Stir. Add meat and cook for 30 minutes. Stir constantly. Cook until desired doneness. Serve over rice.

Rice and Sweet Potatoes

Ingredients

4 cups sweet potatoes, peeled and sliced
1 cup white long grain rice
1 quart water
1 teaspoon salt
1 cup sugar
1 teaspoon vanilla
1 cup molasses

Directions

1. In a large pot, add potatoes, rice, salt and water. Stir and cover. Cook for thirty minutes on medium heat.
2. Add remaining ingredients and continue to cook for ten minutes or until desired don

Wild Rice Pilaf

Ingredients

1 quart water
1 cup wild rice, rinsed and drained
½ teaspoon sea salt
1 tablespoon vegetable oil
1 cup onions, chopped
2 cups celery, chopped
2 cups carrots, chopped
1 clove garlic, minced
2 teaspoon thyme

2 teaspoons marjoram
1 teaspoon black pepper
½ teaspoon salt
½ teaspoon rosemary

Directions

1. In a large sauce pan, bring 1 quart of water to boil. Add the rice and salt. Stir and return to boiling. Lower the heat, cover and simmer for about one hour or until the rice is tender.
2. Drain and set aside.
3. In a skillet, saute heat oil in skillet, add onions, celery, carrots and garlic. Stir seasoning into vegetables. Cook for 2 minutes.
4. Stir vegetables into rice

Geechee Pigeon Peas and Rice

Ingredients

6cups water
1 ½ cups pigeon peas
3 slices salt pork, diced
1 tablespoon shortening
2 medium yellow onions, chopped
1 stalk celery, chopped
½ cup green pepper, chopped
1 clove garlic, minced
½ teaspoon red pepper flakes
½ teaspoon black pepper
½ teaspoon salt
2 cups water
2 cups rice

Directions

1. In a large saucepan, add water, cleaned and washed peas, salt pork and shortening. Bring to a boil. Turn to low heat for 1 ½ hours.

2. Add celery, green pepper, garlic red pepper flakes, black pepper and salt. Stir. Cook for 15 minutes longer. Stir in water and rice. Cook until rice is done.

Peas and Rice (Hoppin' John)

Ingredients

2 cups cooked dry Black eyed Peas
1 cup long-grain white rice
2 cups water
1 teaspoon salt

Directions

1. Cook peas according to directions of the package.
2. In a large sauce pan, cook rice in water with salt.
3. Cook rice until white and fluffy.
4. Add peas and cook for 10 minutes.
5. Serve.

Conch and Rice

Ingredients

½ pound conch, beaten to tenderize, then cut into ½ -inch strips
3 cups water
1/3 cup vegetable oil

1 onion, chopped
1 teaspoon rosemary

1 teaspoon thyme
1 teaspoon black pepper
1 cup long-grain rice
1 teaspoon salt

Directions

1. Simmer conch in water for 1 hour until tender.
2. Place vegetable oil in skillet and saute onion with rosemary, thyme and black pepper.
3. Place in a large sauce pan with conch add 2 cups water, if needed and stir. Stir in rice.
4. Cook until done add salt.

Rice and Okra

Ingredients

4   strips lean bacon, cut into 1 –inch pieces
3 cups thinly sliced okra
¼ up onion, minced

1 cup washed raw long grain rice
2 cups water
1 teaspoon salt
1 teaspoon cracked black pepper

Directions

1. Cut bacon in 1-inch pieces and fry in a heavy skillet until crisp.
2. Add the okra and onion and cook for 5 minutes. Stir in remaining ingredients and cover simmer
3. Simmer for 30 minutes.

Chicken and Rice

Ingredients

1- 2 ½ pound chicken, cut up
1 cups water
1 cup onion, chopped
1 cup rice
1 teaspoon salt

Directions

1. In a large saucepan, cover the chicken with water. Add onions and celery. Cover.
2. Bring to a boil and simmer for 1 ½ hours. Add rice and cook for 50 minutes. Stir and add salt. Simmer for 10 minutes.

Jollof Rice (African Dish)

Ingredients

½ -2 pounds fryer, cut-up or 2-3 pounds meat, cut up in pieces
1   lemons halved
1 teaspoon salt
2 cloves garlic, minced
½ peanut oil
2 onions, finely chopped
1 green bell pepper, chopped
2(303 cans) whole tomatoes, chopped
1 – 8-ounce can tomato sauce
1 teaspoon red pepper flakes or 1 /2 cayenne pepper
2 bay leaves
2 cups rice
1 quart broth

Directions

1. Wash chicken or meat. Pat dry. Rub with lemon halves, season with salt and garlic. Cover and let marinate in refrigerator for 2 hours.
2. In a 4-quart saucepan, add meat and water. Simmer until tender. Drain. Keep liquid. Wash pot and heat oil. Add chopped vegetables and tomatoes to heated oil in pot.
3. Cook for 5 minutes. Add tomato sauce, pepper, bay leaves and rice.
4. Add 1 quart of broth, Cook 15 minutes add meat.
5. Cook for 10 minutes.

RICE AS A DESSERT

Rice Pudding

Ingredients

> 2 cups cooked long grained rice
> 3 cups milk
> 1 ½ cups sugar
> 4 tablespoons butter
> ½ cup raisins
> 2 teaspoons vanilla
> 1 teaspoon salt
> 1 teaspoon cinnamon

Directions

1. Preheat oven to 350 degrees F. Butter a 2 –quart casserole dish. In a large bowl, add all the ingredient and stir well.
2. Pour into prepared casserole dish. Place in oven and bake for 45 minutes or until firm. Cool. Serve.

Rice Pudding with Peaches

Ingredients

> 3 cups Rice, long-grain white rice
> 2 large eggs
> ¼ cup granulated sugar
> ½ cup brown sugar
> 2 cups evaporated milk
> 1 teaspoon vanilla extract
> ½ teaspoon cinnamon
> 2 cups cling peaches, chopped or 2 ½ cups fresh peaches, chopped

Directions

1 Preheat oven to 325 F degrees. Butter a large casserole dish.
2 In a large bowl, whip together all ingredients.

3   Spoon into buttered dish. Bake at 325 degrees F for 45 minutes.
4   Serve hot or refrigerate 2 hours before servings.

Rice Fritters

Ingredients

2¼ cups cold water
1 cup raw long grain rice
2 packages dry yeast
½ cup lukewarm water
4 eggs, well beaten
1 cup granulated sugar
½ teaspoon ground nutmeg
½ teaspoon salt
2 cups flour
4 cups vegetable oil for frying
Confectioner sugar, 4 X

Directions

1. Place the water and rice in a saucepan and bring to a boil. Lower the heat and cook the rice for 25 to 30 minutes or until it is soft and tender.
2. Drain the rice and place in a mixing bowl. Mash the rice with the back of a spoon and set aside. Dissolve the yeast in the lukewarm water and then ad to the cooked rice. Beat the mixture until well blended. Cover the bowl and let rise for 24 hours. Then beaten in eggs, granulated sugar, nutmeg, salt and flour. Beat well and then let rise for 30 minutes. Heat vegetable oil in a heavy skillet at a temperature of 375 degrees F.
3. Drop the mixture by tablespoons into hot vegetable oil. Fry few at a time.
4. Drain on paper towels. Dust with confectioners' sugar

Pineapple-Cheese Rice Casserole

Ingredients

1 (20-ounce) can pineapple, drained
2 tablespoon pineapple juice
3 cups long grain rice, cooked
1 cup grated Cheddar cheese
½ cup sugar
½ cup dark brown sugar
2 cups cracker crumbs, crushed
½ cup butter, melted

Directions

1. In a large bowl, mix together all ingredients, except cracker crumbs and butter.
2. Pour into buttered casserole dish. Top with cracker crumbs and sprinkle butter on top of cracker crumbs.
3. Bake at 350 degrees for 20 to 30 minutes.

TALKING POINTS:

Georgia's Barrier Sea Island:

Tybee Island

African Connection

Tybee Island is located in Chatman County. It is located 20 minutes from Savannah. Tybee Island is the northeastern-most of Georgia's Barrier Islands. Tybee Island has a total area of 2.7 square miles with land 2.6 square miles and water 0.1 square mile. The population is 3,392. Approximately 660 African -Americans live on Tybee Island. In 1733, James Oglethorpe settled on Tybee Island before settling in Savannah. Tybee Island has a Lighthouse station. The Union soldiers stationed on Tybee Island sieged parts of Georgia while stationed on Tybee

Possible Africa Connection:

Central Republic of Africa –The country is in the central of Africa surrounded by other countries. The tribal groups include Baya, Banda, Mandija, Sara, Mboum and many others. Foods introduced to America include Mangos, fried yams, fried chicken fufu and stews made with okra.

Former Georgia Slaves' Sayings:

PLANTATION LIFE:

1. Duties of Overseers

"Pore white folks used to hang around the quarters, and if they could beat you out of anything they did. They'd trade the slaves out of their rations for calico and stuff. Some of the darkies sold their meat and meal, but if it was found out they got a good whipping.

"The overseer on the plantation had a horn". Said Aunt Ciccly, "a great big ram's horn. I never did see such a big horn. It was 'bout two feet long. The overseer blowed it about two hours before day. The darkieshas to get up and cook their breakfast, and curry their mules and start for the field. They had better be in that field by sun-up. When the sun went down, they stuck their hoes up in the field and quit. Then they was free for the day.

"I've seen slaves sold. I just can remember 'em up on a block with the white men making bids. They was a lot of white mens there, and they bid them off, and the highest bidder got 'em, just like they do at auctions.

"Darkies had partic'lar tasks to perform. Now, like if they was gathering up corn, they shucked corn late to get it in the crib to keep it from being rained on. Sometimes, if they didn't get through before dark they held torches to see by.

"Overseers didn't do no more than what Master told him to, "Aunt Cicely said. "He'd come to the field and if he saw a slave sitting under a tree he'd ask if he was sick, and it was all right if he was sick, but if he was well and laying out under a tree, he get a whipping. The overseer would go back and tell marster, and that night he'd give 'em just as many licks as Marster said, but, he was keerful with the darkies. I never seed the overseer have a billie in his hand. His whip was wropped around the horn of his saddle. He'd unwrop it, and put you on the clock and give you whatever Marster said. Overseers didn't have no rules, but if you resisted him, he'd double your whipping. For killing time or being lazy, you got 25 licks; for stealing, 50 licks; and for running away, that was the worst, if they got you back, you got a hundred licks. I had a cousin to run away, and they got her back from Charleston. The overseer give her a hundred licks. One lick cut the blood, and my Mistis got so mad she throwed that long hair back, I can see that long hair now, and quarreled at Marster. He said he had to make a zample for the other slaves. Mistis said it injured the woman to whip her that way so then Marster made 'em be more careful. Even that warn't so bad as going to the chaingang now. Young darkies now gets mad with me for saying that, but the pertected you, and nobody didn't need to bother you. They pertected you wherever you went.

"We had one man to run away to the north," said Aunt Cicely. "He run away because the overseer whipped him because he went to the adjoining planation to see a woman. You had to have a pass to go off the place, and he went off the place, and he went without a pass. They never did hear nothing of him, They put the hounds on his trail but they never did ketch him. Mistis said there was a trick in it somewhere.

"My mother was Marster's house girl. People didn't d like they do now. She'd be called a chambermaid now. I just staid around the house with the Mistis. I was just, you might say, her little keeper. I stayed around, and waited on her, handed her water, fanned her, kept the flies off her, pulled up her pillow, and done anything she'd tell me to do. My mother combed her hair, and dressed her too. Her hair was long, down to here. (She measured below her waist). She could sit on it. It was a light color, and it was so pretty! I'd call it silver."

"Our marsters kept patrollers to keep us straight. There was some hard-headed darkies like the is now who wanted to go without a pass, and if they didn't have a pass, the patrollers got 'em and brought 'em back home. There's a song about the patrollers," Here Aunt Cicely sang in her musical voice, patting one foot all the while: "Run, nigger, run, the paddy-role will catch you, run, nigger, run, the paddy-role will catch you, run,"

Former Slave Aunt Cicely Cawthon pages 183, 184, 185

Bible Verse(s):

1   By the mercy and truth iniquity I purged; and by the fear of the
    Lord men depart from evil,
2   When a man's ways please the Lord men depart from evil.
    Proverbs 16: 6,7

Chapter 6

Okra

Okra is a favorite vegetable of the Geechees. The word "okra" is an African word.

Boiled Okra

Ingredients

    2 pounds small pods okra, stems at bottom removed
    1 teaspoon salt
    Water to cover

Directions

1. Wash and cut stems from okra.
2. Place in large sauce pan and bring to a boil. Cover.
3. Reduce heat and cook for 30 minutes. Add salt.

Fried Okra

Ingredients

    1 pound okra wash and sliced
    2 eggs well beaten
    1 cup water
    3 cups yellow corn meal

1 teaspoon salt
Peanut oil for frying

Directions

1. Prepare okra as indicated. Set aside.
2. Beat together eggs and water. Place in a bowl and set aside.
3. In a second bowl, combine corn meal and salt
4. Add okra to egg wash Coat well. Then coat with corn meal.
5. Heat oil to 350 degrees F. Fry okra until golden brown.

Okra Gumbo

Ingredients

1 ham bone or 2 ham hocks
4 cups water
2 pounds okra, fresh or frozen, cut up
4 cups tomatoes, cut up
2 cups onion, chopped
1 teaspoon salt
1 teaspoon black pepper

Directions

1. In a large saucepan, boil the meat in the water until almost done. Then add the okra, tomatoes, onions, salt and pepper. Bring to s boil and the turn the heat t simmer and cook for 1 ½ hours or until desired doneness.

2. Serve over rice.

Okra Gumbo with Shrimp

Ingredients

½ pound salt pork, chopped
1 cup onions, chopped

1 cup carrots, chopped
½ cup bell pepper, chopped
½ cup celery, chopped
1 (16-ounce) can whole tomatoes, chopped
1 cup tomato paste
1   (16-ounce) can whole kernel corn
1 (16 –ounce) can creamed corn
1 clove garlic, minced
2 pounds shrimp, deveined and shelled
1 ½ teaspoons seasoned salt

Directions

1. Cover the salt pork, onions, carrots, bell pepper and celery with water in a sauce pan.
2. Cook until meat is tender. Add whole tomatoes, tomato paste, whole kernel corn, and creamed corn.
3. Cover and simmer for 30 minutes. Stir in garlic cook for ten minutes. Stir in shrimp and salt. Cook until shrimp turns pink.

Seafood –Okra Gumbo

Ingredients

1 pound shrimp, peeled
¼ cup oil
1 pound okra, cut
2   cups onions, finely chopped
1 ½ cups flour
2 cups whole tomatoes, hopped
4 cups water
2 teaspoons salt
1 clove garlic, crushed
2 red pods of pepper
1 teaspoon Tabasco sauce
½ pound crab meat, picked over Hot cooked Rice

Directions

1. In a large skillet, cook shrimp in the oil until the shrimp turns bright red color. Set aside.
   In large sauce pot add okra, onions, tomatoes water, salt, garlic and red pepper. Cook for 8 to 10 minutes. Add flour stir until smooth. Simmer for 30 minutes add Tabasco sauce and crabmeat simmer for 30 minutes and then add shrimp cook for 10 minutes. Serve over hot cooked rice

Okra and Tomatoes

Ingredients

2 cups okra, washed, chopped or
1- 10 ounce frozen box chopped okra
1 (No. 2) can tomatoes, chopped
1 teaspoon salt
1 teaspoon garlic, minced

Directions

1. Prepare okra and place all ingredients in a large sauce pan. Stir, cover and bring to a boil. Lower heat and then cook on low heat for 15 minutes.
2. Serve over rice.

TALKING POINTS:

Georgia's Barrier Sea Island

Little Tybee Island – is located the south of Tybee island across Tybee Creek to the southwest.

Possible Africa Connection:

Burkina Faso(Formerly Upper Volta) – The country is located in West Africa. Tribal groups include Mossi, Fulani, Bobo, Lobi, Mande and many others. Foods introduced to America include sugar, pinto beans, okra and sesame seeds. Types of food products include fried yams, fried chicken and stews.

Former Georgia Slaves' Sayings:

PLANTATION LIFE:

1.   Slave Sales

"I ain't wu'k in duh fiel's long though 'cause Massa make me a house boy. I waited on duh tables an' shine duh spoons, an' fo'ks. Hab tuh wu'k hard sometime though w'en dey hab duh 'ception.

"W'en I wuz sixteen yeah ol', Massa sol' me an' some mo' Nigger down Sout', 'Cose us ain't want tuh go, but us hab tuh. We wus chained togedder all duh way frum Norfo'k tuh Savannah. An' w'en us got heah dey put us in a slabe pen right under whar B.H. Labey's sto' use tuh be. Duh nex' mornin' wus wus sale day. Dey brung us heah fuh fuh Cntral Railroad. I wus de only one not sol' tuh duh Central. Dey ays I'se too young. Massa McAlpin he done wants me but fuh pres'dent od duh road tell 'em dat Doctor Arnold hab fu'st pick tuh buy me, Doctor Arnold, he want me fuh a house boy. 'Cause ellie, she duh Doctor's wife, done spent some time in Vaginee at Massa Carter's home, an' she know dat I'se a fuse-class waiter on duh table".

"Dere suh, good as if it wuz jist yesterday," "Dere wuz a pen under duh Pulaski House whar de lock up duh Niggers w'enebuh dey got heah in duh night, an' duh man what hab 'em in charge done stop at duh hotel. Duh rag'lar jail wa'nt fuh slabs but dere wuz speck'lator jail at Hab'sham an' Byron Street. Dey look up duh slabs in duh speck'lator jail when dey brought ;em heah tuh de auction. Mos' ob duh speck'lators come in duh night bfo' duh sale an' stop at duh Pulaski House. Duh slabs wus took tuh duh pen under duh hotel."

George Carter pages 156, 157

2. Trading Slaves

"Slaves wuz treated in most cases lak cattle. A man wen about the country buyin' up slaves and the lak, and he wuz called a speculator, then he'd sell 'em to the highest bidder. Oh! It wuz pitiful to see chillum took from their mothers' breast, mothers sold, husbands sold from wives. One 'oman he wuz to buy had a baby, and of course the baby come befo' he bought her and he wouldn't buy the baby; said he hadn't bargained to buy the baby too, and he just wouldn't. My uncle wuz married but he wuz owned by one master and his wife wuz owned by another. He wuz 'lowed to visit his wife on Wednesday and Saturday; that wuz the earliest time he could git off."

Sally Brown Page 96

2. Slaves Droves
"In those days before the War, slaves were moved from place to place and from State to State in droves, known s "speculators" droves. And sold at public auction. Emmaline Heard's father was born in Virginia, but was brought to Georgia and sold to the Harpers as a plow boy, at the age of eleven."

Emmaline Heard, page 118

Bible Verse(s):

1 Unto thee, O Lord, do I lift up my soul.

2 O my God, I trust in thee: let me not be ashamed, let not mine enemies triumph over me.

Psalm 25. 1, 2

Chapter 7

Side Dishes

Geechees enjoy raising, picking and shopping for vegetables. They like to boil, fry, grill, combine, or baked vegetables to get the best taste.

Sides may be vegetables, pastas or rice. Geechees always have a green, yellow or red vegetable for their main meal. Often times, the Geechees donot eat meats at a meal. Popular side dishes are beans, green and butter beans, dried beans, cabbage, collards, corn, cucumbers, eggplant, lettuce, okra, onions, (green, white, yellow and purple), peas, (field and green), peppers, (bell and hot), squash, (summer), tomatoes(green and ripe) turnips (tops and bottoms), rutabagas.

Macaroni and Cheese

(Thomas Jefferson's slave James Hemings allegedly introduced the cooking of macaroni and cheese dish(Macaroni pie) to African –Americans. This is a popular dish among Geechees. James Hemings studied the "art of cookery" in France in the 1800s.) President Thomas Jefferson's slave James Hemings trained with a French Chef in Annapolis, Maryland and President Jefferson carried James Hemings, the slave to France to study how to prepare and serve properly. Jefferson at the time was a Diplomat to France. While Thomas Jefferson served as President, James Hemings was said to help write the recipes and menus for the White House dinners and special events.) The question remains -how did the dish-Macaroni and Cheese get so popular in Georgia?

Macaroni and Cheese

Ingredients

- 1 box Macaroni Noodles
- 1 cup extra sharp cheddar cheese, shredded
- 1 cup medium cheddar cheese, shredded
- 1 egg, well beaten
- 1 teaspoon salt
- 1 can evaporated milk

Directions

1. Prepare macaroni as indicated on the box.
2. Place in a large bowl add remaining ingredients.
3. Stir well. Place in large baking dish and bake for 30 minutes at 350 degrees F.

Grilled Vegetables

Ingredients

- 1 pound Yukon fingerling potatoes, cut into ½ inch cubes with skins
- 1 pound baby carrots
- 1 red bell pepper, cut into 1-inch pieces
- 1 medium yellow onion, cut into 1 inch quarters
- 1 medium zucchini, cut into 1 –inch chunks
- 1 tablespoon olive oil
- 1 tablespoon cracked black pepper
- 1 teaspoon kosher salt
- 2 tablespoons garlic granules

Directions

1. Boil potatoes until tender. Drain.

2. Place potatoes with all remaining vegetables in a large bowl and coat with olive oil, cracked black pepper. kosher salt and garlic granules.
3. Make 4 tents out of aluminum foil and divide vegetables in each tent cover and grill.
4. Cook on grill for 15 minutes or until vegetables or at desired doneness.

Fried Eggplant

Ingredients

2 eggs beaten
¼ cup cold water
1 teaspoon salt
1 teaspoon black pepper
¾ cup corn meal
¾ cup flour
2 medium eggplants, peeled, cut into slices ½ inch thick
Vegetable
oil

Direction

1. In a bowl mix eggs, and water with a whisk.
2. Place flour meal, salt and pepper in a plastic lockable bag.
3. Dip slices of eggplant into egg mixture and then into flour mixture.
4. Pour at least 2 inches of oil in the skillet.
5. Heat oil in skillet for deep-frying. Fry eggplant until golden brown on both sides.
6. Serve hot.

Fried Plantain (Plantains look like green bananas, but they have texture similar to white potatoes.)

Ingredients

4 large ripe, firm plantains
1 cup cooking oil
Salt to taste

Directions

1. Peel the plantains and cut into 1-inch pieces. Heat the oil in a heavy skillet. Fry the plantains until golden brown.
2. Remove the plantains from the oil.
3. Drain and sprinkle with salt.
4. The plantain can be used as a side dish.

Lima Beans and Sausages

Ingredients

2 teaspoons olive oil
½ cup onions, chopped
¼ cup bell pepper, chopped
2 cups beef sausage, chopped
1 -10 ounce frozen lima beans
2 teaspoon thyme
2 cups carrot coins
½ teaspoon salt
1 cup chicken broth

Directions

1. Heat oil in a skillet and saute onions and bell pepper. Stir in sausages and stir well. Place in a medium sauce pan.
2. Add remaining ingredients and cook on medium heat for 15 minutes.

Eggplant Casserole

Ingredients

1   medium eggplants, peeled, boiled and washed
2 tablespoons butter
¼ cup milk
3 eggs, well beaten
1 cup onion, chopped finely

1 teaspoon salt
½ teaspoon black pepper
1 cup buttered cracker crumbs

Directions

1. Preheat oven to 350 degrees F. Butter a3-quart casserole dish. Set aside.
2. In a large bowl add eggplant, butter, milk, eggs, onions, salt and pepper.
3. Stir well. Pour into casserole dish. Top with buttered crumbs.
4. Bake for 30 to 40 minutes.

Fresh Green Beans with Onions

Ingredients

2 pounds green beans, picked and cut
1 teaspoon salt
1 tablespoon butter
2 medium red onions, sliced thinly
1 clove garlic, minced
½ cup vinegar

Directions

1. Use a 6-quart pot of water to boil add salt and green beans.
2. Cook green beans for 5 minutes and then drain. Set aside.
3. In a large skillet melt butter and add red onions and garlic.
4. Stir in green beans and vinegar. Cook for 15 minutes

Baked Potatoes with Sour Cream Topping

Ingredients

1   Idaho Baking potatoes, boiled for 15 minutes, coat with kosher
salt and then baked for 30 minutes

Directions

1. Boil potatoes for 15minute. Cool and then bake for 30 minutes split
in half and serve with special sour cream.

Sour Cream Topping

Ingredients

> 1 ½ cups sour cream
> ¼ cup fresh parsley, minced
> 2 tablespoons green onion, chopped
> ¼ cup cucumber, finely chopped
> 1 large garlic clove, minced
> ¼ teaspoon white pepper
> ½ teaspoon salt

Directions

1. Thoroughly combine all ingredients. Chill for 3 hours and then serve as toppers for baked potatoes.

Boiled Potatoes in Milk

Ingredients

> 4-5 small red potatoes, washed and cut into half
> 1 large onion, chopped
> 4 cups water
> 1   tablespoon butter
> 2 tablespoons flour
> 2 cups milk
> 1 teaspoon paprika
> 1 teaspoon salt
> 1 teaspoon black pepper

Directions

1. In a large sauce pan, cook potatoes and onions in boiling water until potatoes are tender. Drain water from potatoes and onions.
2. In a saucepan, melt butter and add flour gradually. Slowly add milk and stir until mixture thickens. Add to potatoes and onion mixture and then add paprika, salt and black pepper.
3. Cook for 10 minutes, stirring until consistency reaches a thick consistency.

Fried Green Tomatoes

Ingredients

> 4 large green tomatoes, washed and sliced ¼ inch thickness
> 1 tablespoons salt
> 1 ½ teaspoons black pepper
> 1   teaspoon garlic salt
> 2 eggs well beaten
> 1 cup water
> 1 ½ cups self-rising flour
> 1 cup corn meal
> Oil for frying

Directions

1. Wash and slice tomatoes. Pat dry . Season with salt, pepper and garlic salt.
2. Bring to a boil for five minutes.
3. Mix eggs with water and stir well.
4. In a separate bowl, mix together flour and corn meal.
5. Heat oil to 350 degrees F. for frying.
6. Dip each tomato slice in egg mixture and then coat with flour- corn meal mixture and then fry each slice to golden brown.

Stewed Tomatoes

Ingredients

> 4cups fresh tomatoes, peeled and chopped or 2 (No. 303 cans) tomato, chopped
> ¼ cup green bell pepper, chopped
> 1 tablespoon onion, minced
> 1 teaspoon sugar
> 1 teaspoon salt
> ½ teaspoon black pepper

Directions

1. In a 2-quart saucepan, add tomatoes and remaining ingredients. Stir well. Cover,
2. Turn heat to medium high until tomatoes begin to cook. Then turn down to low cook for 20 minutes.

Yellow Squash Casserole

Ingredients

2 cups water
1 pound yellow summer squash, washed and sliced
1 teaspoon salt
½ cup onion, chopped

½ cup evaporated milk
2 eggs, well beaten
1 ½ cups crackers, crushed

1 tablespoon butter

Directions

1. Preheat oven to 325 degrees F and butter a 2 quart casserole dish.
2. In a large saucepan, cook squash in water until tender. Drain and cool. In a bowl, beat together salt onions, milk, and eggs. pour into a 2 quart casserole dish.
3. Top with cracker crumbs and dot with butter. Bake for 30 minutes.

Red Beans and Rice

Ingredients

2 quarts water
3 cups red beans or pinto beans
1 tablespoon sugar
½ teaspoon red pepper flakes
½ tablespoon fat

2 ham hocks
1 teaspoon salt

Directions

1. Wash beans and place in a large sauce pan. Add remaining
   ingredients and boil for five minutes and then lower heat.
3. Cook for one hour or until desired doneness. Serve over rice.

Baked Beans

Ingredients

3   tablespoons shortening
¼ cup green pepper, chopped
¼ cup celery chopped
½ cup onions, chopped
¼ pound ground beef
2   slices bacon, chopped
2 cups ketchup
½ cup molasses

1tablespoon mustard
1 teaspoon seasoning salt
½ cup tomato sauce
No. 2 ½ can pork –n-beans

Directions

1. In a skillet, heat shortening saute green pepper, celery and onions.
   Add ground beef and cook until all redness is gone. Cool and
2. Drain. In a bowl mix all remaining ingredients together in a large
   casserole dish.
3. Bake for 30 minutes and bake at 325 degrees F.

Boiled Fresh Field Peas(choice –Black eye, Purple Hull, Crowder(brown, cream or speckled), or Lady Peas)

Ingredients

    4 cups Fresh peas, shelled and washed
    1 cured pig's tail, chopped
    1 onion, chopped
    1 teaspoon salt
    1 teaspoon red pepper flakes
    1 gallon water
    1   tablespoons fat

Directions

1. Pick through peas and wash.
2. Place all ingredients in a large saucepan, and cover. Bring to a boil for fir minutes.
3. Cook over low heat for 1 hour and serve. Serve over corn bread or with rice.

TALKING POINTS:

Georgia's Barrier Sea Islands:

Whitemarsh Island – Whitemarsh Island is located in Chatman County

The total area is 6.6 square miles; 5.9 square miles in land and 0.7 square miles of water. More than 500 African –Americans live on Whitemarsh Island.

Wilmington Island -Chatman County

Wilmington Island is located on the Atlantic Ocean. The island has a total area of 9.5 square miles, land 8.4 sure miles and 1 square mile of water.

Approximately 400 African descent live on Wilmington Island.

Possible Africa Connection:

Cape Verde –Cape Verde is located in the Atlantic Ocean in the Western area of Africa. Foods introduced include rice dishes, fish, coriander, cloves sweet potatoes, black pepper, curd, cream pumpkin, lard and salt.

Georgia Former Slaves' Sayings:

PLANTATION LIFE:

1.   Books on the Plantation

"We didn't had no schools. Dey wouldn't let de white chllen tell us about books.

One day I axed about sumpin' in a book, and one de chillen say, 'Mama tole me not to learn you nuttin' or she'd whup me'."

Former Slave Shang Harris page 120

2.   Yankees on the Plantation

"George's master enlisted and was made a Captain. He wanted to take George with him as a body guard. He wanted to take George with him as a body guard, but George thought there was too much shouting. The master would come home for a visit about every six weeks and as soon as he reached the place, he called for George. Old George's face beamed with pride as he told us this.

Conditions changed a great deal during the war. The mistress was always worried for fear the master would be injured. The overseer tended the farm, so the slaves were not quite as comfortable as they had been.

Once the Yankees came by the plantation enroute to Macon. They drove into the gate and loaded wagons with hams, shoulders and other food stuffs. Their own mules were about worn out so they took the master's best mules from the stables and left theirs. They ransacked the large house, threw the furnishings out and burned them. While this was taking place, George was hiding I the woods.

After that occurred, the master lost whatever wealth he had. The Confederate money was useless and about the master had left was land. He did not even have money to pay his servants. For this reason, many of the slaves left him as soon as they were freed.

George remained with him for about three months after being freed. Then, Mr. Dudley Hughes went to Virginia to secure laborers for his cotton field in Twiggs County, Georgia."

Former Slave George Caulton page 173

Bible Verse(s)

1 The Lord is my shepherd; I shall not want.

1 He maketh me to lie down in green pastures: he leadeth me beside the still waters.
2 He restoreth my soul: he leadeth me in the paths of righteousness for his name's sake.
3 Yea though I walk through the valley of the shadow of death, I will fear no evil: for thou art with me; thy rod and thy staff they comfort me.
4 Thou prepares a table before me in the presence of mine enemies: thou anointest my head with oil;
my cup runneth over.
5 Surely goodness and mercy shall follow me all the days of my life: and I will dwell in the house of the Lord forever.

Psalm 23

Chapter 8

Grits

Grits are a staples on many breakfast tables in Georgia. Quaker Oats are the world largest producer of grits since 1862. Grits are made from corn.

Fried Grits

Ingredients

    2 cups cooked grits, cold
    1 teaspoon black pepper
    1 teaspoon salt
    1 egg, well beaten
    1 cup flour
    ¼ cup fat for frying

Directions

1. In a bowl, add cold grits, black pepper, salt and egg
2. Stir well. Form into patties and refrigerate. Put flour on a plate. Roll each patty in the flour. Dust off.
3. Heat fat in a skillet and fry each patty until golden brown on both sides.

Grits and Cheese Casserole

Ingredients

- 3 cups cooked Grits
- 2 eggs, beaten
- 1 cup shredded cheddar cheese, mild
- ½ teaspoon black pepper

Directions

1. Preheat oven to 350 degrees F. Cook grits as instructed on package. Grease a two quart casserole dish.
2. In a large bowl add all ingredients and stir well.
3. Pour into a two -quart -greased casserole dish. Cook for 30 minutes. Cool Serve.

Shrimp and Grits

Ingredients

- 1 pound shrimp, cooked, small sized
- 2 ½ cups grits, cooked
- 1 ½ cups grated extra sharp cheese
- 2 large eggs
- ¼ cup milk
- 2 cloves garlic
- ½ teaspoon cayenne pepper

Directions

1. Clean shrimp and boil until done.
2. Cook grits according to package directions
3. Butter 4 quart casserole dish. Preheat oven to 350 degrees F.
4. In a large bowl, combine cooked shrimp, grits, 1 cup cheese, eggs, milk and cayenne pepper. Beat well.
5. Pour into buttered casserole dish. Top with ½ cup cheese.
6. Bake for 30 minutes or until done.

Shrimp 'n Grits in a Skillet

Ingredients

1 ½ cups grits, cooked

1 1/2 cloves garlic
¼ cup onion, minced
¼ cup celery finely chopped
2 slices bacon, crispy fried
2 ½ pounds shrimp peeled and deveined
1 teaspoon ground cracked black pepper
1 teaspoon salt

Directions

1. Cook grits according to package directions.
2. Prepare vegetables. Set aside.
3. Fry bacon. Saute vegetables in bacon fat.
4. Add shrimp and cook for 8 minutes over low heat. Season.
5. Serve over hot grits.

Georgia's way of cooking Grits.

Georgians cook grits in hot water. They usually chose old-fashioned grits. The Georgians like to stir in the grits while the water is boiling. There usually is a 3 parts water to 1 part grits. The grits are seasoned with salt and sometimes, hoop cheddar cheese.

TALKING POINTS

Georgia Barrier Sea Island

Oatland Island-The island is home to the Oatland Island Education Center which has a variety of wild life in their own habitats. These animals include alligators, wolves, bobcats, bears, deer, bald eagles, egrets, and heron. The island is located in Chatman County near Wilmington River.

Possible Africa Connection

Senegal-Senegal is in western part of Africa. Tribal groups include Wolof, Pular, Serer, Mandinka and many others. Foods introduced include guinea fowls, ducks, rabbits, smoked meats and peanuts.

Former Georgia Slaves' Sayings:

PLANTATION LIFE:

1. Naming Slave Babies

   "There was great rejoicing over the birth of a negro baby and the white folks were called upon to give the little black stranger a name."

   Former Slave Adeline Willis page 164

2. Washing Clothes

   "Course evvybody cooked on pen fireplaces dem days, and da was whar us picked out dem cotton seeds,'round datbig old fireplace in de kitchen. All de slves et together up dar in dat old kitchen. Slave quarter was jus' little one room log cabins what had chimblies made of sticks and red mud. de cracks, andsomctimes dey chinked up cracks in de roof wid red mud. Dere warn't no glass windows in dem cabins, and dey didn't have but one window of no sort; it was jus' house, close by de big old spring whar de wash-place was. Dey had long benches for de washtubs to set on, a big old battlin' block whar dey beat de dirt out of de clothes. Dem Niggers would sing, and deir battlin' sticks kept time to de music. You could hear de singin' and de sound of de battlin' sticks from a mighty long ways off.

   Former Georgia slaves

3. Reading and Writing on the Plantation

   "I ain't never heared nothin' 'bout no jails in slavery time. What dey done den was 'most beat

De life out of de Niggers to make 'em behave. Ma was brung to Bairdstown and sold on de block to Marse Joe long 'fore I was borned, but I ain't never seed no slaves sold. Lordy, Mistess, ain't nobody never told you it was agin de law to larn a Nigger to read and write in slavery time? White folks would chop your hands off.' Why, Mistess, a Nigger widout no hands wouldn't be able to wuk much, and his owner couldn't sell him for nigh a much as he could git for a slave wid good hands. Dey jus' beat 'em up bad when dey cotched 'em studyin' readin' and writin', but folks did tell 'bout some of de owners dat cut off one finger evvy time dey cotch a slave tryin' to git larnin'. How-some-ever, dere was some Niggers dat wanted larnin' so bad dey would study by de light of light'ood torches;

But one thing sho, dey better not let no white folks find out 'bout it, and if dey was lucky 'nough to be able to keep it up 'til dey larned to read de Bible, dey kept it a close secret,"

Former Slave Aunt Mary

4. Master's Doctor

When asked if Mr. Willis had the slaves taught to read and write, Henry hooted at the idea, saying emphatically, "No, Mam, 'Ole Marse' wus sho hard about dat. He said 'Niggers' wus sho hard about dat. He said "Niggers' wus made by de good Lord to work, and onct when my Uncle stole a book a and wuz a trying to learn how to read and write, Marse Jasper hd the white doctor take off my Uncle's fo' finger right down to de 'fust jint'. Marster said he fixed dat darky as a sign fo de res uv 'em! No, Miss us wuzn't larned!"

Former Slave Henry Rogers page 144

5. Children Learning

"When asked if she went to school she replied, "Chillun didn't know what a book wus in dem days

Didn' learn us nothin' but to churn and clean up house and tend to dat boy, and spin, and cyard a roll'

Former Slave Easter Jones Page 149

Bible Verse(s):

1 And seeing the multitudes, he went up into a mountain, he went up into a mountain: and when he was set, his disciples, came unto him:

2And he opened his mouth, and taught them, saying,

3Blessed are the poor in spirit: for theirs is the kingdom of heaven.

4Blessed are they that mourned, for they shall be comforted.

5Blessed are the meek: for they shall inherit the earth.

2 Blessed are they which do hunger and thirst after righteousness: for they shall be filled

3 Blessed are the merciful: for they shall obtain mercy.

4 Blessed are the pure in heart: for they shall see God.

5 Blessed are the peacemakers: for they shall be called the children of God.

6 Blessed are they are prosecuted for righteousness' sake: for theirs is the kingdom of heaven.

7 Blessed are ye, when men shall revile you, and shall say all manners of evil against you falsely, for my sake.

Mathew 5:1-11

Chapter 9

Collard Greens and Other Greens

Collard greens are the most popular leafy green eaten in Georgia. Methods of cooking greens vary due to the choices of cooks. Selected variations of cooking methods have been included.

Old -Fashioned Collard Greens

Ingredients

    1 bunch of collards
    1 medium size country cured meat
    3 tablespoons canola oil
    2 tablespoons pickled pepper sauce
    1 teaspoon salt

Directions

1. Wash collards and cut into bite size pieces. Set aside.
2. Wash and bring meat to boil in a quart of water in a saucepan cook until meat is tender. Pour water off.
3. Add one quart of clear water to meat and bring to boil; add collard and stir. Cover and cook 30 minutes and pickled Pepper sauce. Stir, add salt and canola oil. Stir and cover. Continue to cook on medium heat for one hour.

Collard Greens with Bouillon Cubes

Ingredients

1 bunch collard greens

6 cups water
6 bouillon cubes (chicken)
1 teaspoon salt
2 tablespoons canola oil
½ teaspoon red pepper flakes
¼ cup chopped onion

Directions

1. Wash and cut up collard greens. Set aside. In a large 6 quart stock pot, add water and crumbled bouillon cubes to boiling. Stir in remaining ingredients.
2. Cover and boil for 10 minutes. Reduce heat and cook for 1 hour. Stir and cook for desired doneness.

Steamed Collard Greens

Ingredients

1 bunch collard greens, washed and cut up
8 slices ham, cut up

1 cup water
1 teaspoon salt
½ cup onion, diced
1 jalapeno pepper, minced

Directions

1. Wash and cut up greens as indicated
2. In a Dutch oven, cook ham slices until done
3. Gradually stir in collard greens, add water slowly.
4. Cover when collard greens have cooked down.

5. Season with salt, onions and jalapeno pepper
6. Continue to cook until desired doneness.

Collard Greens and Boiled Okra

Ingredients

2bunches collard greens, washed and cut up
2 ham hocks, washed
2 teaspoons salt
1 teaspoon red pepper flakes
10 pods okra, fresh or frozen

Directions

1. Prepare collard greens as indicated.
2. In a large stock pot, fill with 2 quarts of water and boil ham hocks.
3. Remove ham hocks and stir in collard greens. Cover and bring to a boil.
4. Boil for five minute, add ham hocks and then cook on medium heat for 1 hour.
5. Stir add salt, red pepper flakes. Cook for 10 minutes, Place okra pods on top of cooked collard greens and cook for an additional ten minutes.

Turnip Greens with Bottoms

Ingredients

1 Country cured Turkey Wing Drummette
Or 2 country cured neck bones
1   bunch turnip green tops, picked
1 teaspoon red pepper flakes
2 teaspoons salt
2 tablespoons sugar
2 tablespoons olive oil

Turnip green roots (Bottoms) - peeled and washed and sliced

Directions

1. In large stockpot, boil cured turkey wing until done. Remove wing, chop meat and destroy bones.
2. Add one quart of water to broth and meat in the stock pot.
3. Add cleaned greens tops and stir well; add red pepper flakes, salt, sugar and olive oil
4. Cover and bring for a boil for five minutes, turn to low and cook for 45 minutes. Stir well
5. Place turnip bottoms on top of cooked greens cover and continue to cook for 30 minutes.
6. Stir well. Serve.

Turnip Greens and Corn Meal Dumplings

Ingredients

2 bunches turnip greens
½ cup salt pork, diced
1 pint water
1 teaspoon sugar
1/ 2 teaspoon red pepper flakes

Directions

1. Wash turnip greens two to three times to rid the greens from sand and chop greens
2. In a large sauce pan, boil salt pork in water until tender. Stir in turnip greens with the meat.
3. Stir down until all of the greens are covered. Reduce heat and add sugar and red pepper flakes.
4. Boil down. adding dumplings

Dumplings

Ingredients

    3   cups corn meal mix
    ½ cup shortening
    ½ cup water

Directions

1. In a mixing bowl cut shortening into corn meal. Add water.
2. Roll into 1-inch in diameter balls. Drop balls into turnip greens. Cook covered for 20 minutes.

Steamed Cabbage with Ham Hocks

Ingredients

    4   ham hocks
    1 head green cabbage, shredded
    1 onion, sliced
    1 bell pepper, sliced seeds removed
    1 teaspoon seasoning salt
    ½ teaspoon black pepper
    1 tablespoon olive oil

Directions

1. In a saucepan, add water and cook ham hocks until done. Stir in all ingredients, cover and cook for 10 minutes.
2. Stir and cook additional 5 minutes and serve.

Poke Sallet Greens and Eggs

Ingredients

    1 bunch Poke greens
    2 strips bacon

6 eggs, beaten
1 teaspoon salt
½ teaspoon black pepper

Directions

1. Wash greens and boil for 30 minutes Drain and discard water. Set aside.
2. In a sauce pan, cook bacon until crispy add greens and eggs.
3. Beat well cook until eggs are done.

Steamed Spinach

Ingredients

1 bunch spinach
½ cup water
½ cup vinegar
1 teaspoon salt
1 tablespoon olive oil

Directions

1. Wash spinach. Set aside.
2. In a medium sauce pan, add remaining ingredients and bring to a boil.
3. Add spinach and stir well. Turn on medium heat and steam for 10 minutes. Stir well.
4. Serve.

TALKING POINTS:

Georgia Barrier Sea Island

Dutch Island –The island is located in Chatman County.

Possible Africa Connection:

Cote D' Ivorie (formerly known as Ivory Coast) – The county is located of West Africa. Tribal groups are Akan, Mandes, Voltaiques(Gur), Kous and many others. Foods introduced to America are rice dishes, soups, coconut milk, baked sweet potatoes, peanut candy, onions, taro, green beans, eggplants, spices, akee apples and pineapples.

Former Georgia Slaves' Sayings:

PLANTATION LIFE:

1.   Slave cabins

"It wuz 'way off in de woods. Pa cut down trees an' built us a log cabin. He made de chimbly out of sticks an' red mud, an' put iron bars crost de fireplace to hang pots on for to bile our

Vittuls an' made ovens for de bakin'. De bes' way to cook 'tatoes wuz to roas' 'em in de jackets on.

Dey ain' nothin' better tastin' dan ash-roasted 'tatoes wid good home=made butter to eat wid 'em.

An 'us had de butter, 'cause us kep' two good cows. Ma had her chickens an' tukeys an' us raised plenty of hogd, so we nebber wuz widout meat. Our reg'lar Sunday breakfsd'wuz fish what pa

Cotch out of de crick. I used to git tired out of fish den, but a mess of fresh crick fish would sho' be jus' right now.

"Us always kep' a good gyarden full of beans, corn, onions, peas an' 'taters, an' dey warn't nobody could beat us at raisin' lots of greens, 'specially turnips an' colla'd greens. Us saved heaps of dry peas an' beans, an' dried lots of peaches an' apples to cook in winter. When de wind wuz howlin' an' de groun' all kivvered wid snow, ma would make dried frui puffs for us, dat sho' did hit de spot."

"When I wuz 'bout eight years old, day sont me to school. I had to walk from Eps Bridge Road to Knox Institute no. I toted my blue back speller in one hand and my dinner bucket I de other.

CUs wore homespun dresses wid bonnet to match. De bonnets wuz all made in one piece an' had drawstrings on de back to make 'em fit, an' slats in de brims to make 'em stiff and straight. Our dresses wuz made long to keep our legs warm. I don't see, for to save, how dey keeps dese young-uns iron freezin' now since dey let 'em go roun' mos' naked.

"Our reg'lar preacher wuz a colored man named Harrison, but Mr. Cobb preached to us a lots of times. He wuz awould lak to see you try to make boys go 'roun' lookin' lak now. white genman, an' ha may de oulda act all night an' lissen long as us sung den old songs. Some of 'em I done clar forgot, but de one I lak has' goes lak dis:

'I want to us an angel

An' wid de angels stah'

A crown upon my forehead

And a harp widin my han'

"When I jined de church dere wuz 35 of us baptized de same day in de crick back of de church.

While preacher Brown wuz a baptizin' us, a big crowd wuz standin' on de bank a shoutin' an

Singin', Some of 'em wuz a prayn' too. Atter de baptizin' wuz done dey make a big dinner on de

Groun's for de new members, but de didn't see no jugs dat day. Jus' had plenty of good somethin't'eat.

"When us warn't in school, us an' my brudder wukked in de fiel'wid pa. In cotton plantin'time, pa fixed up to rows an; us drap de seeds in 'em. Nex' day us would rake dirt over 'em wid wooden rakes.

"In dem days 'roun' de house an' in de fiel' boys jus' wo' one piece of clo'es. It wuz jus' a long piece

Of clo'es. It wuz jus' a long shirt. Dey didn't know nothin' else den, but I sho' would lak to see you try to make boys go 'roun' lookin' lax dat now.

"Day hired us out to Mr. Mr. Jack Weir's fambly when I wuz 'bout fo'teen years old to do washin', ironin' an' cleanin' up de house, an' I wukked for 'em 'till I married. Dey lemme dat all I wants.

Were at de house an' paid me in old clo'es, middlin', meat, sirup, 'tatoes, an' wheat flour, but a never old git no money for pay. Not nary a cent.

"Dey kep' it up 'til de corn wuz all shucked, an' sey didn't stop eatin' an' drinkin' dat hot coffee

Long as dey could swallow. Ain't nobody fed 'em no better backbones, an' spareribs, turnip greens, 'tato pies, an' sich lak dan my ma sat out for 'em. Old time ways lak dat is done gone for good now.

Folkses ain't lak dey used to be. Dey's all done got greedy an' don't keer 'bout nothin' for nobody else no more.

"Ma combed our hair wid a Jim Crow comb, oracyard, as some folkses called 'em. If our hair wuz bad nappy she put some cotton in de comb to keep it from pullin' so bad, 'cause it wuz awful hard to comb.

"Evvybody tried to raise plenty of gourds, 'cause dey wuz so hand' y to use for dippers den. Water Wuz toted from de spring an' kep' in piggins. Don't spec' you ebber did see a piggin. Dats a wooden bucket wid wire hoops 'roun' it …."

Former Slave Elisha Doc Carey pages 4,5, and 6

Bible Verse(s):

19 Lay not up for yourselves treasures upon earth, where moth and rust doth corrupt, and where thieves break through and steal:

20 But lay up for yourselves treasures in heaven, where neither moth and rust doth corrupt, and where thieves do not break through nor steal:

21 For where your treasure is, there will your heart be also.

Mathew 6: 19, 20 and 21

Chapter 10

Smoke House Meats and Pork

Smoke houses were used to cure and store meats on the plantation. The slaves would kill the hogs, chickens, fish, beef and lamb.

Shrimp and other fish would be dried.

The cured pork sides, tails, hams, ham hocks and skins would be used as seasoning meats for boiled vegetables.

The slaves knew special recipes for sugar curing meats, smoking meats and making country hams.

In this section, some fresh and smoked meat recipes will be used.

Smoked and Dried Shrimp

Ingredients

    5   pounds jumbo shrimp, cleaned and deveined
    1 pound kosher salt

Directions

    1. Clean and devein shrimp place in a large plastic bowl, cover with water and stir in kosher salt. Cover and refrigerate 24 hour.

2. Wash, dry and string shrimp on a cord string with a large knitting needle. Smoke shrimp and hang to dry in smoke house.
3. When completely dry serve as snack.

Fried Center Cuts Pork Chops

Ingredients

6 center cut pork chops
1 teaspoon sea salt
1 teaspoon black pepper
1 teaspoon garlic granules
2 cups self rising flour
3 cups peanut oil for frying

Directions

1. Wash and pat dry pork chops.
2. Season chops and cot both sides of chops with flour.
3. Heat peanut oil for 350 degrees F and fry each chop to golden brown.

Smothered Pork Chops

Ingredients

6 thinly sliced pork chops
1 teaspoon salt
1 teaspoon black pepper

1 cup flour
2 tablespoons shortening
1 cup water
1 onion, sliced

Directions

1. Wash and season pork chops. Coat with flour. Save 1 tablespoon flour.

2. Heat oil in skillet and fry to golden brown.
3. Remove all but 1 tablespoon fat and 1 tablespoon flour to skillet. Stir flour in fat to make a smooth paste. Gradually add water.
4. Stir until thickens add slices on onions cook for 5 minutes add pork chops and stir well cook until bubbly.

Ribs

(Ribs may be selected by slabs, country cuts, regular ribs)

Oven Barbequed Slab Ribs

Ingredients

1 - 5 pound slab ribs
1 teaspoon salt
1 teaspoon black pepper
1 teaspoon cayenne pepper
Barbeque Sauce
2 cups ketchup
1 tablespoon mustard
2 teaspoon hot sauce
2 cups molasses
½ cup vinegar

Directions for barbeque sauce

1. Measure all ingredients in a medium sauce pan.
2. Cook over medium heat until for 1 minutes. Stirring well.
3. Use when needed.

Directions for cooking slab ribs:

1. Clean and wash ribs; pat dry.
2. Season with salt, black pepper and cayenne pepper. Place in a baking dish meat side up.
3. Bake in oven at 375 degrees F for 1 hour.
4. Baste with barbecue sauce.

Baby Back Ribs

Ingredients

2 Pounds Baby Back Ribs
1 recipe marinade
1 recipe Pork Rib Rub

Directions

1. Clean ribs.
2. Marinade over night
3. Discard marinade and season with rub;
4. Smoke for 4 hours.

Rub Recipe

Ingredients

1 tablespoon kosher salt
1 tablespoon black pepper
1 teaspoon thyme
1 garlic clove, minced
½ cup dark brown sugar

Directions

1. Combine all ingredients in a bowl and cover until use.

Marinade
1 cup soy sauce
1 can beer
½ cup light brown sugar.

Directions

1. Combine all ingredients
2. Stir together.
3. Pour over ribs.

4. Refrigerate for 24 hours.
5. Discard marinade and follow recipe.

Pulled Pork

Ingredients

5 pounds Boston Butt
1 tablespoon cracked black pepper
1 tablespoon salt
1 tablespoon garlic granules

Directions

1. Wash and pat dry meat. Place in aluminum foil and season.
2. Place in a 325 degrees F oven for 3 hours.
3. Cool meat and take a fork and shred meat from bone. Place in a roasting pan.
4. Pour barbeque sauce over meat. Cover with aluminum foil and roast in oven for 20 minutes.

Barbeque Sauce

Ingredients

1 cup molasses
1 cup tomato sauce
½ cup soy sauce
1 cup brown sugar
1 cloves garlic minced
1 teaspoon salt
And discard cloves and
1 teaspoon cayenne pepper
2 cups tomato paste
1 cup onion, chopped

1 quart water

Directions

1. In a large saucepan and cook on low heat 45 minutes.
2. Use as directed.

Baked Fresh Ham

Ingredients

1 Fresh Ham
1 tablespoon salt
1 cloves
2 bay leaves

Directions

1. In a large sauce pot cover ham with water and add seasonings. Cover and boil for 1 hour.
2. Remove ham and discard bay leaves and cloves.
3. Bake ham in oven at 325 degrees F. for 1 hour.

Specialty Cuts

Ingredients

Boiled Chitterlings (Chitterlins')
Ingredients
10 pounds bucket chitterlings, cleaned
1   bay leaves
2 medium onions, quartered
1 cup vinegar
3 cloves garlic
1 medium carrot, chopped
2 ribs, celery, chopped
1 teaspoon salt

Directions

1. If frozen, thaw chitterlings, clean and drain. Place chitterlings in large 6 quart stock pot. Cover with water and add remaining ingredients.
2. Bring to a boil for 10 minutes and then cook on low to medium heat for 2 to 3 hours or until done. When done. Drain. The chitterlings may be diced and served over rice, pickled or fried.

(Note on Chitterlings Safety: Research has shown that eating chitterlings may prove to be hazardous for people with diabetes and others who are chronically ill. It has been reported that the bowels may get a type of bacteria called Clostridium perfringens type C, which produces toxins that can cause a severe infection called enteritis necroticans. This infections kills cells in the intestines of humans. Even though, the disease is rare care must be taken for the proper cleaning, the cooking and refrigeration. One doctor reported that diabetic patients, especially those who do not have their illness well controlled, are at an increased risk from such an infection. That is because poor control of the disease leads to protein malnutrition, reduced movement in the intestines and slow emptying of the stomach. All of these symptoms can contribute to the accumulation of toxins and the excessive growth of bacteria cause the body to have difficulty fighting of enteritis necroticans if the bacteria C perfringens were contained. The common name for the disease is pigbel, may lead to surgery for removal of some of the intestines or death.) Taken from New England Journal of Medicine.

Boiled Pig's Feet

Ingredients

4-6 pigs' feet, cleaned and split into halves
1tablespoon salt
4 ribs celery
2 medium onions, quartered
1 teaspoon red pepper flakes
Water to cover

Directions

1. In a large pot, place cleaned and split pigs' feet, salt, celery and onions, red pepper and water to cover.
2. Boil for 5 minutes and cover. Simmer for 2-3 hours or until done. Drain and serve with vinegar and hot sauce.

Pig's Tail Soup

Ingredients

6 pigs tails cut up
1 cup celery, chopped
1 teaspoon salt
1 pound baby carrots
1 onion, chopped
½ pound small red potatoes
2cups frozen green peas
1 teaspoon red pepper flakes
½ teaspoon salt
2teaspoons garlic cloves, minced

Directions

1. In a large sauce pot, add chopped pig's tail and cover with water. Stir in celery and salt. Bring to a boil and cook for 30 minutes.

Discard the water. Retain the pig's tail and add remaining ingredients to the pot and cover with water. Cover and bring to a boil and cook until vegetables are done.

Salt Fat Back, Salt Pork or Streak of Lean,(sometimes thought of as the same cut of meat.

Pork Belly salted down with curing salt and stored for 6 month before use.)

Ingredients

6 slices salted pork side, sliced into 3 inch x 2 inch pieces

water to cover

Directions

1. Boil pork slices in a skillet for 30 minutes. Drain and pat dry.
2. Fry meat in skillet until done. Drain serve. Serve with hot biscuits.

Hog Head Cheese (Souse Meat)

Ingredients

1 hog's head cleaned and eyes removed
1 tablespoon salt
1 onion, diced
1 tablespoons red pepper flakes
1 tablespoon sea salt
1 cup celery, chopped
1 quarts vinegar
2 tablespoons, cracked black pepper

Directions

1. In a large sauce pot, place entire head, tablespoon salt and boil covered until meat falls off the bones.
2. Remove hog's head and retain broth, remove any bones in broth. Chop meat from head. Peel outside from tongue.
3. Discard outer covering of tongue and chop inside of tongue.
4. Place all meat and remaining ingredients in sauce pot. Stir well.
5. Place in a bowl, cover and refrigerate for 24 hours before serving.

Baked Pork Liver

Ingredients

2pounds pork liver, cleaned and membranes removed
1 teaspoon salt
1 teaspoon black pepper
5 tablespoons melted butter

2 cups mashed potatoes flakes

Directions

1. Wash and clean liver as indicated.
2. Season with salt and black pepper.
3. Sprinkle each piece lightly with butter. Place on baking sheet.
4. Coat both sides with mashed potatoes flakes.
5. Bake in oven at 350 degrees F for 20 minutes turn and bake for 10 minutes on opposite side..

Mountain Oysters

Ingredients

2 pounds mountain oysters (male hog organs)
1 quart water
1 tablespoon salt
2 teaspoons black pepper
2 cups cornmeal, yellow
1 cup corn oil

Directions

1. In a medium saucepan, lace mountain oysters and water. Boil for 30 minutes. Drain, pat dry, Remove membranes and discard membranes. Slice mountain oysters. Season with salt and pepper. Roll in corn meal. Dust off and fry in hot corn oil. Turn to golden brown on both sides.

Country Cured Pork

Ingredients

Fresh Pork Sides, Fresh Hams, Fresh Shoulders
1 pounds curing salt
1 wooden box 4 foot x 6 foot cleaned and dried

Directions

1. Meat should be dry.
2. Evenly pour salt over each piece of meat. Pour salt in wooden box.
3. Do not stack meat.
4. Store meat in dark, cool and dry place. Do not refrigerate.
5. Store for six to eight weeks before use.
6. Use as country cured meat after 6 weeks.

TALKING POINTS:

Georgia's Barrier Sea Island

Burnside Island -The Island is located in Chatman County.

Possible Africa Connection:

Niger –The country is landlocked in the northern part of Africa. It has a river Niger. Tribal groups are Hausa, Djerma, Sonral, Peuhl(Fula), Turaeg, and many others. Foods introduced to America grilled meats, coucous, noodles, buttermilk, meat grilled on open fires and meat and fished smoked and dried.

Former Georgia Slaves' Sayings:

PLANTATION LIFE:

1. Praying for Freedom

"folks straight-from-the shoulder that I could not pray along those lines. I told them flat-footedly that, while I loved them and would do any reasonable praying for them, I could not pray against my conscience: that I not only wanted to be free, but that I wanted to be free, but that I wanted to see all the Negroes freed!

"I then told them that God was using the Yankees to scourge the slave-holders just as he had, centuries before, used heathens and outcasts to chastise His chosen people----the Children of Israel."

"It is note that, for a slave way of between approximately 15 and 17 years of age, remarkable familiarity with the Old Testament was displayed.)

The Parson then entered into a mild tirade against Yankees, saying:

"The only time the Northern people ever helped the Nigger was when they freed him. They are not friends of the Negro and many a time, from my pulpit, have I warned Niggers about going North—

Has no business up there, and you may tell the world that the Reverend W.H. Allen makes no where no whens about saying that! He also says that, if it weren't for the influence of the white race in the South, the Negro race would revert to savagery within a year! Why, if they knew for dead in that there was not a policeman or officer of the law Columbus tonight, the good Lord only knows what they'd do tonight!"

Former Slave W. B. Allen page 13

2.   Digging Graves

"When the news of the war finally reached th plantation, the slaves followed the progress with keen interest and when battles were fought near Columbus, and firing of guns was heard, they cried joyfully – "It ain't gonna be long now." Two of their master's sons fought in the Confederate Army, but both returned home before the close of the war. One day news came that the Yankee soldiers were soon to come, and Walton began to hide all valuables. The slaves were sent to the cemetery to dig very deep graves where all manner of food was stored. They were covered like real graves and wooden slabs placed at either end. For three days before the soldiers were expected, all the house servants were kept busy preparing delicacies with which to tempt the Yankees and thus avoid having their place destroyed. In spite of all this preparation, they were caught unawares and when the "blue coats" were seen approaching, the master and his two sons ran. The elder made his way to the woods; the younger made away on "Black Eagle" a horse reputed to run almost a mile a minute. Nearly everything on the place was destroyed by these invaders. One bit of information has been given in every interview where Northern soldiers visited a plantation, they found, before coming, whether the Master was mean or kind and always treated him as he had treated his slaves. Thus, Mr. Walton was 'given the works" as our modern soldiers would say.

When the war ended the slaves were notified that they were free. Just before Rhodus' family prepared to move, his mother was struck on the head by a drunken guest visiting at the "big house". As soon as she regained consciousness, the family ran off without communicating with an elder sister who had been sold to a neighbor the previous year. A year later, news of this sister reached them through a wagoner who recognized the small boys as he passed them. He carried the news to the family's new residence back to the lost sister and in a few weeks she arrived at Cuthbert to make her home with her relatives.

For the past 9 years, Rhodus has been unable to work as he is a victim of a stroke on his left side, both sides have been ruptured, and his nerves are bad. He attributes his long life

To his faith in God."

Former Slave Rhodus Walton page 126

3.   End of the Civil War

"The Northern Soldiers come to town playing Yankee Doodle. When freedom come, they called all the white people in the courthouse first, and told them the darkies are free. Then on a certain day they called all the colored people down to the parade ground. Dey had built a big stand and the Yankees and some of our leading colored men got up and spoke and told the Negroes: "You are free now. Don't steal, now work and make a living. Do honest work, make an honest living an support yourself and children. No more masters. You are free.

Eugene said when the colored troops come in, they sang:

Don't you see the lightning to work,

Don't you hear the thunder

It isn't the lightning

It isn't the thunder

But it's the buttons on

The Negro Uniforms's!

The slaves that was freed and the country Negroes that had been run off, or had run away from the Plantations, was staying in Augusta in Guv'nant houses, great big ole barns. They would all get fre provisions from the Freedmen's Bureau, but people like us, Augusta citizens, didn't get free provisions, we had it spoiled some of them,"

Former Slave Eugene Smith

Bible Verse(s):

16 Then said I, Wisdom is better than strength: nevertheless the poor man's wisdom is despised, and his words are not heard.

17 The words of wise men are heard in quiet more than the cry of him that ruleth among fools.

18 Wisdom is better than weapons of war: but one sinner destroyeth much good.

ECCLESIASTES 9: 16, 17, 18

Chapter 11

Poultry Cooking

Roast Whole Chicken

Ingredients

    1-2 1/2 pounds whole chicken
    1 stick (1/2 cup) butter, softened
    1 clove garlic
    2 teaspoon salt
    1 teaspoon each sage, thyme, rosemary

Directions

1. Preheat the oven to 375 degrees F.
2. Check chicken for pin feathers, clean and wash chicken. Pat dry. Set aside.
3. In a bowl, mix together butter, garlic salt and herb seasonings. Rub inside and outside of the chicken and underneath the chicken's skin.
4. Place chicken in a roasting pan with breast side up and cook for one hour. Basting every 20 minutes with drippings from chicken. Chicken is done when juices are clear.

Oven Fried Chicken

Ingredients

   1   2 ½ pounds chicken cut up
   1 box cracker crumbs
   2 tablespoons canola oil
   2   large eggs
   ½ teaspoon dried thyme
   ½ teaspoon dried oregano
   ½ teaspoon salt
   ½ teaspoon black pepper
   ½ teaspoon garlic powder
   ½ teaspoon cayenne pepper

Directions

   1.   Clean, cut up and wash chicken set aside.
   2.   Crumble crackers to fine in food processor and place in a shallow
        bowl; stir in canola oil and set aside.
   3.   Beat eggs in a bowl and add all spices.
   4.   Prepare a large pan with foil. Heat oven to 375 degrees F.
   5.   Dip each piece of chicken in the egg mixture and then roll in
        cracker crumbs.
   6.   Oven fry chicken skin up for 30 minutes are until done.

Chicken Noodle Casserole

Ingredients

   1 - 2 pounds fryer
   Water to cover
   1(10 ¾ ounce) can cream of chicken soup
   1 (10 ¾ ounce) can cream of mushroom soup
   1 cup chicken broth
   ¼ cup onions, chopped

1/3 cup celery chopped
1 cup carrots, chopped
1 large package thin noodles, cooked according to directions
1 (10 ounce box) frozen peas
1- 8 ounces grated sharp cheese

Directions

1. Boil chicken in large pan of water until done and debone. Save broth and discard bones. Chop chicken.
2. Grease large 4 quart casserole dish. Preheat 350 degrees F.
3. In a large bowl, mix together soup, mushroom soup and broth. Stir in onions, celery and carrots.
4. Alternate layers of cooked noodles with other ingredients.
5. Sprinkle cheese on top,
6. Cook in oven for 35 minutes.

African Chicken with Spinach

Ingredients

2 fryers, cut up into pieces
¼ cup vegetable oil
2 teaspoons salt
1 teaspoon curry powder
1 large yellow onion, peeled and steamed
1 large red bell pepper, seeded and cut into strips
2 cups tomatoes, chopped
1 -10 ounce box frozen spinach, thawed
1 ½ cups uncooked rice
½ cup crunch peanut butter
¼ cup warm water

Directions

1. Wash chicken and season with salt and curry powder. Brown the chicken in the vegetable oil. Remove chicken. Set aside.
2. Stir together onion, red pepper, tomato and spinach in a Dutch oven in vegetable oil. Cover and simmer for 5 minutes.

3. In a small bowl, stir peanut butter and water together. Place in Dutch oven with vegetables and stir.
4. Return chicken to Dutch oven. Cover and simmer for 30 minutes or until chicken is done.
5. Cook rice following the package directions. When rice and chicken are done. Spoon rice onto a large platter and arrange chicken over rice.

Chicken and Tomatoes

Ingredients

4 smoked chicken breasts, skinned, chopped
6 medium-sized ripe tomatoes, peeled, seeded and coarsely chopped
2 yellow onions, thinly sliced
2 cups water
2 hot chili peppers, chopped
2 tablespoons peanut oil
1 teaspoon salt

Directions

1. Place all ingredients in a large sauce pan. Bring to a boil and cover and then simmer for 30 minutes.

Chicken and Dumplings

Ingredients

1 large hen, cut up or 2 fryers, cut up
3   quarts of water
1   large onion, diced
1 teaspoons salt
1 teaspoon black pepper

Directions

1. In a large pot, place chicken, water, onion, salt and pepper. Cover and bring to a boil and lower heat.

2. Simmer for one hour or until meat falls off bones. Drop dumplings in pot one at a time.

Dumplings

Ingredients

    1 cup flour sifted
    1   teaspoons baking soda
    ½ teaspoon salt
    ½ teaspoon paprika
    ½ cup milk
    1 tablespoon oil

Directions

1. In a bowl, add flour, baking soda, salt and paprika. Mix well. Add milk and oil.
2. Make certain to mix until well moistened. Drop by spoonsful over boiling chicken mixture.
3. Reduce heat and simmer for 15 minutes. Serve chicken and dumplings together.

Smothered Chicken and Rice

Ingredients

    1 chicken, cut up
    1 teaspoon salt
    1 teaspoon black pepper
    1½ cups self - flour
    2   tablespoons shortening
    ½ cup onion, finely chopped
    ½ cup celery, finely chopped
    2 tablespoons flour
    1   ½ cups water
    2 ½ cups cooked long grain rice

Directions

1. Wash chicken. Season with salt and pepper. Coat with flour. In a large frying pan, heat shortening. Place chicken in the hot fat and cook on both sides until chicken is done.
2. Remove the chicken and place on a plate. Pour off all fat except about 2 tablespoons. Add onions and celery. Cook until tender. Sprinkle with flour. Gradually add water, stirring constantly until thickened. Add chicken. Cover and continue to cook on low heat for about 20-30 minutes or until desired doneness. Serve over rice.

Chicken and Rice

Ingredients

11/2 pound to 2 pound fryer, cut up
½ cup onion, chopped
½ cup celery
1 quart water
2 cups rice
1 teaspoon salt
1 teaspoon black pepper

Directions

1. Place chicken, onions, celery and water in a large sauce pan. Cover and bring to a boil. Boil for 5 minutes and Lower the heat to medium. Cook for 15 minutes and add rice. Cook for 15 minutes season with salt and pepper.
Cook for 10 minutes. Serve.

Fried Livers or Gizzards

Ingredients

1 pound chicken livers or gizzards
2 cups milk
2 eggs, well beaten

1 teaspoon black pepper
1 1/2 cups flour, self- rising
Peanut oil for frying

Directions

1. In a bowl, mix milk, eggs and black pepper
2. Whip until well mixed.
3. Dip livers or gizzards one at a time in batter and then deep fry until golden brown.

Wild Turkey

Ingredients

1 wild turkey, cleaned remove and discard feathers, feet, necks and innards
1   gallon hot water
1 cup salt
3 onions, sliced
2 tablespoons rosemary

Directions

1. Clean turkey as indicated.
2. Heat water and dissolve sat in water. Pour over turkey in a noncorrosive pan.
3. Cover and marinate 8 hours.
4. Remove turkey from refrigerator and wash.
5. Place whole turkey in a large stock pot and add onions. Cover with water and cook covered for 1 hour.
6. Cool turkey, rub with rosemary and bake in oven for 11/2 at 325 degrees F or until tender.

Stewed Turkey Wings

Ingredients

> 2-3 pounds turkey wings, cut up into 2 –inch pieces
> 2   cups celery, chopped
> 2 cups yellow onions, chopped
> 1 teaspoon salt
> 1 teaspoon black pepper

Directions

1. Wash turkey wings and vegetables.
2. Place turkey wings and vegetables in a large sauce pot with water to cover. Cover with tight fitting lid. Bring to a boil for five minutes. Lower heat and add seasonings. Cook for 1 hour; stirring constantly until done.

TALKING POINTS:

Georgia Barrier Sea Island

Cockspur Island – The Island is located south of the Savannah River. It is located in Chatman County. Fort Pulaski, Cockspur Island Lighthouse and a monument dedicated to the founder of Methodism, John Wesley, who landed on the island on February 6, 1736. The monument marks the spot where John Wesley conducted a service for thanksgiving.

Lazaretto- A small community in Lazaretto Creek was formerly the site of a quarantine station, now on Cockspur Island, and of a hospital to which slave boats brought Negroes to be examined and treated. The slaves who died were buried in unmarked graves near by.

Possible Africa Connection

Sudan-The country is located near the Sahara desert in northern Africa. The tribal groups are Black, Arab, Beja and others. The foods introduced to America include cucumbers, yogurt, goat, turtles and fermented dough.

Also, cowpeas.

Former Georgia Slaves' Sayings:

PLANTATION LIFE:

1. Slave children learning how to pray.

    "Dey had a ole lady stay in de quarters who tuk care of de chillum whilst de mother wuz in de Fiel': Den dey met at her house at dark, and man name, Hickman, had prayers.

    Dey all kneel down. Den de chillum couln' talk till dey got home---if you talk you git a whippin' from de ole lady nes' night. Ole granny whip 'em."

    Former Slave Fannie Fulcher

Bible Verse(s):

45 That ye may be the children of your Father which is in heaven: for he maketh his sun to rise on the evil and on the good, and sendeth rain on the just and on the unjust.

Mathew 6:45

Chapter 12

Beef Cooking

Stewed Oxtails

Ingredients

> 1 pound oxtails
> 3 teaspoons salt
> 1 teaspoon black pepper
> 1 cup flour
> 4 tablespoons oil for frying
> 1 1/2 quarts water
> 1 cup onions, chopped

Directions

1. Wash oxtails. Dry. Season with salt and pepper. Sprinkle with flour. In a large skillet brown oxtails and onions until onions are tender.
2. Place in a large sauce pot and add water. Cover bring to a boil and then turn down and cook for 2 hours
3. Stir occasionally. Test for doneness and serve over rice.

Roast Beef with Gravy

Ingredients

1-5 pounds roast beef, cut of choice
1 teaspoon sea salt
1   teaspoon black pepper

2 onions, sliced
1 garlic clove, minced
1 cup water

Directions

1. Clean, wash and pat dry roast beef. Season with sea salt and black pepper. Place in large
    Roasting pan, place sliced onions and garlic on top of roast. Gradually pour water over roast. Cover with aluminum foil and roast at 325 degrees for 1 hour.

For Gravy:

1. Pour roast drippings into a sauce pan, heating slowly until needed.
2. Mix 1 cup water in a bowl with ½ cup flour. Beat until smooth. Slowly add flour mixture to cooking drippings. Stir quickly to keep from lumping. Taste for seasoning.

Meat Loaf

Ingredients

1 ½ pounds ground beef
1 cup onion, chopped
1 tablespoon bell pepper, chopped
2 eggs, beaten
1 teaspoon salt
1 teaspoon black pepper
½ cup milk
4 cups sliced bread, crumbled

1 cup tomato sauce

Topping

1 (8 –ounce) can tomato sauce
3 tablespoons brown sugar, dark brown
2 teaspoons Worcestershire sauce
1(6 –ounce) can tomato paste

Directions

1. In a large bowl, mix together all ingredients, except for topping. Preheat to 350 degrees F. Mix topping and set aside.
2. Shape into a loaf and place in shallow pan. Bake for 30 minutes, drain and add topping continue to cook for 30 minutes.
3. Remove from oven and let rest for 10 minutes before serving.

Brisket Cooked in a Slow Cooker

Ingredients

1   teaspoons dry mustard
2 tablespoons dried thyme
2 tablespoons chili powder
1 tablespoon smoked paprika
1 teaspoon cumin
¼ cup brown sugar
1 tablespoon kosher salt
¼ cup olive oil
1 teaspoon black pepper
1 (5 pound) beef brisket
2 large yellow onion, peeled and diced
2   medium carrots, peeled and sliced
1 cup celery, chopped
3   cloves garlic, peeled and sliced

Directions

1. Combine first six ingredients in a large bowl and mix well. Rub the brisket with olive oil; salt and pepper both sides of the brisket. Rub spice mixture on both sides of brisket. Place onions, carrots, celery and garlic in a 6-quart cooker. Place the brisket fat side up on top of vegetables, cover and cook on low for 8 hours.
2. Transfer the brisket to a cutting board and cover loosely until brisket is cooled. Let cool and slice. Discard vegetables.
3. Save drippings for reheating or preparing other vegetables.

Beef Stew and Baked Vegetables

Ingredients

2 pounds stew beef, cut into 1-inch cubes
1 teaspoon salt
1 teaspoon black pepper
1 teaspoon garlic granules
1 cup water
4 medium Idaho potatoes cut up
1 cup yellow onions, sliced
1 (15-ounce) can tomatoes, diced
1 (15-ounce) can tomato sauce
1 -10 ounce box green beans
2 cups carrots, cut
11/2 cup sweet peas
2 tablespoons flour
1 teaspoon salt
1 teaspoon black pepper

Directions

1. Season stew beef with salt, black pepper and garlic granules. In a large 4 quart casserole dish, place seasoned stew beef and water. Cover and roast in oven at 350 degrees F for 30 minutes and stir. Add remainder of ingredients and stir. Cover and continue to oven roast until done.

TALKING POINTS:

Georgia Barrier Sea Island

Wassaw Island- was purchased in 1866 for $5,000 by George Parsons as a wedding gift for his bride. The family was from New England they made their money as cotton brokers. Wassaw Island was a family retreat and playground for the rich.

Possible Africa Connection:

Namibia-The country is located near the Atlantic Ocean in southwestern Africa. The tribal groups are Ovambo and others. Foods introduced to America vinegar, cinnamon, cloves, turmeric, curry powder, wild onions, cabbages and carrots.

Georgia Former Slaves' Sayings:

PLANTATION LIFE:

1.   Old Folks Talk

"Whilst us was all a-wukin' away at house and yard jobs, de old folkses

Would tell us 'bout times 'fore us was borned. Dey sold slaves, dealers used to come 'round wid a big long line of slaves a-marchin' to whar dere was gwine to be a big slave sale.

Sometimes dey marched 'em here from as fur as Virginny. Old folkses said dey had done been fetched to dis country on boats. Dem boats was painted red real bright red, and dey went plumb to Africa to get de Niggers. When dey got dare, dey got off and left de bright red boats empty for a while. Niggers laks red, and dey would get us dem boats to see what dem red things was.

When de boats was full of dem foolish Niggers, de slave dealers would sell off wid 'em and fetch 'em to dis country to sell 'em to folkses what had plantations. Dem slave sales was awful had in some ways 'cause sometimes dey sold mammies away fom deir babies and families got scattered some of 'em never showed what comed of deir brudder and sister and daddies and mommas.

"When us warn't out in de fields, us done little jobs 'round de big house, de cabins, barns, and yards. Us used to help de older slaves git out whiteoak splits, and dey larnt us to make cheer bottoms and baskets out of dem splits. De best cheer bottoms what lasted de longest wus dem what us made wid red ellum withes. Dem old shuck bottoms was fine too; dey plaited dem shucks and wound 'em round for cheer bottoms and foots mats. De 'omans mde nice hats out of shucks and wheat straw. Dey plaited de shucks and put 'em together wid plaits of wheat straw.

Dey warn't counted much for Sunday wear, but made sun hats."

Former Slave Paul Smith, page 331

Bible Verse(s):

7But when ye pray, use not vain repetitions, as the heathen do: for they think that they shall be heard for their much speaking.

8 Be not ye therefore like unto them: for your Father knoweth what things ye have need of before ye ask him.

Chapter 13

Root Vegetables Cooking

Geehees enjoy many root vegetables in salads, soups, cobblers and side dishes.

Fresh Beets Salad

Ingredients

    1   medium fresh beets
    1   quart water for boiling
    1 cup vinegar
    ½ cup water
    ¼ cup granulated sugar
    1 teaspoon salt
    2 slices white onions, sliced
    1 teaspoon salt

Directions

1. Rinse beets and trim stems to about 1 inch. Cover beets with water in a saucepan. Simmer covered for 30-40 minutes or until tender.
2. Drain and place beets in cold water until beets cool down. Remove skins from beets. Slice beets and place in a bowl.
3. Stir together vinegar, water, salt and sugar. Stir until sugar is melted. Pour over beets, add onions and vinegar mixture. Cover.
4. Refrigerate for 30 minutes. Serve.

Boiled Carrots

Ingredients

> 4 cups Carrots, chopped
> 1 cup water
> 1 teaspoon salt
> 2 tablespoon sugar

Directions

1. Peel carrots and chop into coins.
2. Place all ingredients in a medium sized sauce pan. Cover. Bring to a boil for 2 to 3 minutes and then cook on low heat until tender.

Carrot Souffle

Ingredients

> 4 cups carrots, cooked and mashed
> 1 cup dark brown sugar
> 2 eggs, beaten
> 1 teaspoon cinnamon
> 1 cup evaporated milk
> ½ cup butter
> 1 teaspoon vanilla

Directions

1. Butter 2 quart casserole dish. Preheat oven to 350 degrees F.
2. In a bowl, combine all ingredients and beat well. Place in the casserole dish and bake for 30 minutes.

   Onions –Onions –white, yellow and red are used for seasonings and as an accompaniment to other dishes.

Mashed Rutabagas

Ingredients

2 rutabagas, peeled and cooked
1 cured pig's tail
½ cup onion, chopped
1 teaspoon salt
1 clove garlic, minced

Directions

1. Wash and peel rutabagas bottoms. Cut into quarters, place in a large saucepan, add remaining ingredients and cover with water.
2. Cook until done. Remove from heat and discard pig's tail. Mash rutabagas and then season to taste. Beat and serve.

Red Potato Salad

Ingredients

16 red potatoes, clean and quartered
3 hard boiled eggs, chopped
½ cup celery
1 cup onions, minced
1 cup mayonnaise
¼ cup mustard
1 teaspoon salt
1 teaspoon black pepper

Directions

1. Clean potatoes and cover with water in a saucepan. Boil until tender. Drain.
2. Boil eggs, place in cold water. Peel and chop.
3. In a large bowl, add all ingredients. Stir and cover. Refrigerate 24 hours and then serve.

New Potatoes and Green Beans

Ingredients

> 4 cups fresh green beans, snapped
> 1 cured ham hock, chopped
> 6 new red potatoes
> 1 onion, chopped

Directions

1. Prepare green beans and new potatoes.
2. Place all ingredients in a large saucepan. Cover with water and bring to a boil. Cook over low heat until done.

TALKING POINTS:

Georgia Barrier Sea Island

Skidaway Island –The Island has been used to study fish habitats.

Possible Africa Connection

Mozambique –The country is in the south of Africa near the Indian Ocean. Tribal groups include Makauna, Makhuwa, Tsonga, Sena, Lomwe and many others. Foods introduced to America shrimp stew boiled rice, methods of marinating, coconut pudding, and many types of shell fish.

Former Georgia Slaves' Sayings:

PLANTATION LIFE:

1.   Girls on one plantation

"dere was some girls, dey wuz witches. At night dey would go out and steal.

Dey would pull off dey skin and put it in a closet what which dey clothes was and dey had some little caps dey put on when they clothes was and dey had some little caps dey put on when dey shook off dey skin an dey dould go out through de keyhold.

"A man was courtin' one of the girls. He peep in de keyhole and seen 'em put on de caps, and shake deyselves, and say:

"Over and under, thru' thick and thin, tech nowhere."

"He put on a cap, tied it under his chin and said:

"Over and under, Through thick and thin

Tech everywhere,

"You see he got de words wrong, and he went buttin' unto everythin' hurtin' his head, crackin' his joints, knockin' unto trees and fences, until de power of de cap wear off. He was so tired he went back to de house and lay down."

"At daylight de girls flew back."

Former Slave Rachel McCoy page 396

Bible Verse(s):

40 For I lift up my hand to heaven, and say, I live for ever.

Deuteronomy 32:40

Chapter 14

Plantation Barbequing

Each year the plantation owners would arrange to have large barbeques for the slaves and others. Usually the meats were whole beef, whole shoats(pigs), sheep, chickens and many other things. These barbecues would be popular on the 4th of July.)

A special big barbeque pit would be built to handle whole cuts for barbequing. Each plantation had special cooks for barbecuing.

Wood for smoking the meat was made from hickory and apple wood. The wood was specially prepared for the pit. Usually, the hickory wood was left in special cut and the apple wood was made into chips.

In this section, the barbequing of whole or half animals methods used by slaves are shown.

Pulled Pork

Ingredients

> 1 whole hog, dressed and washed cleaned. Head and feet may be left on.
> 2 cups lard, melted
> 3 cups rub

Directions

1. Split the hog into half. Rub with lard.
2. Sprinkle rub over entire hog.
3. Smoke for 25 hours. Pull samples from hog butt to check for doneness.
4. Spread Sauce over meat.

Plantation Barbecue Rub

Ingredients

1 pound salt
½ Pound cayenne pepper
2 pounds cracked black pepper
2 pounds dark brown sugar

Directions

1. In a large bucket, stir together all ingredients.

Plantation Barbecue Sauce

Ingredients

3 gallons molasses
4 gallons vinegar
1 quart mustard
1 pound black pepper
1 cup salt
2 yellow onions, chopped
2 cloves, garlic, minced
1 gallon tomatoes, cooked
½ cup cayenne pepper

Directions

1. In large barrel, stir together all ingredients.

2. Bring to a boil, stir with large paddle.

Barbecued Chitterlings

Ingredients

1 pounds boiled chitterlings, chopped
3 cups barbecue sauce, choice

Directions

1. Wash chitterlings and boil until done.
2. Drain chitterlings and transfer chopped
   Chitterlings to baking dish. Ad barbecue
   Sauce and bake at 325 degrees F.
   Until done.

Whole Beef Barbeque from the Plantation

Ingredients

300 pound beef, split in half, heat and feet removed
Spice Rub to cover

Mustard based Barbeque Sauce

Ingredients

1. Clean beef and let rest for 7 days before use.
2. Cover the meat with rub on outside and inside
3. Place in large smoker and cook for 24 hours.
4. Base with sauce after 24 hours and base every 30 minutes for 2
   hours. Let rest 1 hour, slice and serve with sauce.

Mustard –Based Barbecue Sauce

Ingredients

2 gallons ketchup
3 quarts tomato paste
1 gallon prepared mustard
1 gallons apple juice
2 gallons water
1 tablespoon cayenne pepper
1 tablespoon garlic granules
1 tablespoon black pepper
½ cup salt
½ cup Worcestershire sauce
3 yellow onions, chopped
1 quart orange juice
4 garlic cloves, minced

Directions

1. In a large stock pot, combine all ingredients. Stir well and cook on low heat for 1 hour. Stir constantly.
2. Taste for accuracy. Cool. Baste meat.

Barbequed Lamb

Ingredients

½ half side of Lamb
4 cups Rub
Mint Flavored Barbecue Sauce

Directions

1. Clean meat and wash. Pat dry and rub with rub.
2. Smoke for 24 hours over low heat.
3. Baste meat with sauce for 1 hour every 20 minutes. Clean meat and wash. Pat dry and rub with rub.
4. Smoke for 24 hours over low heat.

5.   Baste meat with sauce every 20 minutes for 1 hour.

Mint Flavored Barbecue Sauce

Ingredients

1 gallon molasses
1 quart Mint jelly
2 gallons tomato sauce
1 quart red wine
2 tablespoons dry mustard
2 tablespoons fresh mint leaves
½ gallon vinegar
2 yellow onions, chopped
4 cloves garlic, chopped
1 pound dark brown sugar
2 tablespoons garlic granules
½ cup salt
1 tablespoon black pepper
4 gallons water

Directions

1.   Stir together all ingredients and cook for 45 minutes on low heat until desired taste.

TALKING POINTS:

Georgia's Barrier Sea Island

Isle of Hope – Isle of Hope is located in Chatham County.

The total land area is 2.1 square miles; 1.9 square miles; 16.4 square miles and 0.2 square miles of water.

The area has a community of privately owned antebellum homes overlooking Skidaway River.

More than 200 African-Americans live on Isle of Hope.

Connection to Georgia Barrier Sea Islands

Bryan County -The county was named for Johnathan Bryan and established in 1793.

County seat: Pembroke

Incorporated Communities:

Pembroke, Richmond Hill

Richmond Hill Village located in Richmond Hill Plantation.

Unincorporated Communities

Belfast, Blickton, Brisborn, Daniel, Eldora, Fancy Hall, Fort McAllister, Groveland, Keller, Lanier, Letford, Myrtle Grove, Oak Level, Port Royal, Rabit Hill, Reka, Southward/

Possible Africa Connection:

Ethiopia-The country is known as home to Haile Sellass, an African ruler. The country is in East Africa.

Tribal groups are Oromo, Amara, Tigraway, Somali, Gurage, Sidamo and others. Foods introduced to America include spices-garlic, mustard, hot peppers, leavened breads, beef meat stews and hard boiled eggs.

Georgia Former Slaves' Sayings:

PLANTATION LIFE:

1.   Mother's Religion

"Mammy wuz a 'ligious 'oman an' de fust day of Chris'tmas she allus fasted ha'f a day an' den she would pray. Atter dat everybody would hav eggnog an' bourbon an' effen den dey had de money to buy it. Mammy said whe dey wuz still slaves Marster allus gived 'em Chris'tmas, but atter dey had freedom den dey had ter buy dey own rations. De would have bahjer playin' an' pijen-wing and de shuffle-toe."

Former Slave Susan Mathew page 114

Bible Verse(s):

1 Remember me, O my God, concerning this, and wipe not out my good deeds that I have done for the house of my God and for the offices thereof.

Nehemiah 13:14

Chapter 15

Food Preservation

Popular foods are processed and canned are fruits, vegetables, boiled eggs, pig's feet, jams, jellies, relishes, chow chow, hot pepper and shrimp.

Fresh Canned Tomatoes

Ingredients

> 3 pounds tomatoes
> 1 Tablespoons salt
> 12 pint canning jars, tops and screw tops

Directions

1. Prepare tomatoes - Wash, dip into boiling water 30 to 60 seconds. Immediately drop in cold water and peel away green areas and cut out core.
2. Cut into quarters.
3. Heat jars in boiling water in a canner. Simmer until ready for use. Do not boil. Set bands aside.
4. Pack tomatoes into hot jars, leaving ½ inch head space. Add ½ teaspoon salt to each jar. Remove air bubbles. Clean off top. Place lids on each jar.
5. Process filled jars in a boiling water for 40 minutes. Cool and remove jars. Check lids for seal after 24 hours.

Peach Jam

Ingredients

6 half-pint canning jars, lids and screw top bands
6 cups peach slices, peeled and fresh
¼ cup fresh lemon juice
1 tablespoon butter
1 box (1 3/4 ounce) dry pectin
5 ½ cups granulated sugar

Directions

1. Wash and sterilize canning jars, lids and bands. Set aside.
2. Prepare peaches and place in a large pan. Add butter and dry pectin. Stir well.
3. Carefully cook peaches, stirring constantly.
4. Remove from heat and stir well. Return to heat and stir mixture as it forms a rolling boil
5. Make sure mixture boils quickly; so that foam maybe removed.
6. Cool and skim foam off jam with a large metal spoon. Then fill jars with jam. Fill up to 1" inch from top of the jar.
7. Clean each jar and seal with lids and screw tops.
8. Return jars to boiling water for 10 minutes. Remove from boiling water and allow to stand upright until cooled.
9. Press lightly in the center to check for seal.

Strawberry Preserves

Yield: 10 half pints

Ingredients

1 half-pint canning jars, lids, screw top bands
2 cups (hulled) strawberries, chopped
7cups sugar
1 tcaspoon butter
1 liquid pectin pouch
1 tablespoon vanilla extract

Directions

1. Sterilize canning jars, lids and tops for 5 minutes.
2. Drain well .
3. Combine strawberries, sugar and butter.
4. Stir well. Bring to a boil and stirring well. Add the liquid pectin and Vanilla extract. Return to a boil and boil for 5 minutes.
5. Skim all foam and continue to cook for 10 minutes.
6. Pour into hot, sterilized canning jars. Wipe rims of jars until clean.
7. Secure lids with screw tops and bands.
8. Process in a boiling water bath for 10 minutes.
9. Carefully remove jars from water bath and let cool. Check for seals.
10. Store until use.

Sweet Blackberry Jam

Yield: 6 half pints

Ingredients

6 half pints canning jars, lids and screw top bands
1   ½ cups blackberries, cleaned and washed
1 (1.75-ounce) box powdered pectin

1 teaspoon butter
5 cups sugar

Directions

1. Sterilize canning jars, lids and screw tops in boiling water for a least 5 minutes. Drain well just before filing jars.
2. In a large saucepan combine blackberries, pectin and butter and stir.
3. Bring to a boil for five minutes. Stir in sugar all at once. Stir well. Bring to a rolling boil and skim foam off mixture. Remove from heat.
4. Pour into hot, sterilized jars. Wipe rims clean. Secure lids with screw top bands.
5. Process jars in a boiling water for 10 minutes. Carefully remove jars from water bath and let stand at room temperature to cool.

6. Check later for certain jars are all sealed.

Hot Mango Jam

Yield: 6 half pints

Ingredients

6half-pint canning jars, lids and screw tops
5 cups medium diced fresh ripe mango
5 jalapeno peppers
2 cloves garlic, minced
7 cups sugar
1 teaspoon butter
1 pouch liquid pectin

Directions

1. Sterilize canning jars, lids and screw on tops. Place in boiling water for at least 5 minutes. Drain.
2. Combine mango, jalapenos, garlic, sugar and butter. Stir well. Bring to a boil and cook until reaches a boiling point.
3. The mixture boils so that the mixture can not be stirred down. Add liquid pectin. Stir well. Remove foam.
4. Return ton heat and boil exactly for one minute.
5. Remove from heat. Pour into hot, sterilized canning jars. Wipe rims of jars. Secure lids with screw tops.
6. Process jars and wipe rims of jars clean. Screw tops on bands. Process canning jars in water bath for 10 minutes.
7. Cool and check or seals.

Classic Head Cheese

Yield: 20 servings

Ingredients

1 pig's head, cleaned and split (remove, eggs, brains and tongue) clean well
2 pig's feet
2 pig's ears
1 pig's tail
2 large onions, quartered
6 stalks celery, diced
3 bay leaves
1 teaspoon coarsely ground black pepper
½ teaspoon salt
Onions, celery ½ teaspoon Tabasco sauce
½ teaspoon red pepper
2 cups white vinegar

Directions

1. In a large sauce pot cover the cleaned pig's head, feet, ears, tail, onions, celery and bay leaves. Cover with water.
2. Bring to a boil and cook for 10 minutes and then reduce heat and boil until meat falls off bones.
3. Pick bones off meat. Discard bones and vegetables.
4. Chop meat up finely and place in a large bowl. Stir in remaining ingredients and make a mold.

Chow Chow Relish

Yield: 2 quart jars

Ingredients

4 cups cabbage, chopped
4 Green tomatoes, chopped
2 cups onions, chopped

2 jalapeno peppers, minced
1 teaspoon salt
1 cup sugar
1/3 cup mustard seeds
1   tablespoons celery seeds
2   cups vinegar

Directions

1. Wash and prepare vegetables. Place in large saucepan and pour 8 cups of water over vegetables; stir well.
2. Cook until vegetables are tender. Add salt, sugar, mustard seeds, celery seeds and vinegar.
3. Cook for 35 minutes and stir well. Can in hot sterilized jars.

Yield: 4 large jars

Ingredients

1 pound jalapeno peppers or green hot peppers
1   cups cider vinegar
½ cup water
1 tablespoon salt
1   bay leaves
1 tablespoon pickling spice
2   tablespoons sugar

Directions

1. Wash peppers and place in 4 pint jars. Set aside. In a saucepan, add vinegar, water, salt, bay leaves, pickling spices and sugar. Heat to boiling.
2. Simmer for 10 minutes. Pour over peppers in jars. Screw lids and tight and place in water bath for 10 minutes.

Pickled Eggs

Yield: 2 jars

Ingredients

12eggs
1 large white onion, thinly sliced
2 cups water
2cups distilled vinegar
1teaspoon salt
1 tablespoon pickling spice

Directions

1. Cover eggs with water in a saucepan. Cover with lid. Bring to a boil over medium high heat. Boil for 10 minutes.
2. Drain. Run cold water over eggs. Let stand for 10 minutes. Peel and set aside.
3. Stir together water, vinegar, salt and pickling spice in a sauce pan and boil for 10 minutes.
4. Place eggs in 4 half pint sterilized jars.
5. Strain mixture and pour evenly over boiled mixture.
6. Seal until ready to use.

Hot Pear Relish

Ingredients

4 pounds pears, slightly green, washed, cored
½ pound green hot peppers, washed
2 cups vinegar, white
1 cup water
1 teaspoon pickling spice
1 teaspoon salt
2 ½ cups sugar

Directions

1. In a food processor, chop the pears and peppers.
2. Place in a large sauce pot, add remaining ingredients.
3. Cover and cook over medium heat for 30 minutes.
4. Cook over low heat. Continue to stir to keep from burning.
5. Place in sterilize jars after cooking.

TALKING POINTS:

Georgia Barrier Sea Island

Ossabaw Island – The Island is located in Bryan County. The Island is used as a tourist area.

Possible Africa Connection:

Uganda –The country is located in Africa, in the east central side and bordering Lake Victoria.

Tribal groups are Baganda, Bankyakole, Basogo, Bakiga, Teso and many others.

Foods introduced to America banana pudding, papaya, wild berries, palm oil and peanut oil.

Georgia Former Slaves' Sayings:

PLANTATION LIFE:

1. Master Ingram and Slave Life

"Pattillo's mother was cook and general house servant, an well thought of by the Ingram family that she managed the house as she saw fit and planned the meals likewise. Young Pattillo was considered a pet by everyone and hung around the mistress, since she did not have any children of her own. His job was to hand her the scissors and thread her needles, and my youngest brother was the master's special pet." Mr. and Mrs. Ingram never punished the children, nor allowed anyone but their parents to do so. If the boy became unruly, Mrs. Ingram would call his mother and say, "Harriett, I think G.W. needs to be taken down a button lower."

"Pattillo declared that he had never seen anyone on the Ingram Plantation punished by the owner, who never allowed the "paterrollers" to punish them either.

"Master Ingram placed signs at different points on his plantation which read thus: "Paterollers, Fishing and Hunting Prohibited on this Plantation." It soon became known by all that the Ingram slaves were not given passes by their owner to go any place, consequently they were known as "Old Ingram's Free Niggers."

"Master Ingram could not write, but would tell his slaves to inform anyone who wished to know, that they belonged to J.D. Ingram. "Once," said Pattillo, "my brother Willie, who was known for his gambling and drinking, left our plantation and no one knew where he had gone. As we sat around a big open fire cracking walnuts, Willis came up, jumped off his horse and fell to the ground. Directly behind him rode a "paterroller.' The master jumped up and commanded him to turn around and leave premises. The "pateroller' ignored his warning and advanced still further. The master then took his rifle and shot him. He fell to the ground dead and Master Ingram said to his wife, 'Hell, Lucy, I guess the next time I speak to that scoundrel he will take heed.' The master then saddled his horse and rode into town. Very soon a wagon same back and moved the body."

"The cotton raised was woven into cloth from which their clothing was made. "We had plenty of good clothing and food." Patillio continued. "The smokehouse was never locked and we had free access to the whole house. We never knew the meaning of a key."

"Master Ingram was very strict about religion and attending church. It was customary for everyone to attend the 9 o'clock prayer services at his home every night. The Bible was read by the mistress, after which the master would conduct prayer. Children as well as grownups were expected to attend. On Sundays, everybody attended church. Separate Churches were provided for the Negroes, with White and Colored preachers conducting the services. White Deacons were also the Deacons of the Colored Churches and a colored one was never appointed deacon of a Church. Only white ministers were privileged to give the sacrament and do the baptizing. Their sermons were of a strictly religious nature. When a preacher was unable to read, someone was appointed to read the text. The preacher would then build his sermon from it. Of course, during the conference period, colored as well as white ministers were privileged to make the appointments. The Negroes never took up collections but placed their money in an envelope and passed it in. It was their own money, earned with the master's consent, by selling apples, eggs, chickens, etc."

"Loss of life among slaves was a calamity and if a doctor earned a reputation for losing his patients, he might as well seek a new community. Often his downfall would begin by some such comment as, "Dr. Brown lost old man Ingram's nigger John. He's no good and I don't intend to use him." The value of slaves varied from $500 to $10,000, depending on his or her special qualifications. Tradesmen such as blacksmiths, show makers, carpenters, etc., were seldom sold under $10,000.

Rather than sell a tradesman slave, owners kept them in order to make money by hiring them out to other owners for a sat sum per season. However, before the deal was closed the lesses would have to sign a contract which assured the slave's owner that the slave would receive the best of treatment while in possession.

"Pattillo remembers hearing his parents say the North and South had disagreed and Abraham Lincoln was going to free the slaves. Although he never saw a battle fought, there were days when he sat and watched the long line of soldiers passing, miles and miles of them. Master Ingram did not enlist but remained at home to take care of his family and his possessions.

"After the war ended, Master Ingram called his slaves together and told them of their freedom, saying, "Mr. Lincoln whipped the South and we are going back to the Union. You are as free as I am and if you wish to remain here you may. If not, you may go any place you wish. I am not rich but we can work together here for both our families, sharing everything we raise equally." Pattillo's family remained there until 1870. Some owners kept their slaves in ignorance of their freedom. Others were kind enough to offer them homes and help them to get a start.

"After emancipation, politic began to play a part in the lives of ex-slaves, and many were approached by candidates who wanted to buy their votes.

"Patillo tells of an ex-slave owner named Greely living in Upson County who bought an ex-slave

Owner vote by giving him as payment a ham, a sack of flour and a place to stay on his plantation. After election, he ordered the ex-slaves to get the wagon, load it with his possessions and move away from his Plantation. Astonished, the old Negro asked why. "Because," replied old Greseley, "If you allow wagons to buy your vote and rob you of your rights as a free citizen, someone could hire you to set my house on fire."

"Patillo remembers slavery gratefully and says he almost wishes these days were back again."

Former Slave George Pattillo, pages 164-170

Bible Verse(s):

1 The Lord said unto my Lord Sit thou at my right hand until I make thine enemies they footstool.

Psalm 110:1

Chapter 16

Fruits and Fruit Cooking

Geechees love fresh fruits, such as, apples, oranges, kumquats, mangoes, berries, lemons, limes and many more. Geechee men love to peel green apples with their pocket knives and eat them all day. Geechees like eating pears in the fall and winter that have been specially packed. The Geechees hold secrets to storing watermelons and cantaloupes for a long time.

TALKING POINTS:

Connections to Georgia's Barrier Sea Island

Bryan County is a connection to Ossabaw Sea Island.

Possible Africa Connection:

Rwanda- The country is located in east central Africa. The tribal groups are Hutu, Tutsi and Twa.

Food introduced to America include Sorghum, flatbread, pancakes goat, pumpkin seeds, grilled corn and goat kabobs.

Former Georgia Slaves' Sayings:

PLANTATION LIFE:

1. Getting married

"Then a male slave reached the age of twenty-one he was allowed to court.

The same was true of a girl that had reached the age of eighteen. If a couple wished to marry they had to get permission from the master who asked each in turn if they wished to be joined as man and wife and if both answered that they did were taken into master's home where the ceremony was performed. Mr. Womble says that he has actually seen one of these weddings and this is was conducted in the following manner: "A broom was placed in the center of the floor and the couple was told to hold hands. After joining hands they were commanded to jump over the broom and then to turn around and jump back." "After this they were pronounced man and wife."

A man who was small in statue was never allowed to marry a large, robust woman. Sometimes when the male slave on one plantation was large and healthy looking and the women slaves on some nearby plantation looked like they might be good breeders the two owners agreed to allow the men belonging to the one visit the women belonging to the other, in fact they encouraged this sort of thing in hopes that they would marry and produce big healthy children. In such cases, passes were give freely."

Former Slave George Womble page 190

Bible Verse(s).

1   Every day will I bless thee; and I will praise thy name for ever and ever.

    Psalm 145:1

Chapter 17

Cobbler Cooking

Apple Cobbler

Yield: 10-12 servings

Ingredients

1 cups peeled and sliced (Rome Beauty or Granny Smith Apples)

1 cup sugar
2 tablespoons all-purpose flour
1 teaspoon cinnamon
½ teaspoon nutmeg
1 teaspoon lemon juice
1 cup water
½ cup butter

Directions for cobbler

1. In a 4 –quart saucepan, combine apple, sugar, flour, spices, lemon juice and water. Cook for 10 minutes until thick and bubbly. Pour into baking dish. Top with pie crust and bake for 35 minutes until golden brown.

Pastry:

2 cups sifted all-purpose
1 teaspoon salt
2/3 cup shortening
½ cup cold water

Directions for pastry:

1. Sift flour and salt together, cut in shortening with pastry blender.
   Sprinkl1 tablespoon water over flour mixture.
   Toss with a fork. Repeat procedure. Roll into a ball and roll out.
   Make strips and place on top of apple mixture.

Blackberry Cobbler

Yield: 10-12 servings

Ingredients

2 cups blackberries, picked and washed
1 cup water
¾ cup sugar
1 tablespoon flour
½ teaspoon nutmeg
½ cup butter
1 teaspoon cinnamon
Pie crust for cover

Directions

1. Preheat oven to 325 degrees F. Spray casserole dish 8x 12 inch baking dish.
2. In sauce pan combine blackberries, water, sugar, flour, butter and cinnamon.
3. Slowly cook for 10 minutes. Stir constantly.
4. Pour in the baking pan. Cover with pie crust. Prick holes in top of crust.
5. Bake at 325 degrees F for 30 minutes or until golden brown.

Peach Cobbler

Yield: 12 servings

Ingredients

8 cups sliced fresh peaches or 1 (2 ½ can) sliced peaches
1 cup water
1 cup sugar
½ teaspoon salt
½ teaspoon cinnamon
½ teaspoon ginger
1 teaspoon vanilla
2 tablespoons all-purpose flour
½ cup butter

Pastry for Rectangular Pan:

3 cups sifted all-purpose flour
1 teaspoon salt
2/3 cup shortening
½ cup cold water

Directions

1. Sift flour and salt together. Cut in shortening into flour mixture and roll out dough. Cut for peach cobbler.

Directions

1. Combine all ingredients for fresh peach cobbler in a large saucepan. Cook for 5 minutes. Cool and set aside.
2. Place peach mixture in 13 x 9 x2 pan. Place pie pastry on top of peach cobbler mixture; prick the top of crust. Bake peach cobbler at 350 degrees F until golden brown.

TALKING POINTS:

Connection Georgia Barrier Sea Islands

Liberty County

Midway – Connection to Georgia's Barrier Island

Midway has a village in Liberty County called Seabrook Village, a post-Civil War black settlement. A research project to show how former Slaves lived after the Civil War. About 300 people are scattered throughout the community who are descendants of the original settlers.

The Seabrook Village has 104 acres, started in 1994. The community is reminiscent of the times between 1870 and 1930. The Village is one of the few sites dedicated to the preservation of rural black culture after the Civil War in the United States. The Village shows how the blacks farmed, fished and hunted for food and how they recycled things thrown away by white folks.

LIBERTY COUNTY

Liberty County was established in 1777 and named in the honor of the word "Liberty". African-American population of the county approximately 20,655. Islands in Liberty County are St. Catherine's Island, Isle of Wight, Hampton Island and Wolf Island. African-American slaves interests Midway, Riceboro, Creek Island, Seabrook, Retreat and Seabrook.

Georgia's Barrier Sea Island

St. Catherines Island

-Known for Nicholsonboro Baptist Church built by freed slaves over 140 years ago. When the slaves were freed in 1870, for $15.00 per acre, the 18 freed slaves bought n acre for a proper praying place under pine and brush their first church. The freed slaves used clap boards were nailed until a cabin was formed. The church was covered with wooden shingles and a tiny belfry and faced a street of oyster shells. The church continue to have the original church bell. The church contains the pot belly stove.

The church has four windows with shutters.

At one time, there was an all-black government headed by Tunis G. Campbell. Campbell once worked with the Freedmen's Bureau.

Possible Africa Connection:

Mali-The country is located in West Africa. Tribal groups include Mande, Malinke, Peal, Voltaic, Tuareg and Moor. Also, there are others. Foods introduced to America include Kola nuts, shea nuts, okra, mangoes, rock rabbit and lamb.

Former Georgia Slaves 'Sayings:

PLANTATION LIFE:

1.   Mother's Work

"Mammy was a low hand but us chillen didn't do nothin' much 'cept eat and play and sleep'

In de grass 'til she got in from de fiel' at night."

Former Slave Easter Huff page 244

Bible Verse(s):

1   The earth is the Lord's and the fullness thereof; the world, and they dwell therein.

Psalm 24:

Chapter 18

Goat Meat Products and Other

Specialty Meat Products

Goat Meat Chili

Yield: 25 servings

Ingredients

        1   pounds goat meat, ground
        1 tablespoon vegetable oil
        1 cup onion, chopped
        1 clove garlic, minced
        1 bell pepper, chopped
        2   stalks celery, chopped
        2 (15 ounce) cans tomato sauce
        1 (18 ounce) can tomato paste
        ¼ cup chili powder
        1 (16 ounce) can tomatoes, chopped
        1 teaspoon salt
        1 teaspoon cayenne pepper
        2 tablespoons green chilies
        1 teaspoon garlic salt
        1 teaspoon black pepper
        2 cups tomato juice

Directions

1. In a large sauce pot, place goat meat and vegetable oil. Saute until meat turns pink. Add onion, garlic, bell pepper and celery. Cook for 15 minutes. Add remaining ingredients and cover. Cook for 1 to 1 ½ hours. Serve over rice.

Pulled Goat Barbeque with Spicy Barbeque Sauce

Pulled Goat Barbeque

Yield: 10 to 12 servings

Ingredients

10 pounds lean goat meat
1   cup seasoned salt
½ gallon spicy barbeque sauce

Directions

1. In a large sauce pot boil meat until tender; Drain and shred meat. Season with salt. Place in a large aluminum pan and cover. Smoke meat in smoker for four hours.
2. Remove from smoker and coat with spicy barbeque sauce. Return to smoker and cook for 1 hour. Serve on buns.

Spicy Barbecue Sauce

Ingredients

1 tablespoon olive oil
½ cup yellow onions, chopped
1 cup catsup
½ cup brown sugar
10 tablespoons Worcestershire sauce

½ cup apple cider vinegar
1 teaspoon cayenne pepper
1 gallon tomato sauce
Directions

> In a skillet heat oil, and saute onion until soft, add catsup, brown
> sugar, Worcestershire sauce, vinegar and cayenne pepper. Transfer
> to a large sauce pot and add tomato sauce. Cook for 30 minutes.
> Stir and simmer
> For 15 minutes.

Season pulled goat with sauce.

Grilled Goat Kabobs

Yield: 12 servings

Ingredients

3 teaspoons garlic granules
1 teaspoon ground cumin
1/ teaspoon red pepper flakes
1 teaspoon salt
2 1/2 pounds goat meat, cut into 1-inch cubes
1   cup Italian Salad Dressing
6(12-inch) metal skewers
12 -1 inch cubes green pepper, slices
12 -1 inch baby carrots

Directions

1. Stir together first 4 ingredients in a bowl and place in a large zip-
    top plastic freezer bag. Add goat meat and Italian salad dressing.
    Seal

And coat each piece of meat. Chill 3 hours; turning occasionally.

2. Drain goat meat and thread skewers with goat meat, green peppers and baby carrots.
3. Preheat grill to 350 degrees F and grill goat kabobs until done internally. Serve with dipping sauce.

Dipping Sauce

Ingredients

2 cups pineapple juice
1 tablespoon tabasco sauce

Directions

1. Combine all ingredients in a large sauce pot. Bring to a boil for 5 minutes. Cool and chill until ready to serve.

Raccoon 'n' Sweet Potatoes

Yield: 8 to 10 servings

Ingredients

1 Raccoon, skinned and cleaned
¼ cup salt
½ cup vinegar
6   medium sweet potatoes, quartered
2 tablespoons butter

Directions

1. Clean raccoon and place in a large roaster pan cover raccoon with water. Add salt and vinegar. Cover and let soak in refrigerator for 24 hours. Drain. Wash meat off.
2. Place sweet potatoes around raccoon and dot with butter. Cover. Bake at 350degrees F or 2 hours or until well done.

Fried Squirrel

Yield: 6 servings

Ingredients

1 squirrel, skinned and cut up
2 quart milk
3 teaspoons salt
1 teaspoon black pepper
1 egg, beaten
1 cup water
1 cup self-rising flour
Peanut oil for frying

Directions

1. Clean squirrel as indicated.
2. Place in a large bowl and pour milk over squirrel cover and refrigerate overnight.
3. Discard milk and wash meat.
4. Season with salt and pepper.
5. Beat egg and add water to make an egg wash.
6. Coat meat with egg wash and dredge in flour.
7. Heat oil and fry to golden brown.

Fried Rabbit

Yield: 4 servings

Ingredients

1 rabbit, skinned and cut up
1 tablespoon salt
1 tablespoon black pepper
2 cups self rising flour
2 cups shortening

Directions

1. Prepare rabbit, wash, pat dry and season with salt and pepper.
2. Dredge in flour.
3. Heat shortening to 350 degrees F.
4. Fry rabbit pieces to golden brown. Drain. Serve hot.

Fried Alligator Tail

Yield: 14 servings

Ingredients

2 pounds Alligator tail, skinned and cut into strips
1 cup apple cider vinegar
1 cup milk
1 teaspoon salt
1 teaspoon black pepper
½ teaspoon cayenne pepper
1 teaspoon garlic granules
2 cups flour
1 quart peanut oil

Directions

1. In a large bowl, place alligator strips. Stir in apple cider vinegar and milk. Cover and marinate 24 hours.
2. Discard marinade. Season with salt, black pepper, cayenne pepper and garlic granule. Roll in flour and fry in hot peanut oil.
3. Drain.

Grilled Rabbit

Yield: 4-6 servings

Ingredients

> 1 rabbit skinned and quartered
> 1 cup vinegar
> 1 cup Italian dressing
> 1 teaspoon salt
> ½ cup Worcestershire sauce
> ¼ cup dark brown sugar

Directions

1. Prepare rabbit and place in a flat pan coat with vinegar and Italian dressing. Cover and marinate overnight.
2. Wash meat and season with salt. Set aside.
3. Mix together Worcestershire sauce and brown sugar.
4. Brush a thin layer over rabbit and then grill with skin side down for one-hour. Brush with remaining sauce and slowly cook until done.

'Possum and Sweet Potatoes

Yield: 10 servings

Ingredients

> 1 possum, skinned and cleaned
> 1 gallon water
> 1 tablespoon red pepper flakes
> 1 tablespoon black pepper
> 1 teaspoon cayenne pepper
> 1 teaspoon garlic granules
> 1 teaspoon salt
> 2 pounds sweet potatoes, peeled and sliced

Directions

1. In a large sauce pot, boil possum in water with red pepper flakes over medium heat for about 30 minutes.
2. Drain. Discard water.
3. Season meat with cayenne pepper, black pepper, garlic granules, and salt.
4. Put in roasting pan and place set potatoes around possum and bake at 325 degrees F for 2 hours.

Grilled Venison Burgers

Yield: 10 servings

Ingredients

2 pounds Ground venison
1 tablespoon garlic granules
1 teaspoon salt
1 ½ teaspoon black pepper
¼ cup onion, minced
½ cup celery, minced

Directions

1. In a large bowl, stir together all ingredients.
2. Make into 10 patties and cover. Refrigerate for 8 hours.
3. Grill for 10 minutes on one side and 5 minutes on opposite side.

Venison Barbeque

Yield: 14 servings

Ingredients

1-5 pound Venison side
1 quart milk
1 cup cracked black pepper

2 cups seasoned salt

For barbecue sauce:

4 cups favorite barbecue sauce
1 tablespoon Worchester ire sauce
3 tablespoons dark brown sugar
1 cup onion, chopped
2 teaspoons Tabasco sauce

Direction

1. Clean and wash venison. Coat with milk and cover. Soak for 24 hours.
2. Wash meat and rub with black pepper and salt. Cover and rest for 4 hours in the refrigerator.
3. Smoke for 4 hours. Make sauce and baste for 30 minutes.

For barbecue sauce: Stir together barbecue sauce, Worcestershire sauce, brown sugar, onion and Tabasco sauce. Heat for 30 minutes.

TALKING POINTS:

Georgia Barrier Sea Island

Isle of Wight- The Island is located in Liberty County.

Possible Africa Connection:

Burundi-The country is located in central Africa. Tribal groups include Hutu and many others.

Foods introduced to America are pigs, tea, chicken and bananas.

Georgia Former Slaves' Sayings:

PLANTATION LIFE:

1.   Playing Games

"Games? Well, 'bout de biggest things us played when I was a chap was baseball, softball, and marbles. Us made our own marbles out of clay and baked 'em in de sun, and our baseballs and softballs was made out of rags."

Former Slave James Bolton page 100 Book II

Bible Verse(s):

7 Rest in the Lord, and wait patiently for him: fret not thyself because of him who prospereth in his way because of the man who bringeth wicked devices to pass.

8 Cease from anger, and forsake wrath: fret not thyself in any wise to do evil.

Psalm 37: 7, 8

Chapter 19

Pastas

Shrimp Pasta

Yield: 8 servings

Ingredients

 1 small box pasta shells
 1 tablespoon olive oil
 ½ cup minced onions
 2   cloves garlic, minced
 3   cups chicken broth

 1 pound jumbo shrimp, shelled and deveined
 1 teaspoon seasoned salt

Directions

1. Cook pasta shells as directed on package. Drain and set aside.
2. Heat olive oil in a medium saucepan and cook onions and garlic until clear.
3. Add chicken broth and pasta; stir and cook covered for 10 minutes.
4. Stir shrimp into mixture and cook for 10 minutes. Season with seasoning salt.
5. Serve hot.

Tuna Pasta Salad

Yield: 8 servings

Ingredients

> 2 cups pasta shells
> 1   cups water
> 1 teaspoon salt
> 1-6 ounce can tuna
> 1-10 ounce frozen package peas and carrots, cooked
> 1 cup mayonnaise
> ¼ cup vinegar
> ¼ cup onion, diced
> ½ teaspoon black pepper

Directions

1. Cook pasta in water and salt according to directions on package
2. Drain tuna and flake. Set aside.
3. Cook peas and carrots as to package directions. Drain.
4. In large bowl, mix together all ingredients and stir well.
5. Refrigerate for 30 minutes before serving.

TALKING POINTS:

Georgia's Barrier Sea Islands

Hutchinson Island –The Island is used as a wild life preserve.

The Hampton Island was an important island for development of special seeds, such as, cotton and rice.

Possible Africa Connection:

Mauritania – The country is located on the Atlantic Ocean in northern Africa.

Tribal groups are Moors and many others. Foods introduced to America include goat, mutton, dried meat and fish. Also many types of game.

Former Georgia Slaves' Sayings:

PLANTATION LIFE:

1. Slave Quarters

"All de slave quarters wuz log cabins and little famblies had cabins wid jes' one room. Old Master Sho' did want to see lots of chillum 'round the cabins and all de famblies was 'lowed to live in two-room cabins. Beds for slaves wuz made by nailing frames, built out of oak or walnut planks to de sides of de cabins. Dey had two or three laigs to make 'em set right, and de Mattresses wuz filled with wheat straw. Dere warn't no stu' bought stoves den, and all our cookin' wuz done in the fireplace. Pots wuz hung on iron iron cranes to bile and big pones of light bread Wuz cooked in ovens in de hearth Dat light bread and de biscuits made out of shorts wuz our Sunday bread dey sho' wuz good, wid ur homemade butter. Us had good old corn bread for our evvyday bread, and dere ain't nothin' lak corn bread and buttermilk in healthy Niggers.

Dere wouldn't be so many sick Niggers now if dey et corn bread everyday and let all dis wheat bread.."

Former Slave Willis Cofer Page 203

Bible Verse(s):

1 Deliver me from mine enemies, O my God: defend me from them that rise up against me.

1 Deliver me from the workers of iniquity, and save me from bloody mem.

Psalm 59: 1,2

Chapter 20

Church Gatherings

Church gatherings included regular Sunday services, midweek services, Baptizing,

Revivals, spring and summer, and many other selected meetings.

Baptism –"Take me To The Water"

"Take me to the water, Take me to the Water, I want to be baptized." Before the '50s, African-Americans who lived in the rural areas, baptized the new coverts in the creeks, streams or ponds or rivers. Some were baptized in the Atlantic Ocean. After the new converts were fellowshipped in the church, there was a great big dinner.

    Sample Baptismal Dinner
    Fried Chicken
    Smoke Mullet Fish
    Chicken and Dressing
    Green Peas
    Peach Cobbler
    Pound Cake
    Lemon Ade

Smoke Mullet Fish

Yield: 50 servings

Ingredients

> 100 mullet fish, cleaned and washed

Directions

1. In a large smoker, smoke 25 fish at a time.
2. Serve 2 fish at a time.

TALKING POINTS:

Georgia's Barrier Sea Island

Wolf Island -The Island is located in Liberty County.

Possible Africa Connection:

South Africa -The country is located in the south of Africa. Tribal groups included

Bantus, Zulus, Xhosa, Swazi and Sotho. The black Africans introduced among other dishes.

Barbecue meats, peanut soup and tea.

Former Georgia Slaves' Sayings:

PLANTATION LIFE:

1. Early Church Life

Lucius H. Holsey born into slavery, was elected bishop for the Southern Region before he reached thirty. He was the chief founder of the Paine College.

St. Stephens Episcopal Church was the church for upper class blacks in Savannah.

Early on all of the islands slaves had churches in buildings or in Tree Groves. The slaves sang spiritual songs- anthems, gospel songs or shouters.

Many of the popular church songs sang in present times date back to plantation songs. On all of the island plantations there were the Shouters.

The shouters are religious dancers. A method of the shouters would use they go around and around with a shuffling motion of the feet and a tap of the heel on the floor. The slaves say the dance came from Africa and the dance was performed in the Negro Churches for many years.

The songs and traditions of the islands were written bout by Lydia Parrish – Slave Songs of The Georgia Sea Islands.

Bible Verse(s):

10In God will I praise his word: in the Lord will I praise his word,

11In God have I put my trust: I will not be afraid what man can do unto me.

Psalm 56: 10,11

Chapter 21

Salad Making

Conch Salad

Yield: 4 servings

Ingredients

1 pound Conch
1/3 cup Jalapeno peppers, minced
½ cup lemon juice
2 tomatoes chopped
1 cup celery, chopped
½ cup green peppers, chopped
1 medium tomato, chopped
1   cucumbers, chopped
2 teaspoons salt

Directions

1. Prepare conch as stated. Stir together all ingredient in a bowl.
2. Cover and refrigerated for 4 hours. Serve.

Tuna Salad

Yield: 6 servings

Ingredients

1 (7-ounce) can tuna
4 hard boiled eggs, chopped
¼ cup onions, finely chopped
½ cup celery, minced
½ cup sweet pickle relish
1 cup mayonnaise
1 teaspoon salt
1 teaspoon black pepper

Directions

1. Drain tuna. Place in a boil and flake. Add remaining ingredients and stir well.
2. Cover and refrigerate before serving.

TALKING POINTS:

Georgia's Barrier Sea Islands Connection

Blackbeard Island – The Island was known for the hideouts of pirates.

Possible Africa Connection:

Equatorial Guinea – The country is located on the west coast of Africa. The tribal groups are Fanf, Bubi, Mdowe and many others. Foods introduced to America include cowpeas, eggs, tomatoes and greens.

Georgia Former Slaves' Sayings:

PLANTATION LIFE :

1.   Rations

Food was distributed on Monday night, and for each adult slave, the following staple products were allowed----

Weekly ration: On Sunday:

    3 ½ lbs meat One qt. syrup
    1 pk of meal One gal. flour
    1 gal shorts one cup lard

Vegetables, milk, etc., could be attained at the "big house", but fresh meat ad chicken were never given."

Former Georgia Slave Della Brisco Page 128

Bible Verse(s):

1 O Lord, God of hosts how long wilt thou be angry against thee prayer of thy people?

2 Thou feedest them with the bread of tears; and giveth them tears to drink in great measure.

Psalm 80: 4,5

Chapter 22

Seafood Cooking

(Some Geechees catch fish with nets from the Atlantic Oceans. However, most people buy fish from the fishing boats or ships, fish market or from the grocery stores. For fish preparations, Geechees fry fish, smoke fish on an outdoor grill or make fish based soups.)

Fish Recipes

Fried fish usually is made with corn meal mixed with flour, salt, garlic salt and black pepper. The frying oil is usually corn oil or peanut oil.

Fried Oysters

Yield: 10 servings

Ingredients

    1 pound Oyster picked and shelled
    2 cups yellow corn meal
    ½ cup flour
    1 teaspoon salt
    1 teaspoon black pepper
    ½ teaspoon garlic salt
    Selected vegetable oil for frying

Directions

1. Prepare oysters, drain and set aside.
2. Mix remaining ingredients together.
3. Fill oil in deep skillet up to one inch or use a deep fat fryer.
4. Heat oil to 350 degrees F. Fry oysters few at a time to golden brown.
5. Drain on paper towels. Serve hot.

Deep Fried Shrimp

Yield: 10 servings

Ingredients

1 pound raw shrimp (jumbo, medium or small size) deveined, clean and washed
1 teaspoon salt
2 cups flour
2 cups water
1 egg
Vegetable oil for frying

Directions

1. Wash and prepare shrimp.
2. Season with salt. Set aside.
3. In a separate bowl, mix together flour, water and egg.
4. Dip the shrimp by the tail when battering each piece .
5. Heat the oil for deep frying (350-365 F) for deep frying.
6. Fry each piece of shrimp in hot vegetable oil.

Steamed Shrimp

Yield: 12 servings

Ingredients

> 1 pound jumbo shrimp
> 1 package old bay seasoning

Directions

1. Peel and devein shrimp.
2. Wash. Fill medium saucepan with water add old bay seasoning and bring to a boil. After water boils, add shrimp.
3. Boil in old bay seasoning for 5 minutes.
4. Serve with cocktail dipping sauce.

Grilled Shrimp

Yield: 6 servings

Ingredients

> 1 pound jumbo shrimp, deveined and cleaned
> Seasoning salt
> Oil grill

Directions

1. Clean and oil grill. Heat grill.
2. Devein, clean and wash shrimp.

Grilled Shrimp, Watermelon and Green Cantaloupe Kabobs

Yield: 12 servings

Ingredients

2 pounds (36) unpeeled, jumbo, raw shrimp
12 (12-inch) metal skewers

Marinade(mix together 1 cup red wine vinegar, 2 tablespoons seeded and minced jalapeno pepper, 2 tablespoons sugar, ¼ cup fresh lime juice, 2 tablespoon Dijon mustard, 2 cloves garlic, minced, teaspoon kosher salt and 1 cup olive oil).

24 (2-inch) cantaloupe cubes
24 (2-inch) watermelon cubes

Directions

1. Peel and devein shrimp leaving tails.
2. Marinade shrimp in a large zip top plastic freezer bag. Seal bag. Place in refrigerator and chill for 30 minutes.
3. Preheat grill to 350 degrees F. Remove shrimp from marinade, discarding marinade. Thread shrimp, watermelon and cantaloupe cubes alternately on skewers, leaving a ½ inch space between pieces.
4. Grill kabobs covered with grill lid 4 to 5 minutes on each side or just until shrimp turns pink. Serve on bed of lettuce with Italian dressing.

Crab and Shrimp Spread

Ingredients

1 pound crab meat, can
1 pound shrimp, peeled, deveined and cooked
1 cup jalapeno, minced
1 cup mayonnaise
¼ cup mustard
1 teaspoon dried dill

1 teaspoon salt

Directions

1. Place canned crab in a bowl. Prepare shrimp and chop.
2. Combine all ingredients. Cover. Refrigerate for 1 hour.
3. Serve.

Shrimp Pilaf

Yield: 8 servings

Ingredients

2 slices bacon, chopped
½ cup onions, chopped
1 cup green pepper, chopped
½ cup celery, chopped
1 ½ cups long-grain rice
1(15 –ounce) chicken broth
1 cup water
1 teaspoon salt
1 whole bay leaves
½ teaspoon black pepper
½ teaspoon rosemary

½ teaspoon cayenne pepper
1 ½ pounds shrimp, peeled and deveined

Directions

1. Cook bacon in a large sauce pan over medium heat. Remove bacon and on paper towels then chop bacon. Add onions, bell pepper and celery to the bacon fat; cook until tender.
2. Add rice, water, chicken broth, bacon seasonings and salt to vegetables in large sauce pan. Cover. Cook for 10 minutes and add shrimp. Bring to a boil for 5 minutes and reduce heat and simmer for 15 minutes.

Shrimp Provencal

Yield: 6 servings

Ingredients

    1 tablespoon olive oil
    ½ cup onion, diced
    2 garlic cloves, minced
    3 plum tomatoes, diced
    1 cup dry white wine
    1 pound large shrimp, peeled and deveined
    1 teaspoon thyme
    ½ teaspoon rosemary
    1 bay leaf
    1 teaspoon black peppercorns, cracked
    1 teaspoon salt
    5cups cooked hot brown rice

Directions

1. Heat olive oil in a nonstick skillet and saute onion until clear and tender. Add garlic and cook for 2 minutes.
2. Add tomatoes and cook for 5 minutes. Add wine and simmer for 2-3 minutes. Place shrimp over tomato
    Mixture and add seasonings, except salt. Cover and simmer for 5 minutes.
3. Stir and season with salt.
4. Serve over hot cooked brown rice,

Fried Crab Cakes

Yield: 8 cakes

Ingredients

    2 cups crab meat
    3 eggs, well beaten
    4 cups cracker crumbs, crushed

1 ½ teaspoons black pepper
1 teaspoon salt
¼ cup onions, finely chopped
1 ½ cups flour
4 cups vegetable oil for deep fat frying

Directions

1. In a large bowl, blend together crab meat, eggs, cracker crumbs, black pepper salt and onions. Shape into patties and roll each patty in flour. Shake off excess flour. Chill patties for 30 minutes.
2. Heat the oil to 350 degrees F. Cook the patties for about 3 minute and cook until crisp and brown. Remove and drain.

Deviled Crab Cakes

Yield: 8 cakes

Ingredients

2 tablespoons butter
½ cup onion, minced
¼ cup red bell pepper, chopped
¼ cup celery, chopped
3 eggs
½ sour cream
½ teaspoon dry mustard
½ teaspoon cayenne pepper
½ teaspoon black pepper
½ teaspoon salt
2 tablespoon green onions
½ teaspoon Tabasco sauce
1 cups saltine cracker crumbs, crushed
1 teaspoon lemon juice
½ pound crabmeat, picked over
1 tablespoon oil + 1 tablespoon butter

Directions

1. Place butter in skillet and saute onion, pepper and celery until tender and clear.
2. In a bowl, mix together eggs, sour cream, dry mustard, cayenne pepper, black pepper and salt; stir in sautéed vegetables, green onions, saltine crackers crumbs, and Tabasco sauce.
3. Fold in crab meat and lemon juice. Make into crab patties (8)
4. Heat oil and butter to hot. Fry crab patties to golden brown on both sides. Serve with tarter sauce.

Crab Casserole

Yield: 8 servings

Ingredients

1 tablespoon olive oil
½ cup onions, chopped
½ cup celery chopped
1 clove garlic, chopped
½ cup green pepper, chopped
2 tablespoons flour
1 cup cheddar cheese, shredded
1 cup milk
1 (16 –ounce) can green peas

2 pounds shrimp, peeled, deveined and chopped
2 pounds crab meat, chopped
2 cups bread crumbs
¼ cup butter

Directions

1. Butter a 13 X 9 X2 casserole dish. Set aside until later.
2. In a skillet saute onions, celery, garlic and green pepper until tender. Add flour and stir. Slowly add in milk and stir until mixture thickens. Stir in cheese and green peas.
3. In a large bowl add mixture, shrimp and crab meat. Stir well.

4. Pour into casserole dish. Set aside. Saute bread crumbs in a skillet, Drain and sprinkle on top of mixture in casserole dish.
5. Bake at 350 degrees F for 25 minutes.

Baked Seafood Jambalaya

Yield: servings

Ingredients

1 large onions, chopped
2 bell pepper, chopped
½ cup celery, chopped
½ cup vegetable oil
1 (6-ounce) can tomato sauce
1 (6-ounce) can tomato paste
1 can chicken broth
½ cup green onions, topped
2 cloves garlic, minced
1 cups water
1 teaspoon salt
1 teaspoon black pepper
2 bay leaves
4 cups uncooked long-grain rice
1 pound shrimp, peeled, deveined and chopped
1 pound crabmeat, picked
1 pound oysters, chopped

Directions

1. Butter large Dutch oven and set aside.
2. In a large skillet, saute onions, bell pepper and celery in oil until tender and clear.
3. Add tomato sauce, tomato paste and chicken broth and cook on low heat for 20 minutes. Add remaining ingredients and stir well. Pour into a Dutch oven and cover. Bake at 300 degrees F for 1 hour or until rice is done.

Shrimp Pilau

Yield: 8 servings

Ingredients

1   pounds shrimp, peeled and deveined
1 teaspoon red pepper flakes, crushed
3   cups water
2   slices bacon
½ cup onions, finely chopped
½ cup celery
½ cup green pepper, finely chopped
1(15 ½ ounces) can tomatoes, chopped
11/2 cups rice, long-grain
1 teaspoon Tabasco sauce
½ teaspoon salt

Directions

1. In a large sauce pan, place cleaned shrimp, red pepper and water. Bring to a boil and then turn heat down and simmer for five minutes. Set aside. Cook the bacon in a skillet until crisp. Drain bacon on a paper towel. Save two tablespoons of the bacon fat. Add the onions, celery and green peppers to the fat in the skillet and cook until very soft. Add the chopped tomatoes and cook for 5 minutes, stirring constantly.
2. Add rice and 2 cups of liquid from the shrimp cooking liquid. Stir well. Let simmer for about 20 minutes. Add shrimp and bacon. Season with Tabasco sauce and salt.

Shrimp Creole

Yield: 4 servings

Ingredients

¼ cup butter or margarine
1 cup onions, chopped

1 ½ cups celery, finely chopped
1 cup green pepper, finely chopped
1 clove garlic
2cups tomatoes, canned, chopped
1 (6 ¼ ounce) can tomato paste
3 cups water
1 teaspoon oregano,
2 bay leaves
¼ teaspoon Tabasco sauce
1 pound shrimp, peeled and deveined

Directions

1. In a large skillet, melt butter and add onions. Cook for 5 minutes, stirring constantly. Add celery, green pepper and garlic. Cook until vegetables are soft.
2. Add tomatoes, oregano, bay leaves and Tabasco. Add tomato paste and water. Cook for about 30 minutes over low heat and then add shrimp. Simmer for 30 minutes, stirring constantly.
3. Serve over rice.

Boiled Shrimp

Yield: 4 to 6 servings

Ingredients

1 pound shrimp, peeled and deveined
1 clove garlic
1 bay leaf
1 clove garlic
1 teaspoon salt
1   cups water
1 teaspoon red pepper flakes

Directions

1. In a large saucepan, place all ingredients and bring to a boil.
2. Simmer for 10 minutes,

3. Drain the shrimp.
4. Serve with cocktail sauce.

French Fried Shrimp

Yield: 4 to 6 servings

Ingredients

1 pound shrimp, deveined, peeled and washed
1 cup flour, self-rising
2 eggs, well beaten
1 cup milk
1 cup water
Peanut oil for deep fat frying

Directions

1. Clean shrimp and set aside. In a large bowl, combine self-rising flour, eggs, milk and water. Dip shrimp by the tails into the mixture and deep fat fry.

Conch Fritters

Yield: 8 servings

Ingredients

1 pound conch, picked and separated from any shells
1 medium onion, chopped
1 cup celery, chopped
1 teaspoon cayenne pepper
1 teaspoon black pepper
1 teaspoon salt
1 teaspoon garlic salt
1 teaspoon thyme

1 cup milk
Juice of 1 lime

2 cups water
2 teaspoons baking powder

½ pound flour
Peanut oil for frying

Directions

1. Pick conch and wash. Pat dry.
2. Place conch, onion, and celery in a food chopper and chop well. Place mixture in a bowl and season with cayenne pepper, black pepper, salt, garlic salt, and thyme., Add milk, water, baking powder and flour. Stir well. Drop by tablespoons in hot vegetable oil.
3. Fry until golden brown. Drain.
4. Serve with hot sauce or favorite dipping sauce.

Dipping Sauce for Conch Fritters

Ingredients

½ cup mayonnaise
2 tablespoons catsup
1 tablespoon dark rum
Juice of 1 lime

Directions

1. Mix all ingredients together well. Chill for 30 minutes. Serve.

Sardine Spread

Yield: 10 servings

Ingredients

2-(3 1/2 ounces) cans sardines in oil, drained
1 medium tomato, chopped
¼ cup onions, minced

½ cup celery chopped
¼ cup salad cubes
1 teaspoon black pepper
1 teaspoon hot pepper sauce
1   tablespoons mustard

½ cup mayonnaise

Directions

1. In a bowl, combine all ingredients and toss together.
2. Refrigerate for 1 hour. Serve.

Conch Cakes

Yield: 8 cakes

Ingredients

1   medium conchs, minced
2 tablespoons celery, minced
¼ cup bell pepper, minced
2 tablespoons onion, minced
1 tablespoon jalapeno pepper, minced
Juice of 2 limes
3 eggs, well beaten
2 cups bread crumbs

1 teaspoon salt
1 teaspoon black pepper
1 teaspoon Tabasco sauce

2 cups oil for frying

Directions

1. Place conch, celery, onion, green pepper, salt, hot pepper, thyme and lime juice in a large bowl. Stir well.
2. Add beaten eggs and bread crumbs. Add salt, black pepper and Tabasco sauce.

3. Form into conch cakes about 1 inch in diameter. Place on lightly oiled pan and cover with foil and refrigerate for an hour.
4. Heat oil and fry each conch cake until golden brown. Serve with tartar sauce.

Nile Perch

Yield: 4 servings

Ingredients

1 pound Nile perch, cleaned and cut up
2 teaspoons salt
1 teaspoon black pepper
1 teaspoon garlic salt
2 cups corn meal
1 eggs
2 tablespoons water
Vegetable oil

Directions

1. Clean, cut up and wash fish. beat eggs and add water.
2. Season corn meal with salt. pepper and garlic salt.
3. Coat fish with egg wash and then with seasoned corn meal.
4. Heat up vegetable oil to hot.
5. Fry fish few pieces at a time until golden brown.

Fried Ocean Perch

Yield: 4 servings

Ingredients

1 pound ocean perch
1 teaspoon seasoned salt
1 teaspoon onion powder
2 teaspoons black pepper
½ pound fish frying meal mix

Oil for frying

Directions

1. Clean and prepare fish.
2. Season fish with seasoned salt, onion powder and black pepper.
3. Dredge fish in fish frying meal mix. Dust.
4. Heat oil. Fry fish until golden brown.

Fried Red Snapper(Whiting, Tilapia, Jumbo Perch Fillets)

Yield: 8 servings

Ingredients

2 pounds whole red snapper
1   eggs, well beaten
1   cup milk
2   tablespoons water
3 cups fish fry mix
1 teaspoon salt
1 teaspoon seasoned black pepper
Oil for frying

Directions Perce

1. Clean fish and leave whole.
2. In a bowl, combine eggs, milk and water.
3. In another bowl, stir together fish frying mix, salt and seasoned black pepper. Stir well
4. Heat oil to 350 Degrees F.
5. Dip whole cleaned red snapper in egg mixture and then fish fry mixture.
6. Fry fish in hot oil until golden brown

Buttered Baked Trout
(Perch, Salmon, Shad, Grouper or fish or choice)

Yield: 6 servings

Ingredients

1 pound Trout, cleaned and washed
1 teaspoon garlic salt
1 teaspoon Old Bay Seasoning
1 teaspoon seasoned salt
½ teaspoon lemon pepper
½ cup chopped onions
½ cup butter, melted

Directions

1. Prepare trout whole or fillet. Place on a pan lined with aluminum foil, leave foil open to make enough to close the foil lightly over the fish.
2. In a small bowl, mix together all dry ingredients. Add onions
3. Coat the trout with the mixture inside and out side. Drizzle butter on trout. Close foil over fish and then bake in 375 degrees F oven for 40 minutes.

Jack Mackerel Patties or Salmon Patties (Croquettes)

Yield: 8 patties

Ingredients

1 (303 can) Jack Mackerel or Salmon
2 tablespoons onions, chopped
1 egg well beaten
1 teaspoon salt
1 teaspoon black pepper
1 cup cracker crumbs
1 cup self- rising flour
1 cup peanut oil for frying

Directions

1. Drain canned fish. Place in a bowl and flake. Add onion, egg, salt, black pepper and cracker crumbs. Stir well. Make six patties.
2. Dredge in flour and pan fry.

Baked Flounder

Yield: 8 servings

Ingredients

 2 pounds flounder, split and deboned
 1 cup corn meal
 ½ cup flour
 1 teaspoon salt
 1 teaspoon black pepper
 ½ cup butter

Directions

1. Preheat oven to 350 degrees F. Spray baking dish with nonstick spray.
2. Mix together cornmeal, flour, salt, black pepper and garlic salt.
3. Season flounder on both sides. Sprinkle with butter.

 Place in baking pan and bake for 30 minutes.

Boiled Clams

Yield: 6 servings

Ingredients

 1 pound clams
 1 cup melted butter

Directions

1. Boil clams in large stock pot until clams completely open. Serve with melted butter.

Fried Scallops

Yield: 4 servings

Ingredients

    1   pound scallops
    1 teaspoon cayenne pepper
    1 teaspoon black pepper
    1 teaspoon salt
    2 cups yellow meal
    oil for frying

Directions

1. Clean scallops and season with cayenne pepper, black pepper and salt.
2. Roll in cornmeal and fry in hot vegetable oil.
3. Drain on paper towels.

Steamed Crab Legs

Yield: 8 servings

Ingredients

    4 gallons boiling water
    1 package crab seasoning
    3 pounds whole crab legs

Directions

1. Boil water and add seasonings. Drop crabs into water. Cook for about 10 minutes. Serve.
2. Break crab legs and scoop meat. Dip meat into melted butter or cocktail sauce.

Steamed Lobster Tails

Yield: 6 servings

Ingredients

- 1 lobsters
- 1 large stock pot water

Directions

1. Clean lobsters
2. Boil water and boil lobster until done
3. Separate tails and serve with melted butter.

Geechee Seafood Platter

(1 pc. Whiting, 1pc. Trout, 1 pc. Catfish, 1 pc. Mullet, 6 Oysters, 6 meat, 6 Scallops, Fries, Coleslaw and Hushpuppies)

Crawfish Etoufee

Yield: 6 servings

Ingredients

- ½ cup fat back or salt pork, diced
- 3 pounds crawfish tail meat, picked and diced
- 1 teaspoon salt
- 1 teaspoon black pepper
- ½ cup green pepper, chopped
- ½ cup onions, chopped
- ¼ cup celery, chopped
- 1 cup water
- ½ cup butter
- 1/3 cup flour
- 1 cup water

½ teaspoon red pepper
½ teaspoon garlic

Directions

1. In a large skillet, cook fat back, do not burn. Add crawfish, salt, black pepper, green peppers, onions and celery. Stir and cook until done.
2. Add water, turn to low, continue to cook for a few minutes. Set aside.
3. In another skillet, melt butter and brown flour in butter. Slowly add water. Cook for five minutes until very thick. Then stir in fish mixture. Stir together and add red pepper and garlic. Cook for 5 minutes. Serve over rice.

Salmon Loaf

Yield: 6 servings

Ingredients

1 (16 –ounce) can, salmon, drained and flaked
1 ½ cups bread crumbs
1 tablespoons margarine or butter
1 tablespoons onions, minced
¼ cup celery, minced
1 cup milk
2eggs, well beaten
1 cup green peas, drained
1 teaspoon salt
1 teaspoon black pepper

Directions

1. Spray a loaf pan with non stick spray. Preheat 350 degrees F.
2. In a bowl, combine all ingredients and form into a loaf.
3. Place in the loaf pan and bake for 25 to 30 minutes,

TALKING POINTS:

Connection to Georgia's Barrier Sea Islands

McINTOSH COUNTY

McIntosh County was established in 1793 and named in the honor of William McIntosh, Creek Indian Chief leader of Lower Creeks served in Seminole War 1817-18; he was a brigadier general in the U.S. Army. He was killed by his tribesmen, who considered him a trader.

McIntosh County contains Blackbeard Island National Refuge, Wolf Island National Wildlife Refuge and Sapelo Island National Estuarine Sanctuary.

Darrien is the county seat for the county. County was created in 1793.

Connections to the Barrier Islands:

Meridian –Departure point for Sapelo Island. Sapelo Island is only accessible by boat.

Meridian is the city nearest Sapelo Island's Wild Life Management.

Richmond Hill- an area which was built by Henry Ford.

Connection to Barrier Island:

Darrien the city is a connector to the Sapelo Island and the city is also known for the McIntosh County Shouters who performed slave songs dating back to 1722.

The Shouts The shout is an African slave tradition in which performers form a circle and sing a cappellas they sway, clap, tap their feet and move counterclockwise.

Shouts told stories, from biblical vignettes to tales of daily life in slavery. Some contained coded messages so slaves could communicate secretly in front of the master.

A lead singer starts the shout, which is often improvised and then other shouters join in uses a stick as a drum to control as they rhythmic pace of the shout.

Possible Africa Connection:

Angola –The country is located in southern Africa. The tribal groups include Ovimbundu, Kimbundu Bakongo and many others. Foods introduced to America include pork, salt cod sesame seeds and many more.

Former Georgia Slaves Sayings:

PLANTATION LIFE:

"Rias Body was born the slave property of Mr. Ben Body, a Harris County planter. He states that he was bout fifteen years old when the Civil War started and, many year ago, his old time white folks told him that April 9, 1846, was the date of his birth.

The "paterolers" according to "Uncle" Rias, were always quite active in ante-bellum days. The regular patrol Tin each militia district in the County.

All slaves were required to procure passes from their owner or their plantation overseer before they could go visiting or leave their home premises. If the "paterolers" caught a "Nigger" without a pass, they whipped him and sent him home. Sometimes, however, if the "Nigger" didn't run and told a straight story, he was let off with a lecture and a warning. Slave children, though early taught to make themselves useful, had lots oftime for playing and frolicking with the white children.

Rias was a great hand to go seining with certain clique of white boys, who always gave him a generous or better than equal part of the fish caught.

At Christmas, every slave on the Body plantation received a present. The Negro children received candy, raisins and "nigger-toes", balls, marbles, etc.

As for food, the slaves had, with the exception of "fancy trimmins", about the same food that the whites ate.

No darky in Harris County that he ever heard of ever went hungry or suffered for clothes until after freedom.

Every Saturday was a wash day. The clothes and bed linen of all whites and Blacks went into wash every Saturday. And "Niggers", whether they liked it or not, had to "scrub" themselves every Saturday night.

The usual laundry and toilet soap was a home-made lye product, some of it a soft-solid, and some as liquid as water. The latter was stored in jugs and demijohns. Either would "fetch the dirt, or take the hid off" in short, when applied "with rag and water, something had to come."

Many of the Body slaves had wives and husbands living on other plantations and belonging to other planter. As a courtesy to principals of such matrimonial alliances, their owners furnished the men passes permitting them to visit their wives once or twice a week. Children born to such unions were the property of the wife's owner; the father's owner had no claim to them whatsoever.

"Uncle" Rias used to frequently come to Columbus with his master before the war, where he often saw "Niggers oxioned off" at the old slave mart which was located at what is now 1225 Broadway.

Negroes to be offered for sale were driven to Columbus in droves –like cattle—by "Nawthon speckulatahs".

And prospective buyers would visit the "block" accompanied by doctors, who would feel of, thump, and examine the "Niggers" to see if sound. A young or middle-aged Negro man, specially or even well trained I some trade or out-of-th-ordinary line of work, often sold for from $2000.0 to $4,000.00 in gold.

Women and "runty Nigger men" commanded a price of from $600.00 up, each. A good 'breedin' oman", though, says, "Uncle" Rias, would sometimes sell as high as $1200.00.

Rias Body had twelve brothers, eight of whom were "big buck Niggers," and older than hisself. The planters and "patarolers" accorded these "big Niggers" unusual privileges –to the end that he estimates that they 'wuz de daddies uv least a hunnert head o' chillum in Harris County before de war broke out."

Some of these children were "scattered" over a wide area"

Former Slave Rias Body pages 86, 87, 88

Bible Verse(s):

1 Keep not thou silence, O God: hold not thy peace, and be not still, O God.

Psalm 83:1

Chapter 23

Fresh Water Fish Cooking

Fried Whole Catfish

Serving Number 10 Serving size: 2 whole pieces per person

Ingredients

   10 whole catfish, cleaned
   2 pounds corn meal, yellow
   1 cup flour
   2 tablespoons kosher salt
   1 tablespoon black pepper
   1 tablespoon lemon pepper
   1 quart peanut oil

Directions

1. Clean catfish, leave whole. Set aside.
2. In a large bowl, combine together corn meal, flour, salt, black pepper and lemon pepper.
3. Stir well.
4. Roll whole fish in corn meal mixture. Refrigerate for 30 minutes. Heat oil in deep fat fryer to 350 degrees F.
5. Fry catfish until golden brown. Serve hot.

Baked Catfish

Yield: 6 servings

Ingredients

- 1 pound catfish fillets
- 1 teaspoon salt
- 1 teaspoon black pepper
- 1 teaspoon paprika
- 1   teaspoon onion powder
- 2   tablespoon butter, melted
- 2 onions, sliced
- 1 tablespoon lemon juice

Directions

1. Clean, wash and pat dry catfish.
2. Season with salt, black pepper, paprika and onion powder.
3. Place butter in casserole dish. Roll each piece of fish in butter.
4. Cover with sliced onions and bake at 350 degrees F for 20 minutes.
5. Sprinkle with lemon juice and sere.

Smoked Catfish

Yield: 6 servings

Ingredients

- 1 pound Catfish cut into halves
- Olive oil
- 1 teaspoon salt
- 1 teaspoon black

Directions

1. Prepare catfish and brush with olive oil.
2. Season with salt and black pepper.
3. Smoke for 30 minutes.

4. Serve.

Catfish Nuggets

Yield: 6 servings

Ingredients

 1 pound catfish, cleaned and cut into 1 –inch squares
 1 teaspoon salt
 1 teaspoon black pepper
 1 pound self-rising cornmeal
 Oil for frying

Directions

1. Season catfish with salt and pepper.
2. Coat with corn meal mix
3. Heat oil to 350 degree F.
4. Fry catfish nuggets until golden brown.

Catfish Hash

Yield: 8 servings

Ingredients

 1 pound catfish, deboned, cut up
 11/2 cups water
 1 cup chopped onions
 1 cup bell pepper, chopped
 1 teaspoon garlic salt
 ½ cup celery, chopped
 1 teaspoon black pepper
 ½ teaspoon salt
 1 tablespoon butter or margarine

Directions

1. Clean and debone fish. Place with water in a sauce pan. Simmer for 15 minutes.
2. Add onions, bell pepper, garlic salt and celery.
3. Add remaining ingredients, stir and cook for 10 minutes.

Fried Whole Mullet (Trout, Croaker or Bream)

Yield: 10 servings

Ingredients

1 pound whole mullet fish (small), cleaned and fins removed
1 ½ pounds corn meal
1 tablespoon salt
1 tablespoon black pepper
1 teaspoon cayenne pepper
1 egg
1 cup water
½ gallon peanut oil

Directions

1. Clean fish as indicated.
2. Place corn meal, salt, black pepper and cayenne pepper in a bowl and mix well. Set aside.
3. In a second bowl, make an egg wash; beat together egg and water. Set aside.
4. Deep fish in egg wash and then in corn meal mixture.
5. Heat peanut oil in deep frying pan to 350 degrees F.
6. Fry in peanut oil until golden brown. Drain on paper to towels. Serve hot with mustard, dipping sauce or hot sauce.

Fried Mullet Fish Roe(fish eggs)

Yield: 4 servings

Ingredients

1 pound fish roe

1 teaspoon salt

1 teaspoon black pepper

2 cups yellow corn meal

2 cups vegetable oil for frying

Directions

1. Season fish roe with salt and black pepper. Roll in corn meal.
2. Heat oil in skillet to hot. Fry roe until golden brown.
3. Remove from skillet with a spatula and drain. Serve,

TALKING POINTS:

Georgia's Barrier Sea Island

Sapelo is located in McIntosh County.

Brunswick –Home to Hofwyl-Broadfield Plantation –Historic site –Large plantation area that is more than 200 years old rice plantation. Now the plantation is a nature preserve, museum and antebellum home.

Sapelo Island is accessible only by boat. There are 10,000-acres in the island. There are descendants of slaves who live at Hog Hammock community. The Island is located 40 miles south of Savannah.

Sapelo Island – Many descendants of slaves continue to live on the island. Sapelo Island is also home of the Sapelo Island Estuarine Reservation (Formerly owned by millionaire R.J. Reynolds). The Department of Natural Resources and the University of Georgia operate the Estuarine Reservation in Sapelo in McIntosh County.

First African Baptist Church was built by freed slaves in the Raccoon Bluff area of the Island in 1866. The church has been restored by the Sapelo Island Cultural and Revitalization Society.

Sapelo Island is the home to the Gullah culture Isee-The heritage of an Island Hog Hammock- The area is located on Sapelo Island where it has been said that the African-Americans are descendants of Thomas Spalding's slaves of the island's original plantations. These descendants chose to remain on the island after Emancipation.

Hog Hammock School was closed in 1978. Students have to take the ferry from Sapelo back- and forth to Brunswick. A Sapelo Island Cultural and Revitalization Society (SICARS) has been developed. –The goal is to develop a Cultural Village were Geechee descendants can make a living demonstrating and selling traditional crafts -cast –net maker for catching shrimp crafts and basket weaving.

Additional building possible on Sapelo are Farmer Alliance building. Reynolds Mansion

Yesteryear Activities – legends of traditions and heritage of home folks allegedly on Sapelo Island

1– fishing on Raccoon Bluff
2- fishing with a drop line and cane pole from a batteau boat
3– fishing at night for alligators with a flambeau
4- plowing with mules
5- dancing Buzzard Lope

Possible Africa Connection:

Angola- abolition of the slave trade in 1836, Angola served as the chief supplier of slaves sold in Brazil and other parts of South America.

Georgia Former Slaves' Sayings:

PLANTATION LIFE:

1.Place in baking pan and bake for 30 minutes.Ring the Bell

"What de slaves done when dey wuz told dat dey wuz free? I wuz too little to know what dey meant by freedom, but Old Master called de overseer and told him to ring de bell for de Niggers to come to the big house. He told 'em dey wuz free devils and dey could go whar dey pleased and do what de pleased-dey could stay wid him if dey wanted to. Some stayed wid Old Marster and some went away. I never seed no yankee sojers, I heared tell of 'em comin' but I never seed none of 'em".

"No'm I don't know nothin' bout Abraham Lincoln, Booker T. Washington or Jefferson Davis. I didn't try to ketch on to any of 'em. As for slavery days some of de Niggers ought to be free and some oughn't to be. I don't know nuttin much 'bout it. I had a good time den and I gits on pretty good now,"

Former Slave Easter Brown pages 4 and 5

Bible Verse(s):

1   Show us thy mercy, O Lord, and grant us thy salvation.

2   I will hear what God the Lord will speak: for he will speak peace unto his people, and to his saints; but let them not turn again to folly.

Psalm 85:1, 2

Chapter 24

Corn, Cornbread and Other Breads

Corn serves as a very important staple item. It is eaten as a side dish, in soups, puddings, cereal and breads. There are many types of bred Geechees enjoy. They re the first to introduce most breads made from corn meal. Hoe cake gets its name from the idea that slaves would cook the bread wrapped in collard green leaves and put them on a hoe and cook it in the fireplace.

Usually each plantation had a gristmill. The slaves harvested the corn and carried it to the grist mill to be grounded.

Corn was ground using a Gristmill that was water powdered . Slaves usually built the mills on the plantations. The gristmill had sections an earth portion and a dam portion. The slaves constructed the earth portion of the dam by bringing in dirt with ox carts and wheel barrows. The water spins the turbine before spilling the water into a creek, which may flow into a river or a stream. The turbine turned a shaft attached to grooved millstones, which ground the corn.

The water underneath the dam was responsible for the milling of the corn and wheat. The corn was milled into meal and grits.

Hush Puppies(recipes were made by slaves for confederate soldiers to eat during the Civil War)

Yield: 12 hush puppies

Ingredients

    1 ½ cups cornmeal
    ½ cup flour
    2 teaspoons baking powder
    1 egg well beaten
    ¾ cup milk
    ½ cup onion, minced
    Vegetable oil for frying

Directions

    1. In a bowl, sift together cornmeal, flour, baking powder and salt.
    2. Mix together egg, and milk in a small bowl.
    3. Combine dry mixture and milk mixture. Make into small balls.
    4. Heat oil and fry balls and drain.

Cracklin' Corn Bread

Yield: 6 servings

Ingredients

    ½ cup cracklins
    2 cups cornmeal mix
    1 cup water
    Oil for frying

Directions

    1. Mix together cracklins', cornmeal mix and water.
    2. Heat oil in skillet. Fry cornmeal mixture into patties to make crackling patties.

Hot Water Cornbread Patties

Yield: 6 patties

Ingredients

> 2 cups white cornmeal self-rising
> 1 ½ cups hot water
> 1 egg, well beaten
> Oil for frying

Directions

1. In a bowl, combine cornmeal mix, hot water and egg. Stir well.
2. Heat oil and fry corn patties until golden brown.
3. Drain. Serve hot.

Old Timey Cracklin' Bread

Yield: 6 servings

Ingredients

> 1 ½ cups corn meal
> 1 teaspoon baking powder
> 2 tablespoons sugar
> 1   beaten eggs
> 1 cup cracklins', chopped
> 1 teaspoon salt
> 1 cup water

Directions

1. In a mixing bowl, add all ingredients together. Stir well. Pour into baking pan.
2. Bake in hot oven for15 minutes at 400 degrees.

Sunday Corn Bread

Yield: 6 servings

Ingredients

2 cups corn meal
1 cup flour
2 tablespoons sugar
3 teaspoons baking powder
1 cup milk
1 egg, well beaten
1 tablespoon butter, melted

Directions

1. Heat oven to 400 degrees F. Spray large baking pan with non stick vegetable spray,
2. In a bowl mix together cornmeal, flour, sugar and baking powder. Add milk, beaten egg and butter.
3. Mix well and pour into pan. Cook for 10-15 minutes or until done,

Buttermilk Corn Bread

Yield: 6 servings

Ingredients

1 cup corn meal
1 cup all purpose flour
¼ cup sugar
½ teaspoon salt
1 teaspoon baking powder
1 ½ teaspoons baking soda
2 eggs, well beaten
1 cup buttermilk
¼ cup shortening

Directions

1. Preheat oven to 425 degrees F. Place 2 tablespoons shortening in a rectangular pan and heat up.
2. In a large bowl, sift together corn meal, flour, sugar, salt, baking powder, and soda. Stir together eggs, buttermilk and shortening.
3. Pour in baking pan and bake until golden brown.

Corn Sticks or Corn Pone (Use cast iron corn stick pan)

Yield: 6 servings

Ingredients

1 cup corn meal
½ cup all purpose flour
2   teaspoons baking powder
½ teaspoon salt
3   tablespoon sugar
1 egg, well beaten
1 cup milk

Directions

1. Heat cast iron corn stick pan in oven for 450 degrees F for 3 to 5 minutes.
2. In a large mixing bowl, sift together corn meal, flour, baking powder, salt and sugar.
3. Make a hole in center of cornmeal mixture. Add egg and milk. Stir until well mixed.

Corn Meal Hoe Cake Patties

Yield: 8 patties

Ingredients

1 cup yellow meal corn meal
1 cup flour
½ teaspoon salt
½ teaspoon baking powder
¼ teaspoon sugar
1 cup water
½ cup shortening

Directions

1. Combine all dry ingredients and stir in water. Make a soft batter.
2. Heat shortening in a heavy black 10 –inch skillet until hot.
3. Make 3 –inch in diameter patties cook in skillet until golden brown on both sides.

Corn Pone

Yield: 6 servings

Ingredients

2 cups plain white cornmeal
1 teaspoon salt
1 tablespoon fat
1 cup boiling water
½ cup shortening

Directions

1. In a large mixing bowl, combine corn meal, salt and fat. Stir in boiling water. Stir well.
2. Heat shortening up in skillet. Drop pones by ¼ cup into hot shortening. Brown on both sides.

Corn Muffins

Yield: 12 muffins

Ingredients

    1   cups yellow corn meals
    1 cup all-purpose flour
    1 teaspoon baking powder
    1 teaspoon salt
    1 tablespoon sugar
    ½ cup shortening melted

    1 cup whole kernel corn (optional)
    ½ cup milk
    1 egg beaten

Directions

1. In a bowl, sift corn meal, flour, baking powder, salt and sugar. Make whole in the middle and add remaining ingredients.
2. Spoon butter in prepared muffin pans. Fill muffin cups two thirds full. Bake at 425 degrees F or until lightly browned.

Baking Powder Biscuits

Yield: 8 biscuits

Ingredients

    2½ cups all purpose flour, sifted
    2teaspoons baking powder
    1 teaspoon sugar
    ½ teaspoon salt
    ½ cup shortening
    1 cup buttermilk

Directions

1. In a large bowl, sift together flour, baking powder, sugar and salt.
2. Cut in shortening in flour mixture and stir in buttermilk.
3. Turn dough out on a floured cutting board and gently knead
4. Roll dough out to ½ inch thickness. Using biscuit cutter, cut dough into biscuits.
5. Place on baking pan and bake at 400 Degrees F for 15 minutes.

Hoe Cake Patties (Biscuits)

Yield: 6 hoecakes

Ingredients

1 ½ cups all purpose flour
1 ½ teaspoons baking powder
1   teaspoon salt
2 tablespoons sugar
½ cup shortening
½ cup milk
½ cup shortening for frying

Directions

1. Sift together dry ingredients, cut in shortening and add milk. Stir well.
2. Heat shortening in large black skillet. Drop the batter by spoonsful in hot shortening. Fry until golden brown on both sides.
3. Drain. Serve hot with molasses or fish.

Fry Bread

Yield: 12 small patties

Ingredients

2   packages of yeast

¼ cup lukewarm water
4 ½ - 5 cups all-purpose flour
¼ cup sugar
1 teaspoon salt
1 cup shortening
1 egg, beaten
1 cup milk
2 cups shortening

Directions

1. Soften yeast in lukewarm water. Combine shortening, sugar, and salt. Add egg and milk. Add half of mixture in the mixture.
2. Mix well. Add the remaining flour. Place in greased bowl and grease the entire ball. Cover and let rise for 2 hours.
3. Punch dough down and flatten on dough board. Roll dough out and make into flat patties. Fry each patty in small amount of fat until golden brown on both sides.

Spoon Bread

Yield: 8 servings

Ingredients

3   cups milk
1 ½ cups cornmeal
¼ cup butter
1 tablespoon sugar
1 teaspoon salt

3 eggs, well beaten

Directions

1. Heat oven to 350 degrees F. Oil large casserole dish.
2. In a large bowl add the milk, corn meal, butter, sugar and salt.
3. Pour into greased dish.
4. Bake for 45 minutes until browned.

Flap Jacks (Pancakes) -Recipe similar to the one made famous by Aunt Jeminia.

Yield: 12 pancakes

Ingredients

> 2   cups sifted all purpose flour
> 1 teaspoon baking powder
>
> 1 ½ tablespoons sugar
> ½ teaspoon salt
> 1 egg, beaten
> 1 cup milk
> ½ cup vegetable oil

Directions

1. Combine the first four ingredients and add egg. Make a batter. Spoon batter on griddle or put shortening in skillet and make the desired sizes of pancakes. Fry on both sides.

Angel Biscuits

Yield: 12 biscuits

Ingredients

> 2 packages dry yeast
> ¼ cup warm water
> ¼ cup granulated sugar
> 1 cup oil
> 2 cups buttermilk
> 6 cups flour, self rising
> 2 ½ cups butter or margarine, melted

Directions

1. In a large bowl, dissolve yeast in warm water. Add sugar. Stir very well and stir in oil and buttermilk. Add flour and stir until well blended.
2. Turn out on a lightly floured dough board and knead gently until dough is smooth.
3. Pat down dough to ¼ to ½ inch thickness and cut out with round biscuit cutter. Let stand for 30 minutes.
4. Dip cut biscuits in melted butter, fold in half slightly off center and place on an ungreased baking sheet.
   Bake in 400 degrees F oven for 10 to 15 minutes.

Hot Rolls

Yield: 24 rolls

Ingredients

1   packages active dry yeast
¼ cup warm water
½ cup shortening
2 cups milk, scaled
2 eggs
5 cups sifted flour, self –rising

Directions

1. Soften yeast in warm water, In a large bowl, combine sugar, shortening and milk
2. Cool to lukewarm. Add yeast and egg; stir in 2 cups of flour. Beat well. Stir in remaining flour to make a soft dough.
3. Knead on lightly floured surface until dough is smooth. Put into lightly greased bowl and let rise to double.
4. Shape into roll dough shape desired. Let rise doubled Bake in hot oven 400 degrees F 10 to 12 minutes.

Starter

    1   package active dry yeast
    2 cups warm water
    2 cups all-purpose white flour

Directions

1. and milk to form a soft dough. Dissolve yeast in warm water. Stir in flour. Pour into a stone crock or stone bowl. cover. Place in a warm place for 3 to 4 days.
2. Refrigerate tightly covered.
   (When making rolls, doughnuts or other yeast raised dough use 1 cup starter.)

Doughnuts or Beignets(made from starter)

Yield: 12 doughnuts

Ingredients

    4cups flour, all-purpose
    2 teaspoons salt
    2 tablespoons sugar
    4 teaspoons baking powder
    1 cup shortening
    1 cup starter

    1 cup milk
    2 cups oil for frying
    1 box powdered sugar

Directions

1. In a large bowl, combine flour, salt, sugar and baking powder. Cut in shortening with fork or pastry blender.
2. The mixture should look like fine peas after shortening is added.
3. Add starter and milk to form a soft dough. Turn onto a floured surface. Knead slightly. Roll dough to ½ inch thick.
4. Cut into doughnuts or make beignets. Let rise until double.

5. Fry in skillet. Drain. Sprinkle with powdered sugar.

4TALKING POINTS:

Georgia's Barrier Sea Island

Butler's Island

Located - Altamaha River Delta —US 17 South

Major Pierce Butler established one of the world's greatest rice plantation in 17888 and wrote slaver into the Constitution in 1788 and while a South Carolina delegate to the U. S, Senate, he invited Vice President Aaron Burr to his plantation in Georgia. Burr killed Alexander Hamilton

Pierce Butler was known to direct his slaves to develop the rice and cotton plantation. He was known to have the most organized plantation in the early 1800s. His first plantation included main house, with separate kitchen and store house, smoke house an overseer's house with a separate kitchen, a smokehouse, poultry house, wash house, cotton ban, corn house, horse mill, two store houses, the hospital, stable and six duplex slave cabins, and other slave settlements built near the fields.

Butler was very mean to his slaves. He did not let them attend church or associate with slaves from other plantations. The slaves made certain that Butler averaged profits of $50,000 per year from the 1780s up to 1835 of his Georgia holdings. Butler named his plantation Hampton.

His grandson's wife – Fanny Kemble, an English actress, wrote about slavery on the Hampton Plantation and the Butler's Island.

In her diary book, she wrote about the shock of slavery. Her published diary of 1863, was said to have begun the abolition of slavery movement

In the United States, England and the rest of the World.

Butler Island –Presently Butler Island is a Waterfowl Management Area – Butler Island was the first rice plantation where slaves worked the rice plantations. This area was known as the "Rice Capital" of

Georgia. Butler was the rice plantation on the Delta of the Altamaha River. The Flail song was made popular on the Island. Rice harvested by blowing of the wind.

There were nine plantations that were rice plantations on Islands before the Great Hurricane. Butler, Champney, Cambers, General's, Broughton, Rhett, Vivians, Wrights and Carrie Islands. The Old Rice Mill can still be seen standing in the Waterfowl Management Area. Rice grows wiled in the area.

The knowledge and backbreaking labor of the slaves were responsible for the rice plantation owners to become rice and stay rich from the 1700s to the late 1860s.

The slaves did not receive money nor good housing, food nor good medicine. The slaves made meals on the meager food they could find to eat.

Fanny Kemble Diary

Possible Africa Connection:

Egypt-Egypt is a country that bordering the Red Sea and the Mediterranean Sea. The country is in northeast Africa. The tribal groups include Arab, Berber and Bedouin and many others. Foods introduced to America include beef, goat water buffalo, prawns, fish and cheese.

Former Georgia Slave Sayings:

PLANTATION LIFE:

1. Man Servant

"An ex-slave's description of the real cause of the Civil War, deserves a place here.

It seems that Lincoln had sent several messages to Davis requesting that he free the slaves.

No favorable response was received. Lincoln had a conference with Mr. Davis and to this meeting he a gun and the Bible, so he finally throw the two upon the table and asked Davis to take his choice. He chose the gun. Lincoln grasped the Bible and rushed home. Thus Davis began the war but Lincoln had God on his side and so he ended it.

"One of Gov. Towns' sons went to the army and Phil was sent to care for him while he was there;

An aristocratic men never went to the war without his Valet. Phil duty was to cook for him, keep his clothes clean, and we bring the body home if he was killed —the poor soldiers were either buried when they fell or left lying on the field for vultures to consume. Food was not so plentiful in the army and their diet of flapjacks and canned goods was varied only, coffee and whiskey which was given when they were not on the battlefields. All cooking was done either between two battles or during the lull in a battle. John Towns was soon sent back home as they he was too valuable a Southerner to be killed in battle. His services were needed at home.

Near the close of the war, Sherman made a visit to this vicinity. As was his usual habit, he had obtained the reputation of Gov. Towns before he arrived at his home. He found conditions so ideal that not one thing was touched.

He talked with them all and went gaddy on his way. Phil was so impressed by Sherman that he followed his army and camped with the Yankees about where Central City Park is now. He thought that anything a Yankee said was true. One gave him a knife and told him to go and cut the first man he met, he followed instructions even though he knew the men. Realizing how foolish he had acted he readily apologized and explained why. These soldiers seemed to fear nothing —but lizards. They had never seen such animals and would run in terror at the sight of one.

The Confederates never discovered this. After the close of the war, they were stationed in the towns to keep order.

Union flags were placed everywhere, and a Southerner was accused of not respecting the flag if he even passed under one without bowing. Penalties for this offense were, to be hung up by the thumbs, or carry greasy poles for a certain time, and numerous other punishments which caused a deal of discomfort to the victims but sent the soldiers and ex-slaves into peals of laughter. The sight of a Yankee soldier was enough –to-send a Confederate one into hysteria.

"The slaves laughed when told they were free, but Gov. Towns was almost indifferent. His slaves, he said, were always practically free, as a little legal form did not own very much. Nearly every one remained there and worked for wages"

Former Slave Phil Towns pages 45 and 46

1.   Hoe-Cakes

"I worked under four overseers, "Mary continued. "One was named Sanders, one named Saxon, one Bush, and the other I can't 'member. One of them was mean, and had a big deep voice. When the niggers was at the feed lot, the place where they carried the dinner they brought to the fields, he would hardly give 'em time to et before he hollered out" "git up and go back to work!"

"When the slaves got hungry before dinner time, they would ask the nursing mothers to bring them back hoe-cake "corn dodgers", when they went to nurse the babies. Those hot-hoe cakes were eaten in mid-morning, "to hold us till dinnertime."

"Soap was made at certain time of year and left in the hollowed out trough of a big log. Indigo was planted for blucing. Starch was made out of wheat bran, which was put in to soak. The bran was squeezed out and used for hogs, and the starch water was saved for washing.

"Cider was made by hollowing a hole in the top of a tree stump, which was filled with apples. A hole was bored in the middle of the front, and a lever put inside, which would crush the apples. As Mary put it, "You put apples in the top, press the lever, the cider come out of the spout, and my, it was good!"

Former Slave Mary Child

Bible Verse(s):

1 I will sing of the mercies of the Lord for ever; with my mouth will I make known thy faithfulness to all generations.

1   For I have said Mercy shall built up for ever: thy faithfulness shall thou establish in the very heavens.

Psalm 89: 1,2

Chapter 25

Stews and Soups

Brunswick Stew – (Legend in Georgia has it that a slave made Brunswick stew for his confederate master from Georgia, however, when the confederates fought in Virginia the slave was captured and cooked the stew in Brunswick, Virginia. This is a Geechee original stew. (The meat for formerly squirrels, raccoons, fish and rabbit.) There is a special plaque naming Brunswick, Georgia the beginning of Brunswick Stew. The plaque is on St. Simons Island.

The Virginians say that the Brunswick stew was a stew created by a slave named Jimmy Matthews in 1828.

Ms. Mary's Brunswick Stew

Yield: 12 servings

Ingredients

    1 hog head cleaned and scraped
    1 tongue skinned and cleaned
    1 tablespoon salt
    Water
    ½ large yellow onions, chopped
    3 pounds white potatoes, diced
    3 (14-ounce) bottles catsup
    2   (15 ¼ ounce) can whole kernel corn

1 (15 ¼ ounce) can creamed corn
1   (14 ½ ounce) cans whole tomatoes, chopped
2   cups apple cider vinegar
1 tablespoon black pepper
1 teaspoon cayenne pepper

Directions

1. Clean hog's head as stated. Skin tongue. Place in a large stock pot, cover with water, add salt and boil until tender.
2. Remove from pot and debone head, Cut all meat up into small bites. Strain stock from boiling pot and place back in pot. Add water to make 1 gallon stock add all remaining ingredients stir and add meat.
3. Cover and stir well. Cook over low heat for one hour.
4. Season with vinegar, salt and pepper.

Brunswick Stew

Yield: 14 servings

Ingredients

1 pound salt pork, chopped
3   cups celery chopped
2 cups onions, chopped
1 cup green pepper, chopped
3 cloves garlic, chopped
2 pounds boneless chicken breasts cut into 2 inch pieces
2 cups potatoes, chopped
4 quarts boiling water
11/2 pounds shrimp, cleaned, deveined and chopped
1 pound crabmeat, chopped
2 (16-ounce) cans tomatoes, chopped
2 cups tomato paste
1 cup tomato sauce
1 tablespoon cayenne pepper

2 cups frozen whole kernel corn, thawed

2 cups frozen cut okra, thawed
2 cups frozen baby lima beans, thawed
2 cups frozen green peas, thawed
1 tablespoon Tabasco sauce
1 tablespoon salt
1 tablespoon black pepper
1 teaspoon Worcestershire sauce

Directions

1. In large 6 gallon stock pot, cook salt pork and add celery, onions, green pepper and garlic. Cook until tender and clear.
2. Add chicken breast and water. Cook until tender. Stir in remaining ingredients, cover and cook for 1 ½ hours.

Slave's Brunswick Stew

Ingredients

Yield: 12 servings

1 cup salt pork
1 squirrel cleaned and cut up
1 raccoon cleaned and cut up
1 rabbit, cleaned and cut up
1 wild turkey, cleaned and cut up
2 tablespoons salt
Water to cover
1 tablespoon black pepper
1 tablespoon cayenne pepper
1tablespoon sage
4 pounds tomatoes, cut up
2pounds butter peas
2cups yellow onions, chopped
1 cup yellow meal
4 cups creamed corn cut from corn
3   pounds shrimp, cleaned and deveined
¼ cup salt

Directions

1. In large barrel cover with water, add salt and boil all meat until all is tender. Debone, discard bones and chop meat. Save stock.
2. Place all remaining ingredients with stock in barrel and cook for 4 hours. Stir well. Add shrimp for the last 30 minutes. Serve.

Brunswick Stew

Yield: 8 servings

Ingredients

1 pound salt pork, chopped
2 cups onion, chopped
1 cup chopped green pepper
3 cloves garlic, chopped
2 cups potatoes, diced

1-2 pounds shrimp, cleaned, deveined, chopped
1 pound crabmeat, chopped
1   (16 ounce) cans tomatoes, chopped
2 cups tomato paste
1 cup tomato sauce

1   tablespoon cayenne pepper
4 quarts boiling water
2 cups frozen whole kernel corn (thawed)
2 cups frozen cut okra, (thawed)
2 cups frozen baby lima beans (thawed)
2 cups frozen green peas (thawed)
2 cups chicken breasts, cooked and cut up
1 pound pork, cooked and chopped
1 pound beef, chopped and cut up
1 package cooked thin spaghetti

Directions

1. In a large saucepan, cook salt pork until tender. Add celery, onions, green pepper, garlic and potatoes. Cook until tender.
2. Add Shrimp and crabmeat and cook just until pink. Add tomatoes, paste and sauce; cook for 10 minutes. Add cayenne. Gradually add boiling water. Stir in corn, okra, lima beans and green peas. Simmer over low heat for 30 minutes. Add chopped chicken, breast, beef and pork.
3. Simmer for 35 minutes. Add cooked spaghetti and cook for 10 minutes.

Brunswick's Stew

Yield: 14 servings

Ingredients

1 -3-pound pork roast, cut into 1-inch squares
1   2 1/2 pound chicken, cut up
4 -16 ounce cans green peas
1 large bag frozen whole kernel corn
4   medium potatoes, diced
1 large butter beans, frozen
5 cups catsup
3 medium onions, chopped
4 cups tomatoes chopped
1 tablespoon salt
1 tablespoon red pepper
2 teaspoons seasoning salt
2 cups tomato sauce

Directions

1. In a large saucepot, add water to cover pork and cut up fryer and boil till done.
2. Debone chicken and roast, Reserve broth. Discard bones. Add remaining ingredients to meat and broth. Bring to a boil for 1 minute. Cover and reduce heat and simmer for 2 ½ hours.

Brunswick Stew

14 servings

Ingredients

1   pounds Boston Butt
2   pounds cut up chicken
2 pounds boneless beef, cut into 1-inch pieces
Water to cover
large onions, chopped
1   stalks, celery, chopped
2 large bell pepper, chopped
1 quart tomato sauce
1 number 10 can tomatoes, chopped
1   pounds white potatoes, chopped
1 teaspoon rosemary
1 tablespoon salt

Directions

1. In large 5 gallon stock pot, add all meat and cover with water. Bring to a boil. Cook until tender. Debone chicken. Discard bones. Chop all meat. Return meat to stock pot and liquid add remaining ingredients and cook for 1 ½ hours stirring constantly.
2. Season to taste.

Catfish Stew

Yield: 12 servings

Ingredients

½ cup salt pork, diced
1 cup onions, chopped
1 cup potatoes, diced
2 (16-ounce) cans tomatoes, whole, chopped
1 can tomato sauce
2 pounds catfish fillets, cut into 1 –inch pieces

1 teaspoon Tabasco sauce
½ teaspoon Worcestershire sauce
½ teaspoon salt
½ teaspoon black pepper

Directions

1. In a large saucepan, brown salt pork; remove meat and drain on paper towel. Set aside.
2. In a large sauce pan add fat and cook onions and potatoes until tender.
3. Add tomatoes, tomato sauce and drained salt pork. Cook covered for 20 minutes. Add catfish and remaining ingredients and cook covered
4. Over low heat for 45 minutes to 1 hour or until desired doneness. Serve over rice.

Catfish Gumbo

Yield: 12 servings

Ingredients

¼ cup butter
1 cup celery, chopped
1 cup onions, chopped
¼ cup green pepper, chopped
1 clove garlic, minced
1 tablespoon flour
½ teaspoon chili powder
1 teaspoon black pepper
1 teaspoon salt
1 (16 ounce) can whole tomatoes
1 (8 ounce) can tomato sauce
½ Tabasco sauce
2 cups water
1 pound catfish, cut into 1 ½ inch cubes
1 (10 ounces) package frozen okra, thawed

Directions

1. In a large saucepan, melt butter and saute celery, onion, green pepper and garlic until tender. In a small bowl, add flour, chili powder, black pepper and salt. Stir into vegetables add tomatoes, tomato sauce, Tabasco sauce and water. Stir well. Bring to a boil for about 5 minutes and then simmer for about 15 minutes. Add catfish and okra and cook for 30-35 minutes or until done. Serve over rice.

Fish Chowder

Yield: 8 servings

Ingredients

¼ cup butter or margarine
½ cup celery
¼ cup onion, chopped
1 cup whole kernel corn
2 cups potatoes, diced
2 cups carrots coins
2 cups milk
1 tablespoon corn starch
1 teaspoon salt
2 cups crab meat
4 cups shrimp, cleaned, deveined and chopped

Directions

1. Saute celery and onion in butter or margarine. Transfer to a large sauce pan and add corn, potatoes and carrots.
2. Add 2 cups of water. Cover and cook until tender. Add milk, stir in cornstarch, salt, crabmeat and shrimp. Cook covered for 45 minutes.

She Crab Soup

Yield: 10 servings

Ingredients

2 quarts fish stock(made from 1 cup clam shells, 1 cup whole shrimp and 3 quarts water)
4 cups whole kernel corn
½ cup onions, diced
3 cups potatoes, diced
1 teaspoon thyme
1 teaspoon rosemary
1 tablespoon olive oil
1 ½ pounds crabmeat, picked and chopped
2 tablespoons flour
2 cups milk
1 teaspoon black pepper
1 teaspoon salt
Few drops hot sauce

Directions

1. Make fish stock by boiling 1 cup crab shells(cleaned) and 1 cup whole shrimp in 3 quarts of water for 3 minutes. Drain and discard crab shells and shrimp. Set broth aside.
2. In a gallon size sauce pot, bring fish stock to a boil.
3. Add corn, potatoes and onions. Reduce heat to simmer. Cover and cook for 15 minutes. Add thyme, rosemary, olive oil and crab meat.
4. In a small bowl, combine flour and milk with 1 cup of the liquid from the sauce pot. Stir well and gradually add to the sauce pot.
5. Add black pepper, salt and hot sauce. Stir well. Boil until mixture thickens. Continue to simmer until desired doneness.
6. Stir and serve hot.

Jambalaya

Yield: 12 servings

Ingredients

1 cup fat back, cut into small cubes
4 cups onions, finely chopped
3 cups celery, finely chopped
3 tablespoons garlic, chopped
1 cup green peppers, chopped
4 cups hot link sausages, chopped
3 pounds ham, chopped into 1-inch squares
3 bay leaves, chopped
1 teaspoon thyme, crushed
2(no.2) cans tomatoes, chopped

¼ cup Tabasco sauce
1 quart shucked oysters
1 pound clams
8 cups water
1 pound jumbo shrimp, cleaned and deveined

Directions

1. In a large sauce pot cook fat back and add onions, celery, garlic and green peppers.
2. Cook until tender. Drain fat. Add remaining ingredients, except shrimp.
3. Stir and cook on medium heat for 30 minutes. Cover simmer for 10 minutes.
4. Sir in shrimp and cook until shrimp urns pink.

Oyster Stew

Yield: 8 servings

Ingredients

½ pound red potatoes cooked and cut into 1 –inch cubes
1 tablespoon olive oil
2   tablespoons butter
3   cups green onions, chopped
1 cup mushrooms, chopped
1 teaspoon Tabasco sauce
12 small oysters, shucked
1 tablespoons garlic, minced
4   cups heavy cream
1 teaspoon tarragon
1 teaspoon salt

Directions

1. Parboil potatoes until done. Drain and set aside.
2. Heat oil and butter in a heavy pan. Saute onions and mushrooms until softened. Add tabasco.
3. In a large sauce pan, add oysters, garlic, potatoes and heavy cream. Simmer until cream has thickened
4. Add tarragon and salt. Stir. Serve hot.

Fish Stew or Bouillabaisse

Yield: 8 servings

Ingredients

1 cup tomatoes, chopped
2 cups tomato juice
3 cups carrots, peeled and chopped
2 cups celery, chopped
1 cup onions, quartered
¼ cup tomato paste
1 teaspoon each thyme, rosemary, savory, sage, and basil

¼ teaspoon cayenne pepper
1 teaspoon salt
5   cups water
1 bottled clam juice
1 pound grouper, boneless, skinless cut into fillets
3   ounces sea scallops
8 ounces medium shrimp, peeled and deveined
6 small hard shell clams, soaked and scrubbed

Directions

1. Combine tomatoes, tomato juice, carrots, celery, onions, tomato paste, seasonings and salt. Add water and clam juice. Cover and cook slowly for one hour.
2. Cut fish into bite size pieces and stir into soup. Stir in remaining fish. Cover and cook for30 minutes. Serve hot with slice bread in a soup dish.

Low Country Boil

Yield: 10 servings

Ingredients

1 bag Old Bay Seasonings
12 Cobbetts yellow corn
10 small red potatoes, cleaned
5 pounds crab legs, cleaned
3 pounds sausages, cut into 3" lengths
3 pounds shrimp, deveined and washed

Directions

1. In a large sauce pot, stir in Old Bay Seasonings
2. Bring to a boil add corn and potatoes. Cover and cook for 10 minutes.
3. Add crab legs and sausages. Cook until done.
4. Add shrimp and cook until shrimp turns pink.
5. Serve with melted butter or cocktails sauce.

Seafood Gumbo

Yield: 10 servings

Ingredients

    1 tablespoon oil
    2 tablespoons flour
    1 ½ cups water
    1 ½ cups, onions, chopped
    ¼ cup celery, chopped
    ½ cup green peppers, chopped
    1   (No.2 ½) can tomatoes, chopped
    3 cups okra, chopped
    1 pound fish, boneless
    1 can tomato paste
    1 teaspoon salt
    1 teaspoon black pepper
    ½ teaspoon cayenne pepper
    1 cup uncooked rice

Directions

1. In a large stock pot, heat oil and add flour. Stir and add water in slowly. Add chopped vegetables and cook for 10 minutes.
2. Add tomatoes. Gradually add fish and tomato paste, salt and pepper. Cover and let simmer for an hour. Add water, if needed, stir in rice. Cook for 30 minutes

Seafood Stew

Yield: 8 servings

Ingredients

    1 pound fish fillets (cod, bass, snapper or grouper), cut in bite-size pieces
    1 pound medium shrimp, shelled and deveined
    ¼ cup lime juice
    1 ½ teaspoons Tabasco sauce

½ teaspoon salt
2   teaspoons vegetable oil
1 1/2 cups onion, chopped
1 cup green pepper, chopped
3   garlic cloves, minced
1 (16 –ounce can) whole tomatoes and juices
½ cup coconut milk
1 cup green onion, chopped
Hot cooked rice

Ingredients

1. Marinate in refrigerator- fish, lime juice, tabasco sauce and salt for 30 minutes.
2. In a large skillet heat oil and saute onion, green pepper and garlic until clear and tender.
3. Chop tomatoes. Stir tomatoes, juice and coconut milk into large skillet with vegetables. Cook covered for 10 minutes. Add marinated fish and cook for 10 minutes. Stir in shrimp and green onion. Cook for 10 minutes. Season to taste. Serve hot over rice.

Rabbit Stew

Yield: 6 servings

Ingredients

1 rabbit, cut up
1 teaspoon salt
1 teaspoon black pepper
2 cups water
2 medium onions, chopped
2 cups carrots, cut up
2 cups celery, chopped
4   medium white potatoes, diced
1 bay leaf
1 teaspoon thyme
2 cups green peas

Ingredients

1. Clean rabbit and season with salt and black pepper. In a large sauce pot, cover cut up rabbit with water. Cover. Bring to a boil and reduce heat. Cook over medium heat until rabbit can be deboned. Debone rabbit and discard bones. Save liquid from boiled rabbit add 2 cups water to make stock. Place meat, stock and all remaining ingredients in sauce pan and cook over low heat for 1 hour and 30 minutes.
2. Serve over rice.

TALKING POINTS:

Connection to Barrier Sea Island and Georgia's Barrier Sea Island:

Glynn County

"Liberty Ship" - The ship is located at the U.S. 17 at the foot of the St. Simons Island Causeway. The ship depicts the major role played in World War II. Ninety-nine percent of the 447 foot long cargo vessels were built in the Brunswick ship yard from 1942-45.

Possible Africa Connection:

Eritrea - A small country in East Africa. Tribal groups include Tigrinya Tigre and Kunama, Afar and Saho.

Foods introduced to America include frittata, pasta, millet, lamb and mutton.

Former Georgia Slave' Sayings:

PLANTATION LIFE:

1. Horse Finds the Gold!

"Aunt" Mary's young master—her owner's son—was John Nunnally. In 1865, while all the Nunnally men were away at the front, and "Miss"

Annie—Mr. John's wife— (except for the slaves), she heard that the Yankees were coming and had two of "Aunt" Mary's uncles dig a pit behind the smokehouse and bury all the family plate and money in it. But, when the Yankees came, their leader, who was riding a "great" big, nits an lice hoss"(a flea-bitten gray or pied roan)

Which he had trained to "seek out" and find things the Southern Whites had hidden, "circled the Nunnally house three times" and then that "Hoss" stopped right over the pit where Miss Annie had had had the family valuables hidden, and began to "stomp"! The Yankees then made the "Niggers"

Dig thee and unearth everything hidden, which they confiscated.

Former Slave Mary Carpenter page 143

Bible Verse(s)

15To show that the Lord is upright: he is my rock, and there is no unrighteousness in him.

Psalm 92:15

Chapter 26

Cake Baking and Other Desserts

Pound cakes and ginger cakes were poplar with the Geechees. Molasses were used as sweetening agents in many of the cakes and desserts.

Simple Pound Cake

Yield: 1 pound cake

Ingredients

    1 pound butter or margarine
    1   cups all purpose flour
    1 cup self –rising flour
    8eggs
    2 cups sugar
    1 teaspoon vanilla

Directions

1. Cream butter in a large mixer. Sift flours together twice. Add gradually to butter.
2. In a small bowl, beat eggs, add sugar. Blend; add to flour mixture.
3. Beat at medium speed for 5 minutes. Add vanilla.
4. Bake in greased tube pan for 1 ½ hours at 300 degrees F.
5. Cool in tube pan. Turn out on cooling rack.

Chocolate Cream Cheese Pound Cake

Yield: 1 pound cake

Ingredients

    1 cup butter, room temperature
    4   ounces cream cheese, room temperature
    3cups sugar
    6 eggs, room temperature
    2 ½ cups all-purpose flour
    ½ cup cocoa powder
    2 tablespoons vanilla extract

Directions

1. Preheat oven to 325 degrees F. Grease and flour a 10-inch tube pan.
2. In a large mixing bowl, using an electric mixer, cream butter, cream cheese and sugar until light and fluffy.
3. Add eggs, one at a time. Sift together flour and cocoa. Add to creamed mixture 1 cup at a time.
4. Beat well after each addition. Stir in vanilla extract and mix well. Pour mixture into cake pan.
5. Bake for 2 1/1 hours until tester comes out clean. Cool on cooling rack.
6. Remove from pan to completely cool on cooling rack. Place on plate when thoroughly cooled.

Egg Custard Pie

Yield: 1-9 inch pie

Ingredients

    4well- beaten eggs
    1 cup sugar
    ½ teaspoon salt
    1 teaspoon vanilla
    1 teaspoon cinnamon
    2 ½ cups milk, scaled
    1 -9-inch unbaked pastry shell

½ teaspoon ground nutmeg

Directions

1. In a bowl combine the first five ingredients. Blend well. Gradually add milk. Stirring very well.
2. Keep eggs from scrambling. Pour mixture into pastry shell. Sprinkle with nutmeg. Bake at 350 degrees F. for 30 to 40 minutes or until knife inserted in the center and the knife comes out clean. Cool.

Caramel Cake

Yield: 1 large cake

Ingredients

3cups sifted flour
4 teaspoons baking powder
1 teaspoon salt
1 ½ cups sugar
¾ cup butter or margarine
3 eggs
1 cup milk
1 teaspoon vanilla extract

Directions

1. Sift together flour, baking powder, and salt. Set aside. Dream together sugar and butter.
2. Add eggs, one at a time. Alternate flour with milk. To the egg mixture. Stir well. Pour batter into 3 floured 9 inch pans. Bake at 350 degrees F. for 20 minutes. Cool. Frost with Caramel Icing.

Caramel Icing

Ingredients

¼ cup granulated sugar

¼ cup hot water

3cups granulated sugar

1/8 teaspoon soda

1 ½ cups evaporated milk

¾ cup margarine

Directions

1. In a saucepan, brown ¼ cup sugar. Add ¼ cup of hot water. Cook approximately 1 minute and stirring often.
2. This mixture makes a syrup. Set aside.
3. In a large sauce pan, mix together sugar, soda and milk. Cook over medium heat until mixture is very thick, do not scorch.
4. After the mixture thickens, remove from heat and beat to desired spreading thickness. Spread on cooled layers of caramel cakes.

Banana Pudding

Yield: 1 large pan of pudding

Ingredients

1 package vanilla wafers

1   cups milk

1 cup sugar

1 tablespoon corn starch

1 teaspoon vanilla extract

2 eggs, separated save egg whites

4 cups ripe bananas

Directions

1. Line a 13 x 9 x 1 ½ dish with vanilla wafers. Set aside.
2. In a large bowl, combine milk, sugar, and corn starch.
3. Stir together well. In a medium saucepan, bring milk mixture to a simmer.
4. Stir well until mixture thickens. Add vanilla. Gently add eggs, stir well so that eggs want scramble.

5. To make pudding, pour part of mixture over wafers and alternate pudding and wafers wwith pudding on top.
6. Make meringue and spread on pudding.

Meringue

Ingredients

2 egg whites
¼ cup granulated sugar
1 teaspoon vanilla

Directions

1. In a mixing bowl, beat egg whites to form small peaks, gradually add sugar until stiff peaks form.
2. Stir in vanilla. Spread meringue over banana mixture.
3. Bake in a 350 degrees F. oven until meringue is golden brown.

German Chocolate Cake

Yield: 1 large cake

Ingredients

2   cups flour
1 tablespoons soda
1 teaspoon salt
½ cup butter
3cups sugar
1 teaspoon vanilla extract
1 cup buttermilk
1/3 cup melted unsweetened chocolate

Directions

1. Prepare 3 -9-inch cake pans.
2. Preheat oven to 350 degrees F.
3. Sift together flour, baking soda, and salt. Set aside.

4. In a mixing bowl, cream together butter and sugar.
Add vanilla extract. Add eggs one at a time.
5. Beat for 20 minutes and equally divide filling between baking pans,
6. Bake in oven until done,
7. Cool cakes and frost each cake.

Ginger Bread Cake

Yield: 24 servings

Ingredients

    3cups flour
    1   teaspoons soda
    ½ teaspoon salt
    1 cup butter
    1 cup sugar
    3 eggs
    1 cup molasses
    1 cup butter milk
    1 teaspoon vanilla
    ½ teaspoon ginger, ground

Directions

1. Prepare a 13" x 9" x 2" inch pan (Use oil and grease pan and then dust with flour). Set aside. Preheat oven to 350 degrees F.
2. Sift together flour, soda and salt. Set aside.
3. Cream together butter and sugar.
4. Add eggs; one at a time. Beating well after each addition.
5. Stir in molasses. Beat well.
6. Stir in flour mixture small amounts at a time and add buttermilk alternately with flour mixture.
7. Stir in vanilla and ginger into batter.
8. Pour batter in prepared pan and bake for 1 hour or until springs back to touch. Cool slice and eat.

TALKING POINTS:

Connection to Georgia's Barrier Sea Islands and Georgia's Barrier Sea Island

Glynn County

Jekyll Island – During the slave trade Jekyll Island was used as a quarantine place for the slaves.

Jekyll Island is known for the playground for the rich and famous. Rich families, such as, the Morgans, Goulds and the Rockefellers bought the entire island. They formed the Jekyll Island Club in 1886 and for 55 years they spent time in Jekyll Island and they built cottages on the Island. Other families joining the Jekyll Island Club were the Goodyears, Pulitizers and many more. The Jekyll Island Club closed down at the beginning of World War II.

Possible Africa Connection:

Sierra Leone-Sierra Leone is located in West Africa along the Atlantic Ocean. The tribal groups include Mende, Temne, Creole and many others. Foods introduced to America include lemons, chili peppers, onions, peanuts, peanut sauce, coconut and many more foods, Former Georgia Slaves' Sayings

PLANTATION LIFE:

1. No Cotton Gins

"Durin' de war, we had hard times, an' had to keep things hid out to keep the Yankee's f'um gittin' 'em. I 'member one night I had a cold an' was coughin' mighty bad. Us was hid out wid de horses, an' all of us was so 'fraid de Yankee's would hyar me cough an' fine de horses, so I got sont back to de house.

"I 'member one time de Yankees come by an' us all hid out 'fraid dey would kill us. Dey jes' to'e up things as fas' an dey could fine 'em. Dey tuk de meat outen de smoke'ouse an' wheat, an' oats, an' muss up what dey didn't want. Dey buss up all de soap barrels an' was'e all mist'ess soap what from everlastingshe done made. We had to hide out Marster so dey couldn't find 'im, cyase dey sho' would a kilt 'im.

"We had to bury all de silver an' things so as dem Yankees couldn't fine 'em.

Dey didn't leave nuffin dey could tote."

"Us had to make everything us had. Us couldn't buy nothin'. Dare won't no gins on our place den, so us had to pick de cotton offen de seeds, wash it, an cyard an' spin it.

Former Slave O. Williams page 643

Bible Verse(s):

1 The Lord reigneth, he is clothed with majesty; the Lord is clothed with strength, wherewith he hath girded himself: the world also is stablished, that it cannot be moved.

1   Thy throne is established of old: thou art from everlasting.

Psalm 93:1,2

Chapter 27

Cookies

Tea Cakes

Yield: 12 tea cakes

Ingredients

    1 cup shortening
    ¾ cup granulated sugar
    1 teaspoon vanilla
    1 egg
    ¼ cup milk
    2cups sifted all-purpose flour
    1 ½ teaspoons baking powder
    ¼ teaspoon salt

Directions

1. Cream shortening and sugar together. Add vanilla. Add egg, beat till light and fluffy. Stir in milk.
2. Sift together dry ingredients. Gradually and the dry ingredients to creamy mixture. Chill for 30 minutes.
3. Drop dough in 2-inch mounds on greased cookie sheets. Bake at 375 degrees F. for 6 to 8 minutes.

Ginger bread Cookies

Yield: 24 cookies

Ingredients

> 2 cups flour
> 1 teaspoon salt
> 1 teaspoon baking powder
> 1 teaspoon soda
> ½ teaspoon cinnamon
> 2eggs
> 1 cup dark brown sugar
> 1 cup sorghum syrup
> ½ cup butter
> 1 cup buttermilk

Directions

1. Preheat oven to 375 degrees F. Grease cookie sheets.
2. Sift together flour, salt, baking powder, soda and cinnamon. Set aside.
3. Cream together brown sugar, syrup and butter. Add eggs one at a time.
4. Add flour mixture and milk alternately to the butter mixture. Make a dough.
5. Refrigerate for 10 minutes. Drop cookies 2 inch a part on the cookie sheets.
6. Bake for 6 to 8 minutes. Serve hot.

Peanut Cookies

Yield: 24 cookies

Ingredients

> 3cups flour
> 1   teaspoons baking powder
> 1 teaspoon salt
> 1 cup peanut butter, smooth
> 1 cup brown sugar

½ cup granulated sugar
1 egg
1 cup cocktail peanuts
½ cup milk
1 teaspoon vanilla

Directions

1. Sift flour, baking powder and salt together. Set aside.
2. Cream together brown sugar, granulated sugar and peanut butter. Stir in egg.
3. Gradually add flour mixture to peanut butter mixture. Stir in milk, vanilla and cocktail peanuts.
4. Drop 1 tablespoon of dough unto cookie sheets, make a crisscross with a fork in the cookie. Bake at 375 degrees F. for 6 to 8 minutes.
5. Roll in sugar.

TALKING POINTS:

Georgia's Barrier Sea Island

Little St. Simons Island – The Little St. Simons Island is located 5 miles east of St. Simons Island. The Little St. Simons Island is privately owned near the Atlantic Ocean. The island has 10,000 acres.

Possible Africa Connection:

Senegal –Senegal is located in West Africa near the Atlantic Ocean. Tribal groups include Wolof, Pular, Serer, Mandinka and many others. Foods introduced to America are palm oil, coconut oil, okra, cowpeas and sweet potatoes.

Former Georgia Slaves' Sayings

PLANTATION LIFE:

1. Young Children Meals

"The younger children were fed from a trough that was twenty feet in length. At meal time each day the master would come out and supervise the cook whose duty it was to fill the trough with food. For breakfast the milk and bread was all mixed together in the trough by the master who used his walking cane to stir it with. At dinner and supper the children were fed pot liquor and bread and sometimes milk that had been mixed together in the same manner. All stood back until the master had finished stirring the food and then at a given signal they dashed to the trough where they began eating with their hands. Some even put their mouths in the trough and etc. There were times when the master's dogs and some of the pigs that ran round the yard all came to the trough to share these meals. Mr. Womble states that they were not permitted to strike any of these animals so as to drive them away and so they protected their faces from the tongues of the intruders by placing their hands on the sides of their faces as they ate. During the meal the master walked from one of the trough to the other to see that all was as it should be."

Former Slave George Womble page 187

Bible Verses(s):

164 Seven times a day do I praise thee because of thy righteous judgments.

Psalm 119:164

Chapter 28

Sweet Potatoes and Yam Cooking

Sweet potatoes are very important to Geechees cooking. They bake, boiled, fry, and roast sweet potatoes. They make desserts such as pones, souffles, pies, puddings, candied yams and many more dishes. However, George Washington Carver made the sweet potato famous.

The slaves had special methods for curing sweet potatoes and storing sweet potatoes so the potatoes would last year around.

Ash Roasted Sweet Potatoes

Yield: 10 servings

Ingredients

(On the plantations, sweet potatoes were roasted in the fire places or outdoors.)

    10 sweet potatoes
    ¼ cup butter

Directions

1. Make a bed of hot ashes in a fire place or a hot pit of ashes. Dig spaces in ashes, place sweet potatoes about an inch apart.
2. Cover with hot ashes and bake for one-hour.

3. When done, clean sweet potatoes; split and eat with butter.

Baked Sweet Potatoes

Yield: 10 sweet potatoes

Ingredients

10 small sweet potatoes, scrubbed and washed.
½ cup butter melted

Directions

1. Wash, scrub and dry off wash sweet potatoes. Prick holes in sweet potatoes.
2. Spread thin layer of butter on each sweet potatoes.
3. Place in a baking pan and bake for 1 hour and serve with cinnamon butter.

Cinnamon Butter

Ingredients

1 cup butter, softened
½ teaspoon cinnamon
2 tablespoons dark brown sugar

Directions

1. Stir together all ingredients.
2. Refrigerate for 30 minutes.

Fried Sweet Potatoes

Yield: 6 servings

Ingredients

2 sweet potatoes, medium
1 teaspoon cinnamon
2 tablespoons sugar
¼ cup butter or margarine, melted

Directions

1. Peel and rinse sweet potatoes. Slice into thin slices. Sprinkle potatoes with cinnamon and sugar.
2. Heat butter in a large skillet. Heat to very hot. Place potatoes in skillet. Cook until done, turning every 5 minutes.

Sweet Potato Croquettes

Yield: 6 servings

Ingredients

2 cups sweet potatoes, cooked and mashed
1 tablespoon butter, melted
1 teaspoon salt
½ cup milk
2 tablespoons brown sugar
¼ cup nuts, chopped
½ cup raisins
1 cup dry bread crumbs
2 eggs well beaten

Oil for frying

Directions

1. In a large bowl, add sweet potatoes, butter, salt, milk, sugar, nuts and raisins. Mix well. Make into balls.
2. Roll in bread crumbs, then beaten eggs and then crumbs again, until all croquette balls are coated.
3. Fry in deep fat until golden brown.

Sweet Potato Pone

Yield: 6 servings

Ingredients

 4 cups sweet potatoes, cooked and mashed
 ½ cup butter, melted
 2 eggs, beaten
 ½ cup brown sugar
 ½ cup molasses
 ½ cup evaporated milk
 1 ½ tablespoons vanilla flavor
 ½ teaspoon salt
 ½ teaspoon cinnamon
 ½ teaspoon nutmeg
 ½ teaspoon ground cloves

Directions

1. Preheat oven to 350 degrees F and butter a 2 quart casserole dish. Set aside.
2. In a large bowl add sweet potatoes and remaining ingredients. Place in the buttered Casserole dish, cover with foil and bake for 1 hour. Cool and serve.

Sweet Potato Custard

Yield: 1- 9 inch pie

Ingredients

 1 -9 –inch unbaked pie shell
 1   cups sweet potatoes, mashed
 1 cup sugar
 1 cup brown sugar
 1 cup condensed milk
 1 teaspoon cinnamon
 2 eggs, well beaten

1 teaspoon vanilla extract

Directions

1. Preheat oven to 400 degrees F. In a large mixing bowl, combine sweet potatoes, sugars, condensed milk and cinnamon.
2. Beat with an electric mixer. Add cinnamon, eggs and vanilla extract.
3. Pour into unbaked pie shell. Bake at 400 degrees F for 10 minutes and reduce heat and bake until well done. A knife blade should come out clean when inserted.

Candied Yams on Top of Stove

Yield: 6 servings

Ingredients

6 sweet potatoes, washed and peeled and cut into slices
1 cup water
1 teaspoon salt
1 ½ cups brown sugar
½ cup granulated sugar
1 cup water
2 tablespoons butter
2 teaspoons vanilla
½ teaspoon cinnamon

Directions

1. Clean, peel and slice. Place the sweet potatoes and salt in a sauce pan and add water. Cook covered on medium heat until tender.
2. Add remaining ingredients, stirring constantly. Cook for an additional 15 minutes.

Old Fashioned Candied Yams

Yield: 6 servings

Ingredients

3cups mashed sweet potatoes
1 1/2 cups sugar
4 tablespoons butter, melted
1 teaspoon vanilla
1 1/2 teaspoons cinnamon˙
½ teaspoon cloves ground
½ teaspoon nutmeg, ground
6 cups miniature marshmallows

Directions

1. In a large mixing bowl, combine all ingredients except marshmallows.
2. Pour into a baking dish, place miniature marshmallows on top.
3. Bake at 350 degrees F for 45 minutes.

Candied Sweet Potatoes

Yield: 6 servings

Ingredients

6 sweet potatoes, boiled and mashed
2 cups sugar
1   eggs, beaten
2 cups evaporated milk
½ cup butter, melted
1 tablespoon vanilla flavor
¼ teaspoon salt
1 teaspoon lemon flavor
½ teaspoon cinnamon

Ingredients

1. Boil potatoes until tender. Drain and mash.
2. Place in large bowl and thoroughly mix all ingredients. Pour into a casserole dish and bake at 325 degrees F.

Grated Sweet Potato Pudding

Yield: 8 servings

Ingredients

1 cups uncooked sweet potatoes, grated
1 ½ cups evaporated milk
½ cup corn syrup, dark
½ cup granulated sugar
½ cup brown sugar
½ cup butter, melted
2 eggs, well beaten
½ teaspoon cinnamon
¼ teaspoon nutmeg
½ teaspoon vanilla flavor
½ teaspoon lemon flavor

Directions

1. Preheat oven to 350 degrees F. In a large bowl, place grated uncooked sweet potatoes. Stir in milk,
Corn syrups, butter and eggs. Beat very well. Add spices and flavors. Mix well. Turn unto butter casserole dish.
2 .Bake for 45 minutes or until done.

Candied Yams and Orange Juice

Yield: 6 servings

Ingredients

4cooked sweet potatoes
1 cup butter or margarine, melted
1 cup granulated sugar
1 teaspoon salt
1 teaspoon vanilla flavor
½ teaspoon lemon flavor
Juice of one orange
1 teaspoon cinnamon
1 bag miniature white marshmallows

Directions

1. Preheat oven to 350 degrees F. In a large bowl, add first 10 ingredients. Stir well.
2. Pour into 2-quart casserole dish, top with marshmallows. Bake for 30 minutes or until marshmallows are golden brown.

Sweet Potato Pudding

Yield: 6 servings

Ingredients

1   medium sweet potatoes
1 cup evaporated milk
½ cup butter or margarine
1 teaspoon vanilla flavor
½ teaspoon lemon flavor
1 teaspoon cinnamon
2 cups sugar
1/3 cup flour
2 eggs, well beaten
1 package small marshmallows

Directions

1. Peel sweet potatoes, place in large saucepan cover with water and boil until done. Drain and mash. In a large bowl, stir together all ingredients, except marshmallows. Put marshmallows on top. Bake in oven for 30 minutes and serve.

Boiled Sweet Potato Pie

Yield: 2 – 9 inch pies

Ingredients

1-9 –inch pie crusts
4 sweet potatoes
½ cup evaporated milk
2 eggs, beaten
2 tablespoons vanilla flavor
2 cups granulated sugar
¼ cup dark brown sugar
1 teaspoon cinnamon
1/3 teaspoon nutmeg
2 tablespoons lemon juice
¼ cup flour

Directions

1. Boil sweet potatoes, in skins. Cool. Peel and mash. Add milk, eggs and vanilla flavor. Mix well. Add sugars and remaining ingredients. Stir well. Divide evenly between the two pie crusts. Bake for 50-60 minutes until done.

Sweet Potato Pie

Yield: 1-9 inch pie

Ingredients

    1 -9 inch pie crust
    1 ½ cups mashed sweet potatoes
    ¾ cup sugar
    1 ½ teaspoons cinnamon
    ½ teaspoon salt
    ½ teaspoon ginger
    ½ teaspoon ground allspice
    2   eggs, slightly beaten
    1 ¼ cup milk

Directions

1. Preheat oven to 350 degrees F. Prick crust slightly. In a large bowl, mix together all ingredients and pour into pie crust.
2. Bake pie for one hour and test for doneness.

Sweet Potato Souffle

Yield: 8 servings

Ingredients

    4 cups mashed sweet potatoes
    1 cup brown sugar
    ¼ cup butter, melted
    4 eggs, well beaten
    1/3 cup orange juice
    ½ teaspoon cinnamon
    ½ teaspoon vanilla extract

Directions

1. Butter a large casserole dish and preheat oven to 350 degrees F.
2. In a large bowl, combine all ingredients.
3. Beat well.
4. Pour mixture in casserole dish and bake for 45 minutes.

Shredded Sweet Potato Souffle

Yield: 6-8 servings

Ingredients

3 cups sweet potato, grated
1 teaspoon fresh lemon juice
2 eggs well beaten
1 cup brown sugar
1 cup granulated sugar
1 cup raisins
½ teaspoon vanilla
1cup evaporated milk
½ teaspoon cinnamon
¼ teaspoon nutmeg

Directions

1. Butter casserole dish and preheat oven to 350 degrees F.
2. Peel and shred sweet potatoes
3. Place in a bowl and add remaining ingredients.
4. Bake in casserole dish at 350 degrees F for 45 minutes or until tender.

Mashed Sweet Potato Souffle

Yield: 8 servings

Ingredients

3 cups sweet potatoes, cooked and mashed
1 ½ cups sugar
½ cup butter, melted
½ cup raisins
2 eggs, beaten
1 tablespoon vanilla flavoring
½ teaspoon lemon flavoring

Directions

1. In a large bowl, mix together all ingredients and beat. Pour into a casserole dish and top with topping.

Recipe for topping:

Ingredients

1 cup brown sugar
½ cup flour
1 teaspoon vanilla flavoring
1/2 cup butter
1 ½ cup pecans, chopped

Directions

1. Stir together brown sugar and flour. Add butter, vanilla flavoring and pecans.
2. Sprinkle on top of casserole.

Directions for baking.

1. Preheat oven to 350 degrees F. Bake for 30 minutes or until done.

Sweet Potato Souffle

Yield: 6 servings

Ingredients

¼ cup butter or margarine
3   tablespoons flour
1 ½ cups milk
1 teaspoon nutmeg
1 teaspoon salt
½ teaspoon cinnamon
1   eggs separated, beat whites until fluffy

2 cups sweet potatoes, grated

1 cup granulated sugar

Directions

1. In a 2-quart saucepan, melt the butter or margarine, add the flour and mix well. Add the milk slowly, and stir over medium heat until the mixture is thick. Add spices.
2. Beat the egg yolks until very light. Add a small amount of hot mixture to the egg yolks. Then add egg yolks too mixture, beat well after each addition. Cook until thick.
3. In a large mixing bowl, add grated sweet potatoes to egg mixture. Fold egg whites into mixture. Add sugar gradually.
4. Pour into casserole dish and bake at 325 degrees F for about 1 ½ hours or until lightly browned.

Sweet Potato Souffle

Yield: 8 servings

Ingredients

4 cups sweet potatoes, mashed

½ cup butter or margarine, melted

1 eggs, separated-beat egg whites after separating

1 cup milk

¼ cup brown sugar

½ teaspoon nutmeg

1 teaspoon salt

Directions

1. In a large mixing bowl, add potatoes melted margarine and egg yolks. Beat well. Add milk, sugar, nutmeg and salt.
2. Beat the egg whites until very stiff and fold into sweet potatoes mixture. Pour into baking dish. Bake at 325 degrees F for 30 to 35 minutes or until light brown and firm.

Sweet Potato Pie I

Yield: 1 – 9 inch pie

Ingredients

    2   cups cooked, mashed sweet potatoes, cooled
¾ cups sugar
½ teaspoon salt
½ teaspoon cinnamon
¼ cup melted butter or margarine
2 eggs, well beaten
¾ cup milk
1 teaspoon vanilla extract
1 unbaked 9-inch pastry shell

Ingredients

1. In a large bowl combine the first six ingredients. Mix well. Remove all lumps or strings.
2. Add to eggs, milk and vanilla. Stir well. Add egg mixture to sweet potato mixture.
3. Mix well. Pour filling into shell.
4. Bake at 350 degrees F for 1 hour or until a knife inserted into the center comes out clean. Cool.
5. Serve with Cool Whip.

Sweet Potato Pie II

Yield: 1 -9 inch pie

Ingredients

4cups cooked, mashed, sweet potatoes, cooled
1cup butter or margarine, melted
1 teaspoon cinnamon
½ teaspoon allspice
½ teaspoon salt
¼ cup granulated sugar

½ cup evaporated milk
1   large eggs
1 teaspoon flavor
1 unbaked 9 inch pastry shell

Ingredients

1. In a large bowl, add potatoes, butter, spices, salt, sugars and milk. Beat until light and fluffy.
2. Add the eggs, one at a time, heating well after each addition.
3. Add the lemon flavor. Mix well. Pour the filling into the pastry shell.
4. Bake at 400 degrees F for 10 minutes. Reduce heat to 350 degrees F.
5. Bake until a knife inserted in the middle comes out clean. Cool.

Sweet Potato Pie III

Yield: 1 – 9 inch pie

Ingredients

1   cups cooked, mashed sweet potatoes
½ cup sugar
½ cup brown sugar
¼ teaspoon salt
½ ground allspice
1 teaspoon cinnamon
¼ teaspoon ground ginger
1/2 cup melted butter or margarine
1 teaspoon vanilla extract
½ cup coconut, grated
½ cup pecans
½ cup milk
2 eggs, beaten
1 unbaked 9 inch pastry shell

Directions

1. Mix the first 7 ingredients in a large mixing bowl. Mix well. Stir in melted butter or margarine and vanilla extract.

2. Set aside. Add in q separate mixing bowl coconut, pecans, milk and eggs. Mix well. Add to sweet potato mixture. Stir
3. Well until all ingredients are evenly mixed. Pour filling into pastry shell. Bake at 450 degrees F for 10 minutes and reduce heat to 350 degrees F and bake 45 minutes or until a knife or toothpick inserted in the center comes out clean. Cool.

Sunday Best Sweet Potatoes

Yield: 12 servings

Ingredients

1 cups sweet potatoes, cooked and mashed
1 cup sugar
½ milk
2 eggs, well beaten
1 tablespoon vanilla extract
1 cup margarine, melted
1 cup coconut
1 cup pecans, chopped
1 cup brown sugar, packed
½ cup flour

Ingredients

1. Preheat oven at 325 degrees F. In a large bowl combine sweet potatoes, sugar, milk, eggs and vanilla extract.
2. Add cup margarine. Pour into casserole baking dish.
3. In a separate bowl combine cup or margarine, coconut, pecans, brown sugar and flour.
4. Stir well. Sprinkle mixture over the op of potatoes and bake for 20 minutes or until golden brown sugar.

Sunday Best Sweet Potatoes with Topping

Yield: 12 servings

Ingredients

> 3 cups cooked and mashed sweet potatoes
> 1 cup sugar
> 3 eggs, well beaten
> ½ cup butter
> 1 teaspoon vanilla
> ½ cup milk

Directions

1. Preheat oven to 350 degrees F. In a bowl, combine sweet potatoes, sugar, eggs, butter, vanilla and milk.
2. Pour into buttered casserole dish.
3. Top with topping and bake for 5 minutes

Topping

Ingredients

> 1 cup brown sugar
> ½ cup self-rising flour
> 1 teaspoon butter, melted
> 1 cup coconut

Directions

1. In a bowl, combine, flour, butter and coconut.
2. Sprinkle on top of casserole of sweet potatoes.
3. Bake in oven for 10 minutes.

Sweet Potato Pie IV

Yield: 2 – 9 inch pies

Ingredients

> 2 - 9-inch unbaked pie shells
> 2 baked medium sweet potatoes, peeled
> 3 eggs
> 1 ½ cups sugar
> 1 teaspoon cinnamon
> 1 teaspoon vanilla
> 1 cup margarine or butter
> 1 can condensed milk

Directions

1. Place all ingredients in mixer or food processor
2. Mix well. Pour into pie shells.
3. Bake 350 degrees F until firm. Cool.

Sweet Potato Pie V

Yield: 1-9 inch pie

Ingredients

> 3 cups uncooked sweet potatoes, melted
> 1 cup sugar
> ¼ cup sugar
> ½ teaspoon salt
> 1 teaspoon cinnamon
> 1 cup evaporated milk
> 2 eggs, well beaten
> 2 teaspoons vanilla
> 1 cup pineapples, crushed
> 1 unbaked 9 –inch pie crust

Directions

1. In a large bowl combine, first 9 ingredients. Mix well. Pour into unbaked pie crust.
2. Bake at 350 degrees F for 1 hour 20 minutes or until a knife inserted into the center comes out clean. Cool.

George Washington Carver Sweet Potato Pie

Yield: 1 -9 inch pie

Ingredients

1 9-nch unbaked pie shell
3 medium sweet potatoes
½ cup butter
1 cup brown sugar, packed
3 eggs, well beaten
¼ teaspoon salt
½ teaspoon vanilla extract
¼ teaspoon cinnamon
¼ teaspoon cloves, ground
¼ teaspoon ginger
¼ teaspoon nutmeg
¼ teaspoon allspice
¼ teaspoon mace
1 cup evaporated milk

Directions

1. In a saucepan, cook potatoes in water until done. Pout off water, mash and set aside. Preheat oven to 350 degrees F.
2. In a large bowl, cream together butter and sugar Add eggs one at a time. Add all remaining ingredients except milk.
3. Add sweet potatoes mixture and then milk. Pour filling into pie shell. Bake for 1 hour.

Cakes

Yield: 1 large cake

Georgia Sweet Potato Cake with Cream Cheese Icing and Filling

Ingredients

 2   cups flour
 2 teaspoons baking powder

 1 teaspoon cinnamon
 1 teaspoon nutmeg
 ½ teaspoon salt
 1 ½ cups oil
 2   ¼ cups sugar
 3   eggs separated
 ¼ cup water, hot
 2 cups sweet potatoes, grated
 1 ½ cups pecans, chopped
 2 teaspoons vanilla extract

Cream Cheese Icing

Ingredients

 1- 6-ounce package cream cheese, softened
 ¼ cup margarine, softened
 1 teaspoon vanilla
 1 cup pecans, chopped

Directions

 1. Preheat oven to 350 degree F. Spray pans with non stick spray and flour three 9-inch cake pans.
 2. Sift together flour, baking powder, cinnamon, nutmeg and salt unto waxed paper. Set aside. In a large mixing bowl, combine oil, sugar, egg yolks and water. Mix well. Add flour mixture to eggs mixture.

3. Stir in sweet potatoes, chopped pecans and vanilla extract. Beat egg whites to stiff but not dry. Fold into batter.
4. Pour into prepared cake pans. Bake for 30 to 35 minute or until cake is done.
5. Cool for 20 minutes then spread layers with cream cheese frosting.

Cream Cheese Frosting

Ingredients

½ cup butter or margarine, softened
1 (8-ounce) package cream cheese, softened
¼ teaspoon salt
1 teaspoon vanilla
2 tablespoons milk
4   cups sifted powdered sugar
½ cup chopped pecans

Directions

1. Cream the butter and cheese until light and fluffy; Add salt and vanilla. Stir well.
2. Add one tablespoon of milk. Add powdered sugar, ½ cup at a time, beat until fluffy after each addition.
3. Add remaining tablespoon milk. Add pecans. Spread over cake.

Sweet Potato Cake I/ Cream Cheese Frosting

Yield: 1 cake

Ingredients

¾ cup shortening softened
2 cups sugar
3 eggs
1 teaspoon vanilla extract
3 cups cake flour
1 ½ teaspoons baking powder
½ teaspoon salt

½ teaspoon ground cinnamon
½ teaspoon nutmeg
2 cups sweet potatoes, cooked and mashed
½ cup milk
1 ½ cups raisins
2 tablespoons brown sugar
1 cup pecans, finely chopped
3 prepared 9 –inch round cake pans
1 recipe Cream Cheese frosting

Directions

1, Place softened shortening in a large mixing bowl, cream until fluffy. Gradually add sugar beating well with the electric mixer. Add eggs, one at a time beating after each addition. Add vanilla extract. Set aside.
2. Sift together measured flour, baking powder, salt, cinnamon and nutmeg unto waxed paper; add flour mixture and sweet potatoes alternately to creamed shortening mixture. Add flour mixture at first and end with flour mixture. Add milk at last and mix well. Stir in raisins, brown sugar and pecans.
3. Pour batter into 3 greased and floured 9-inch round cake pans. Do not use butter to grease pans. Spray with non stick vegetable spray.
4. Bake at 350 degrees F for 35 to 30 minutes or until toothpick inserted in the center comes out clan. Cool cake on a cooling rack and remove from pans.
5. Spread cream cheese between layers and on top and on sides. Makes one 3 layer cake.

Sweet Potato Cake with Pineapples

Yield: 1 cake

Ingredients

¾ cup butter or margarine

1 cup sugar
1 cup brown sugar

2 eggs
1   cups all-purpose flour
1 ½ teaspoons baking powder
1 teaspoon baking soda
½ teaspoon salt
1 teaspoon cinnamon
½ teaspoon ginger
1 teaspoon vanilla
1 cup buttermilk
2 cups grated sweet potatoes
1 cup crushed pineapples
1 cup raisins
2 9-inch prepared cake pans or
1 prepared 13 x 9x 2 –inch pan

Directions

1.   Cream butter or margarine, gradually add sugars. Add eggs one at a time. Sift together in a bowl flour, baking powder, baking soda, salt, cinnamon and ginger.
2.   Add Flour mixture and buttermilk alternately to creamed mixture. Add about ¼ cup of flour mixture and about 1 tablespoon of buttermilk when adding to creamed mixture. Beat well after each addition. Add grated sweet potatoes, pineapples and raisins.
3 Pour batter into 3 prepared 9 –inch round cake pans or 13 x 9 x 2-inch pan. Bake at 350 degrees F for 25 to 30 minutes or until wooden toothpick inserted into the center of each cake comes out clean.
3.   Cool and frost with cream cheese frosting.

Sweet Potato Candy

Yield: 36 pieces of candy

Ingredients

2   medium sweet potatoes
1 pound light brown sugar
1 teaspoon fresh lemon juice

½ teaspoon cinnamon

2 cups Granulated sugar

Directions

1. Peel sweet potatoes cut up and cover with water. Bring to a boil and boil until tender.
2. Remove from water and cool. Put sweet potatoes in food processor and make a small pulp.
3. Sift brown sugar to remove all lumps. Stir together sweet potatoes, brown sugar and lemon juice in a large saucepan.
4. Cool for 25 minutes and cool. Stir in cinnamon. Cover and refrigerate for one hour. Make into 36 small balls and roll in granulated sugar.
5. Wrap each candy with waxed paper.

TALKING POINTS

Georgia Barrier Sea Island

St Simons Island is part of the Golden Isles with islands such as Sea Island, Jekyll Island, privately owned Little St. Simons Island, privately owned Little St. Simons Island). St. Simons Slaves assisted in developing rice cotton and food dishes. The slaves on St. Simons assisted in creating the Geechee/Gullah culture. St. Simons is located in Glynn County. The total are land 16.6 square miles and water 1.3 square miles and a total of 17.9 miles.

There are approximately 400 African-Americans living on St. Simons Island. Most are descendants from slaves.

Possible Africa Connection:

Nigeria-(second reference) – The country is located in West Africa. Tribal groups include Hausa, Fulani, Yoruba, Igbo, Ijaw and others. Foods introduced to America stews, fried fish, tomatoes, chickens, peas and beans

Former Georgia Slaves' Sayings

PLANTATION LIFE:

1.   Work Time

"Slaves on the Harper plantation arose when the horn was sounded at four o'clock and hurried to the fields, although they would sometimes have to wait for daylight to dawn to see how to work.

The overseer rode over the plantation watching the slaves at work and keeping account of the amount of work performed by each. Any who failed to complete their quota at the close of the day were punished."

Former Slave Emmaline Heard

Bible Verse(s)

5   Trust in the Lord with all thine heart; and lean not unto thine own understanding.

6   In all thy ways acknowledge him, and he shall direct thy paths.

7   Be not wise in thine own eyes; fear the Lord and depart from evil.

PROVERBS 3:5, 6, 7

More About St. Simons Island:

St. Simons Island – Popular for moss-draped oaks and historic light house

Popular plantations worked by Negroes on St. Simons – The Retreat Plantation, was once owned by James Spalding Family, Major William Page and later Thomas Butler King. The slaves on the plantation came in the early 1750s. Hamilton Plantation where the noted 'sea island cotton' was planted and shipped by the slaves. Research on agricultural products were done by two Scottish friends –John Couper and James Hamilton.

On John Couper's plantation-Cannon's Point- Couper developed research on sea island cotton seeds, provided a place for a lighthouse on his property and planted orchards or groves of lemons, oranges, dates and olives.

Slavery was on St. Simons Island from 1749 until after the Civil War in 1865.

The St. Simons Island has many attractions:

-Bloody Marsh Battle Site. Demere Rd. A monument marks the site where British forces defeated the Spanish troops in 1742 and was a turning point in the Spanish invasion of Georgia.

- Christ Church – Church was built for spiritual guidance in 1700s and missionary guidance of John Wesley, who headed the Methodist Church. Church was defiled in the Civil War. Located on Frederica Rd. founded by John and Charles Wesley, ordained clergyman of the Church of England who around on St. Simons in 1736. The first congregation services present structure was built in 1884 by Anson Phelps Dodge, Jr.

-Tabby houses- Houses built out of oyster shells, lime and sand.

Epworth-By-The-Sea – Methodist center on the site of former Hamilton Plantation. Former slave cabins open to the public.

Retreat Plantation – An antebellum plantation known for superior sea island cotton and extensive flower garden.

During the Civil War, the slaves gained some land on St. Simons Island and settled in the center of the island along Frederica Road. Their community was known as Harrington after a Demere homestead. Some of the descendants of the former slaves still exist there today.

Fort Frederica – The fort was built by the founder of Georgia, James Oglethorpe in 1736. It is located on Frederica Road.

Most of St. Simons was given by the federal jurisdiction to over five hundred freed slaves settled at Retreat Plantation and Gascoigne Bluff. Negro Troops, who served in the US Colored Troops during the Civil War were stationed on the island.

Lighthouse keeper's cottage. Campground for Native Americans. Gascoigne Bluff, named for the man who first surveyed Georgia's coastline for England, served as a shipping port for cotton to all around the world from plantations on the sea islands. Exports were stopped during the Civil War.

The United States Navy Headquarters were set up at the Bluff. Later on a sawmill was set up to make ships from the Live Oaks Tree.

Neptune Park – Named in honor of a slave, who cared for his confederate masters in the Civil War, is on the south end of the island.

Neptune Small was born in 1831. He was a slave of Henry Lord Page King family. Neptune was assigned as a manservant to his master King who was a soldier in the Confederate Army during the Civil War. King was killed at the battle of Fredericksburg and Neptune went out on the battle field during the war and found King's body and carried it back(toted it) to the plantation in Georgia for burial. Neptune went back to the war and served the youngest King son until the Civil War ended. The King family gave the freedman Neptune Small property and he lived out his life on the property. On the King's plantation, a bronze tablets has been imprinted with the heroism of Neptune Small.

Georgia Sea Island Singers and Festival

1- Gullah Language Demonstration- Gullah language a mixture of English and African dialect that bears the characteristics of some African tribes.
2- Beating The Rice
3- Plantation Demonstration
4- Rice Dance and Songs
5- Slave Games such as Hambone and speaking with the hands and other parts of the body made up on the rice and cotton plantations
6- Work songs of the Georgia Sea Islands
7- Sea Chanties —Call and Reponses

1   —The Shout —"A Slave Dance" seen only in the low country of Georgia and South Carolina.

The shouts and songs are the same ones African slaves sang when they arrived by ship in Virginia in 1722, before being sent to the rice and cotton plantation in the barrier islands off Georgia and South Carolina. Songs in original Gullah, a mixture of African dialect and English. The shouts are said to be an old fashioned way African-Americans way of singing where the performers form a circle and sing a Capella, as they sway. They clap their hands, tap their feet and move counter clockwise. A lead singer starts the shout and then other singers join in. Often times, this is called a 'call and response'. Sometimes, a drummer uses a stick to control the rhythm pace of the shout.

The shouts tell stories from biblical vignettes of daily life in slavery. At one time, some of the shouts contained coded messages so slaves could communicate directly in front of the masters. Shouts oftentimes, were performed in churches, fields and rural worship services.

Ebo Landing —a place in St. Simons where 18 tribesmen from Nigeria drowned themselves. They chose death over servitude.

"The importation of Negro slaves into the English colonies began in 1619 when they were brought into Virginia. Founded as a military colony, Georgia prohibited Negro slavery since it was desired that all men brought into the Colony should bear arms and no Negro slave was ever allowed a gun. This was the only one of Britain's Colonies in North

America to prohibit slavery and for the first twenty years of the life of the Colony there were no Negroes in Georgia.

"In 1798, Georgia prohibited the importation of Negroes direct from Africa and about a decade later the United States passed similar laws.

From that time all Negroes from Africa were smuggled into the country and kept hiding until they could be disposed to plantation owners.

"The winding creeks and waterways of Coastal Georgia afforded ideal landing places for such cargoes, just as in a previous century they had harbored pirates, and a century later they were to provide safety for bootleggers, Ebo Landing on Dunbar Creek was one of the best of these.

Shelters from view of traffic in Frederica River by the dense growth on Hawkins Island, Ebo offered these slave traders a haven for there illicit merchandise. Traditions says that a group of Ebo Negroes who were being held here walked into the water and drowned themselves rather than be slaves saying "The water brought us here; the water will take us away."

"The Ebos were described as having "a sickly yellow tinge in their complexion, jaundiced yes and prognathous faces like baboons' The women were said "to be diligent but the men lazy, despondent and prone to suicide." Slave traders avoided cargoes of these Ebo Negroes and freighted them only when no others were available.

"So, be it fact or fiction, the story of Ebo Landing, fits into the known characteristics of this tribe and name Ebo has been attached to this site for a century and a half. In the olden days no Negro would drop a hook to fish at Ebo. It was "ha'nted"!"

Page 67

Lydia Parrish wrote down the words from the slaves singing of the Slave Songs down on St. Simons Island.

Thomas Wentworth Higginson recorded similar spirituals in South Carolina during the Civil War.

Georgia White, a Georgian introduced a group of Negro Spirituals to America in 1874 when he toured with Fisk University singing Negro spirituals.

Spiritual Songs first heard on St. Simons Island and written down and put to music by James Weldon and J. Rosamond Johnson.

1. A Little Talk wid Jesus Makes It Right
2. All God's Chillen Got Wings
3. All I Do, de Church Keep A-Grumblin'
4. By an'By
5. Calvary
6. Can't You Live Humble?
7. Chilly Water
8. Come, Here, Lord!1.
9. Crucifixion
10. Daniel Saw de Stone
11. De Angel Roll de Stone Away
12. De Angel in Heab'n Gwinter write My Name
13. Death Come to My House He Didn't Stay Long
14. De Band o'Gideon
15. De Blin' Man Stood on de Rod an'Cried
16. Deep River
17. De Ol' Ark's A-Movering and I'm Goin Home
18. De ol' Sheep Done know de Road
19. Deres a Han' Writin' on de Walls
20. Dere's No Hidin' Place Down Dere
21. Didn't My Lord Deliver Daniel?
22. Didn't Old Pharoah Get Los'?
23. Die in de Fiel'
24. Do Don't Touch −A My Garmet
25. Good Lord I'm Gwine Home
26. Ev'ry Time I Feel de Spirit
27. Father Abraham
28. Give Me Dat Ol' Time Religion
29. Gimme Yo' Han'
30. Git on Board, Little Chillun
31. Give Me Jesus
32. Go Down MosesFit de Battl
33. God's A-Gwineter Trouble De Water
34. Great Day
35. Gwineter Ride Up in de Chariot soon-a in de Mornin'
36. Gwine Up
37. Gwinter Sing All Along de Way
38. Hallelujah
39. I am on the Battlefied For My Lord
40. I Couldn't Hear Nobody Pray
41. I Done Done What Ya'Tol Me To Do

42. I Feel Like My Time Ain't Long
43, I Gonna Sing
44. I Got A Home in Dat Rock
45. I Heard de Preachin of de Wordo' God
46. I Know de Lord His Hands on Me
47. I'm A Rollin
48. I'm Gwine Up to Heab'n Anyhow
49. I'm Troubled in Mind
50. In Dat Great Gittin' Up Mornin'
51. I Th.Mynk God I'm Free At Last
52. It's Me. O.   Lord
53. I Want God's Heab'n Anyhow
54. I Want to Die Easy When I Die
55. John Saw The Holy Number
56. Joshua Fit de Battle ob Jerico
57. Jubole
58. Keep A-Inchin' Along
59. Li-a How Dey Done My Lords'em to de Lam's
60. Lit'le David Play on Yo' Harp
61. Look —a How Dry Done My Lord
62. Lord Do Remember Me
63. Lord, I want to Be a Christian in My Heart
64. Mary an' Martha Jes' Gone 'Long
65. Mary Had a Baby, Yes, Lord
66. Member, Don't Git Weary
67. Mos' Done Toilin' Here
68. My Lord Says He's Gwinter Rain Down Fire
69. My Lord, What a Mornin'
70. My Ship is on the Ocean
71. My Soul's Bein Anchored in de Lord
72. My Way's Cloudy
73. Nobody Knows de Trouble I see
74. O, Gambler, Git Up of o' Yo' Knees
75. Oh, My Good Lord, Show Me de Way
76. O Rocks don't Fall on Me
77. O Wasn't Dat a Wide River'
78. Oh, Hear Me Prayin'
79. Oh, My Good Lord, Show Me de Way
80. Oh, Yes! Oh, Yes! Wait 'til I Git on My Robe
81. Peter, Go Ring Dem Bells
82. Pa' Mourner's Got a Home at Las'

83. Religion is a Fortune I Really Do Believe
84. Ride on Moses
85. Rise, Mourner, Rise
86. Rise Up Shepherd an' Foller
87. Roll de Ol' Chariot Along
88. Roll Jordan, Roll
89. Run, Mary, Run
90. Same Train
91. Singin' Wi'da Sword in Ma Han'
92. Sinner, Please Don't Let fid Harres' Pass
93. Somebody's Knockin' at Yo' Do'
94. Sometimes I Feel Like a Motherless Child
95. Stan' Still Jordan
96. Steal Away to Jesus
97. Swing Low Sweet Chariot
98. Too Late
99. To See God's Bleen din 'Lam'
100. Until I Reach Ma Home
101. Up on de Mountain
102. Walk in Jerusalem Jus' Like John
103. Walk, Mary Down de Lanc
104. Walk Together Children
105. We Are Climbin' Jacob's Ladder
106. Weary Traveler
107. Were You There When They Crucified My Lord
108. What Yo Guine To Do When Yo' Lamp Burn Down?
109. When I Fall on My Knees
110. Where Shall I be When De' Firs Trumpet Soun'
111. Where was Peter?
112. Who Dat A Comin' Ovah Yondah?
113. Who'll Be A Witness For My Lord?
114. You go, I'll Go With You
115. Yo u Got a Right
116. You May Bury Me in the Eas'
117. You Mus' Hab Dat True Religion
118. Zekiel Saw de Wheel

Possible Africa Connection:

Burkina Faso and Gabon -Gabon is a country in central Africa located near the Atlantic Ocean. Tribal groups include Bantu tribes, Fang, Nzebi, Obamba and many others. Foods introduced to America include starchy roots cocoa, peanuts, tomatoes, watermelons, corn and other grains.

Former Georgia Slaves' Sayings"

PLANTATION LIFE:

Bible Verse

1 Make a joyful noise unto the Lord, all ye lands.

2Serve the Lord with gladness: come before his presence with singing.

Psalm 100:1,2

Chapter 29

Black Pot Cooking

On the plantation, big black pots were used to cook for a lot of slaves. Geechees now use the big black pots for reunions and parties. Popular dishes cooked are fried fish, low country boil, Brunswick stew, Gumbo and pig's skins. Using a long and large paddle for stirring.

Fried Fish

Yield: 20 servings

Ingredients

> 2 gallons peanut oil
> 25 pounds Tilapia fish fillet
> 2 tablespoons salt
> ¼ cup black pepper
> 5 pounds yellow corn meal

Directions

1. Heat oil in big black pot
2. Clean fish and fillet
3. Season with salt and pepper.
4. Coat with yellow corn meal
5. Fry fish for golden brown
6. Drain on paper towels

Low Country Boil

Yield: 20 servings

Ingredients

10 gallons water
¼ cup seasoning salt
¼ cup garlic salt
5 pounds potatoes, cut in half
3 pounds sausages, cut into links
2 pounds crab legs
3 large bags of cobbets
5 pounds jumbo shrimp

Directions

1. Clean pot and build fire under pot. Stir in seasoning salt and garlic salt in water.
2. Add potatoes and sausages. Cook for 15 minutes. Then add crab legs and shrimp.
3. Cook for 30 minutes or until desired doneness.
4. Serve with melted butter.

Brunswick Stew

Yield: 25 servings

Ingredients

2 cups butter
1   large onions, chopped
2   cloves garlic, minced
1   tablespoons cayenne pepper
2   tablespoons freshly ground cracked pepper
2 tablespoons sea salt

¼ cup barbeque sauce
1 ½ cups dark brown sugar
1 pound pulled chicken
1 pound chopped smoked brisket
2 ½ cups chicken broth
10 ounces chopped smoked turkey
36 ounces crushed tomatoes
2 cups chopped tomatoes
2 cans (303 cans) creamed corn
4 cups frozen butter beans
1 gallon water
¼ cup Tabasco sauce
2 pounds shrimp, deveined and cut up

Directions

1. In large black pot, melt butter and onions and garlic. Stir well.
2. Stir in remaining ingredients, except shrimp. Cook well. Stirring constantly.
3. Cook for 30 minutes then 2 pounds shrimp and cook until shrimp turns pink
4. Serve hot or over rice.

Fried Turkey

Yield: 10 servings

Ingredients

For Frying:

Peanut Oil
1   pound turkey, thawed
½ cup seasoning salt
1 tablespoon black pepper
5gallons peanut oil

For marinating

Brine
1 cup salt
1   gallons water
½ cup vegetable oil

Directions

1. In a large pot, dissolve salt in water and boil for 5 minutes. Cool and stir in vegetable oil. Cool down and submerge cleaned turkey, with turkey parts and gizzard removed.
2. Pace in refrigerator in brine for 24 hours.

To Fry:

1. Remove turkey from brine and was three times. Dry off inside and outside.
2. Season turkey with salt and black pepper
3. Place turkey carefully in hot vegetable oil. Fry turkey, carefully browned and cooked through. The process takes about 45 to 50 minutes.
4. The turkey will rise to the top of the vegetable oil when it is done.
5. The internal temperature should be 180 degrees F.
6. Carve turkey and serve.

Gumbo cooked in Black Pot

Yield: 25 servings

Ingredients

1 cup vegetable oil
3 cups onions, chopped
2 cups green pepper, chopped
2 cups celery, chopped
2 cups okra, chopped
½ cup garlic, minced
3 pounds shrimp, cleaned and deveined

4 pounds chopped chicken, cooked
2 pounds cooked hams, chopped
1 (–no. 10 cans) tomatoes, chopped
1(no. 10 can) tomato sauce
2 bay leaves, crushed
1 (no. 10 can) whole kernel corn
1 (no. 10 can) creamed style corn
1 teaspoon file
1 gallon water

Directions

1. Heat the oil in the bottom of the black pot and cook onions, green pepper and celery until tender and clear.
2. Add okra and garlic. Cook for 5 minutes. Add the shrimp and cook slowly for 10 minutes. Then add remaining ingredients. Simmer for 45 minutes.
3. Stir constantly until desired doneness.

Fried Pig's Skins

Yield: 15 servings

Ingredients

10 pounds pig's skins cut into 3" X 2" pieces
1   gallons peanut oil
1   cups kosher salt

Directions

1. Wash skins and cut into pieces.
2. Heat oil in black pot to 350 degrees F.
3. Fry each piece of skin until the skin puffs out.
4. Drain skins on paper towels and season with kosher salt.

TALKING POINTS:

Connections to Georgia's Barrier Sea Island:

Sea Island

Possible Africa Connection:

Chad – Chad is located in North Africa. Tribal groups include Sara, Arab, Mayo-Kebbets, and many more.

Foods introduced to America include many rice dishes, fish-perch, talpia, shea butter, sweet potatoes, cane rat and tomatoes.

Former Georgia Slaves' Sayings:

PLANTATION LIFE:

1.   Going to School

"Going to school wasn't allowed, but still some people would slip their children to school. There was an old Methodist preacher, a Negro named Ned Purdee, he had a school for boys and girls going on it his back yard. They caught him and put him in jail. He was to be put in stack and got so many lashes except for a month. I heard him tell many times how the man said: "Ned, I won't whip you. I'll whip on the stock, and you holler." Ned, I won't whip you. I'll whip on the stock, and you holler."

So Ned would holler out loud, as if they were whipping him. They put his feet and hands in the holes, and he was stopped to he was supposed to be whipped across his back."

Former Slave Eugene Wesley Smith page 231

2.   Going to a Wedding

"When Marster's chillum got married, we all seed the wedding. From the yard back down to what you call the first orchard, all the darkies gathered. Every darkey fom the quarters was there, men and women too. After it was through, all the darkies passed by the bride and groom and each one, men and women, said, 'Oh! God bless you, Marster!', and squat. That's what we called dropping a curtsey. If the wedding was at a church, all the darkies come, and when the bride and groom come out and stood on the steps, all the darkies passed by and dropped curtsey.

It make 'em feel good for all the darkies to say that to 'em."

Former Slave Aunt Cicely Cawthon Page 191

Bible Verse(s):

1   Now faith is the substance of things hoped for, the evidence of things not seen.

2   For by it the elders obtained a good report.

Hebrews 11:1,2

Chapter 30

Confederate Ladies Tea Party

Usually before the end of the Civil War, the Geechee cooks would prepare foods for the Confederate ladies' tea party.

Menu

Chicken Salad
Watercress finger sandwiches
Cheese Straws
Hot Tea

Chicken Salad

Yield: 10 servings

Ingredients

8cups chicken breasts, chopped
2 cups celery, diced
1 medium onion, diced
1 ½ teaspoons salt
1 pound seedless red grapes
1 cup chopped pecans
½ cup delicious apple unpeeled, chopped
1 cup mayonnaise

1 teaspoon sugar
2 tablespoons fresh lemon juice
¼ teaspoon red pepper
½ teaspoon black pepper

Directions

1. Combine all ingredients in a large bowl and cover. Refrigerate 2 hours before use.

Watercress Sandwiches

Yield: 10 sandwiches

Ingredients

1 cup water cress, chopped finely
1 -8ounce cream cheese softened
½ cup butter, melted
1 loaf white bread
1 loaf brown bread

Directions

1. In a bowl, whip watercress and cream cheese together.
2. Make checkerboard sandwiches. Cover and refrigerate.
3. Serve.

Cheese Straws

Yield: 2 dozen cheese straws

Ingredients

1   ½ cups all-purpose flour
1 teaspoon salt
½ teaspoon cayenne pepper
1 ½ cups extra sharp cheddar cheese, shredded

½ to ¾ cup ice- cold water

Directions

1. Measure ingredients and pulse in food processor.
2. Roll into a dough. Make into 3 inch strips.
3. Bake at 350 degrees until golden brown.

Hot Tea

Yield: 10; 1/2 cups servings

Ingredients

Tea or choice

1 quart of hot water

Directions

1. Steep tea in hot water.
2. Serve with sugar cubes, lemon juice and cream.

TALKING POINTS:

Georgia's Barrier Sea Island

Sea Island- The island is located in Glynn County.

Connections to Barrier Islands:

Darrien – Georgia's second oldest town, founded in 1736. Oglethorpe's Second. Highlanders Historic Squares, district of timber barons homes and the Ridge – area of sea captains residences, shrimp fleets, caviar processing.

Georgia Sea Island Connections:

Camden County-The County was established in 1777. It was named in honor of Charles Lord Pratty, Earl of Camden. Member of British parliament who opposed the Stamp Act and tax of American colonies as unconstitutional. He was Lord Chancellor-1766-70 and Lord President of Council, 1782, 184-94.

County seat is Woodbine. Cities/Town: St. Marys, Kingsland, Woodbine Unincorporated Communities: Billyville, Bullhead Bluff, Burnt Fort, Cabin Bluff, Ceylon, Clarks Bluff, Colerain, Colesburg, Dover Bluff, Dungeness, Elliots Bluff, Flea Hill, Forestview, Glencoe, Greenville, Greyfield, Halifax, Harrietts Bluff, Halzehurst, Hickory Bluff, High point, Hopewell, Jefferson, Jerusalem, Kinlaw, Kings Bay Base. Mays Bluff, Midriver, PineyBluff, Rain Landing, Red Bluff, Scarlet, Scotchville, Seats, Shellbine, Silco, Spring Bluff, Stafford, Taraboro, Tompkins, Wavery, White Oak

Kingsland – Kingsland is the gateway to two national attractions, Cumberland Island National Seashore and the Okefenokee National Wildlife Refuge.I-95 Coastal Connection.

Kingsland also is known for the Catfish Festival.

St. Marys – There are preserved slave cabins located near John McIntosh Sugar Mill. The slave cabins are made from tabby. Tabby is a material unique to southern coast and is made of oyster shells, sand and water.

The Mill is located on Spur Road 40 across from Kings Bay Naval Submarine Base main gate. The John McIntosh Sugar Mill has a structure shows rooms devoted to cane grinding, boiling and processing sugar products.

St. Marys is known as the oldest city in the United States.

Possible Africa Connections:

Congo-Congo was formerly known as Zaire is located in central Africa with parts of the country borders the Atlantic Ocean. Tribal groups include Bantu, Mongo, Luba, Kongo and Mangbetu Azande(Hamitic).

Foods introduced to America include chicken stew, fufu, pumpkin, potatoes, and yams.

Former Georgia Slaves' Sayings:

PLANTATION LIFE:

1.   Yankees

"Mr. Simons, however, did not go to the war and, evidently "dreaded" one Yankees. He had a pit in the "cow swamp", he use as a hiding place—should the Yankees come. And when they did finally arrive, Mr. Simon "too to his pit"" After a few days of hiding, however, he came out and acted as host for the Union soldiers.

And it was these soldiers that told the negroes that they were free. But, even so, the majority of them elected to remain with Mr. Simon"

Former Slave Peter Wells

Bible Verse(s):

2 He only is my rock and my salvation, he is my defense; I shall not be greatly moved.

Psalm 62:2

Chapter 31

Diabetic Cooking

For Geechee diabetics, as well as all diabetics, twenty major points should be followed:

1. Follow doctors' orders for foods to eat.
2. Buy and use measuring cups and spoons. These are cheap.
3. Follow menus and diets.
4. Do not drink sweet tea or other sugary drinks.
5. Do not use sugar in seasoning greens, peas, vegetables or meats.
6. Drink plenty of water- 8 -8 ounce glasses per day.
7. Eat a serving not helping. Control want for excess food.
8. Cooking methods are important – roast, grill, raw, steam or boil foods
9. Read the labels.
10. Learn about breads and other starches.
11. Use measuring cups and spoons in cooking vegetables and side dishes.
12. Cut out eating too many sweet potatoes.
13. Season collard greens with onions and red pepper flakes.
14. Do not add any fat or pork products to collard greens cooking.
15. Use cured turkey wings or chicken breasts if you need meat to season.
16. Use garlic in place of salt.
17. Do not eat the whole pound cake.
18. Try not to drink alcohol and wines –homemade or store bought.
19. Do not eat and drink together. Take small bites and Sip!
20. Eat at the table.

TALKING POINTS:

Georgia's Barrier Sea Island

Cumberland Island – is located in Camden County.

Cumberland Island - Cumberland Island National Seashore access by the way of a passenger ferry, the Cumberland Queen, from downtown St. Mary's waterfront. Cumberland Island has wild horses and many other types of wild life. The beach can be used for shell collecting and viewing the pristine waters. Ruins from old homes can been seen. Also, there is a plum orchard on the island.

The National Seashore Museum houses artifacts from Native Americans, African –Americans and the Carnegie Family. Is located on 129 Osborne St.

Cumberland Island has the ruins of McIntosh Sugar Mill Tabby which was built in the late 1820s for making sugar.

Cumberland Island is Georgia's largest barrier island accessible by ferry from St. Marys.

Waycross –A city "Where All The Ways Cross" . The city is located near the Great Okefenokee Swamp -"Land of the Trembling Earth".

Possible Africa Connection:

Botswana –The country is located in southern Africa. The tribal groups are Tswana Kalanga, Basarwa, and many others. The foods introduced to America included chicken beef, lamb, goat, muslim sausages locusts, termites and corn.

Former Georgia Slaves' Sayings:

PLANTATION LIFE:

1. Father's Family

"Mary related her father's long-continued efforts to have his owner buy her mother and the children.

"One day, Mr. Tom Perry(or Perrin) sont his son-in-law to buy us in. You had to get up on what they called a block, but we just stood on some steps. The bidder stood on the ground and called out prices. There was always a speculator at a sale. We was brought all right, and moved over to the Perry place. The man who 'tried' the sale was Mr. Link. Mommer had ten children. We went to church then at Cedar Springs, and they had a balcony for cullud folks. I had another young marster there, he had his own hands, and didn't sell them at all. Wouldn't none of us been sold from the Roof place, except for my father begging Mr. Perry to buy us, so we wouldn't be separated."

"Mary said Mr. Perry gave his slaves patches to earn money, "so they'd have something for themselves."

"I went to the patch many nights with my father. I'd hold the kindling light while he worked the patch. He'd know I was sleepy when the light began to fall down. He'd holler at me: "If you don't wake up, I'll knock you in the head…"

Former Slave Aunt Cicely Cawthon page 200

Bible Verse(s)

1   For the eyes of the Lord are over the righteous, and his ears are open unto their prayers: but the face of the Lord is against them that do evil.

1 Peter3:11

Chapters 32

Food Safety and Food Borne Illnesses

Food Safety should be practiced in the handling of foods, especially fish, poultry and dairy products.

Common Germs Spreading Game Players

Scratching, Sneezing, Storing, Tasting, Touching, Wiping Surfaces improperly.

1. Scratching – Do not scratch your head, sores or other body parts without washing hands and cleaning finger nails.
2. Sneezing –Do not sneeze directly into food, dishwater, the range or near raw food
3. Storing –Germs may spread when storing food in unclean refrigerators, storage containers, storing food in a warm oven, and storing unclean vegetables and fruits in the refrigerator.
4. Tasting – Germs may spread if you taste with spoons or forks used to stir he big pot of food. Tasting with finger or tasting with a spatula used in the food preparation.
5. Touching unclean surfaces, parts of the body, cleaning children or children bodies.
6. Wiping surfaces-Germs may spread when wiping surfaces such as table tops, chairs and ranges with unclean cloths or wiping areas with aprons or wiping dishes with wet soiled cloths.

TALKING POINTS:

Georgia's Barrier Sea Island

Little Cumberland Island - The Island is located in Camden County.

Former Georgia Slaves' Sayings:

FOLK MEDICINES AND SUPERSTITION

"Belief in charms and conjurs is still prevalent among many of Augusta's older Negroes. Signs and omens play an important part in their lives, as do remedies and curses handed down by word of mouth from generation to generation.

If a wrestler can get dirt from the head of a fresh grave, sew it up in a sack, and tie it around his waist, no one can throw him.

To make a person leave town, get some dirt of one of his tracks, sew it up in a sack, and throw it in running water. The person will keep going as long as the water runs.

To take a hair out of a person's head and put it in to live fishes mouth will make the person keep traveling as long as the fish swims.

If someone dies and comes back to worry you, nail some new lumber into your house and you won't be bothered any more.

When the hands of a dead person remain limp some other member of the family will soon follow him to death.

When a spider builds a web in your house, you may expect a visitor the same color as the spider.

A singing fire is a sign of snow.

If a cat takes up at your house it's a sign of good luck; a dog-bad luck.

If a spark of fire pops on you, it is a sign that you will receive some money or a letter.

To dream of muddy water, maggots, or fresh meat is a sign of death. To dream of caskets is also a sign of death.

To dream of blood is a sign of trouble.

To dream of fish is a sign of motherhood.

To dream of eggs is a sign of trouble unless the eggs are broken. If the eggs are broken your trouble is ended.

To dream of snakes is a sign of enemies. If you kill the snake, you have conquered you enemies.

To dream of fire is a sign of danger.

To dream of a funeral is a sign of a wedding.

To dream of a wedding is a sign of a funeral.

To dream of silver money is a sign of bad luck; bills-good luck.

To dream of dead folks is a sign of rain.

Wear a raw cotton string tied in nine knots around your waist to cure cramps.

To stop nosebleed or hiccoughs cross two straws on top of your head.

Lick the back of your hand and swallow nine times without stopping to cure hiccoughs.

Tea made from rue is good for stomach worms.

Corn shuck tea is good for measles; fodder tea for asthma.

Goldenrod tea is good for chills and fever.

Richet weed tea is good for a laxative.

Tea made from parched egg shells or green coffee is good for leucorrhoea.

Black snuff alum, a piece of camphor, and red Vaseline mixed together is a sure cure for piles.

To rid yourself of a corn, grease it with a mixture of castor oil and kerosene and then soak the foot in warm water.

Sulfur mixed with lard is good for bad blood.

A cloth heated in melted tallow will give relief when applied to a pin in any part of the body.

Take a pinch of sulfur in the mouth and drink water behind it to cleanse the blood.

Dog fern is good for colds and fever; boneset tea will serve the same purpose.

Catnip tea is good for measles or hives.

If your right shoe comes unlaced, someone is saying good things about you; left shoe-bad things.

If a chunk of fire falls from the fireplace a visitor is coming. If the chunk is short and large the person will be short and fat, etc.

Don't buy new things for a sick person if you do he will not live to wear it out.

If a person who has money dies without telling where it is, a friend or relative can find it by going to his grave three nights in succession and throwing stones on it. On the fourth night he must go alone, and the person will tell him where the money is hidden.

If a witch rides you, put a sifter under the bed and he will have to count the holes in the sifter before he goes out, thus giving you time to catch him.

Starch your sweetheart's handkerchief and he will love you more.

Don't give your sweetheart a knife it will cut your love in two.

If it rains while the sun is shining the devil is beating his wife.

To bite your tongue while talking is a sign that you have told a lie.

Persons with gaps between their front teeth are big liars.

Cut your finger nails on Monday, you cut them for news;

Cut them on Tuesday, get a new pair of shoes

Cut them on Wednesday, you cut them for wealth,

Cut them on Thursday, you cut them for health;

Cut them on Friday, you cut them for sorrow;

Cut them on Saturday, see your sweetheart tomorrow;

Cut them on Sunday its safety to seek;

But the devil will have you the rest of the week.

If you start some place and forget something don't turn around without making a cross mark and spitting in it, if you do you will have bad luck.

To stump your right foot is good luck, but to stump your left foot is bad luck. To prevent the bad luck you must turn around three times.

It is bad luck for a black cat to cross you to the left, but good luck if he crosses you to the right.

If a picture of a person falls off the wall it is a sign of death.

To dream of crying is a sign of trouble.

To dream of dancing is a sign of happiness.

If you meet gray horse pulling a load of hay, a red haired person will soon follow.

If you are eating and drop something when you are about to put it in your mouth someone wishes it.

If a child never sees his father he will make a good doctor.

To dream that your teeth falls out is a sign of death in the family.

To dream of a man's death is the sign of some woman's death.

If a chicken sings early in the morning a hawk will catch him before night.

Always plant corn on the waste of the moon in order for it to yield good crop. If planted on the growing of the moon there will be more stalk than corn.

When there is a new moon, hold up anything you want and make a wish for it and you will get it.

If you hear voice call you and you are no sure it is really someone, don't answer because it may be your spirit,

And if you answer it will be a sure sign of death.

Cross eyed women are bad luck to other women, but cross eyed men are good luck to women and vice-versa for men.

To wear a dime around your ankle will ward off witch craft.

To put a silver dime in your mouth will determine whether or not you have been bewitched. If the dime turns black, someone have bewitched you, but if it keeps its color no one has bewitched you.

To take a strand of a person's hair and nail it in a tree will run that person away.

If a rooster crows on your back steps you may look for a stranger.

Chinaberries are good for wormy children.

The top of a pine tree and the top of a cedar tree placed over a large coal of fire, just enough to make a good smoke, will cure chillblain feet.

Former Georgia Slaves

Possible Africa Connection

Kenya –Kenya is an East African country. Tribal groups include Kikuyu, Luhya, Luo, Kalenjin, Kumba and many more. Foods introduced to America include leafy vegetables, potatoes and lentils.

Bible Verse(s):

8I am Alpha and Omega, the beginning and the ending, saith the Lord, which is, and which was, and which is to come, the Almighty.

REVELATION 1:8

REFERENCES

Clements, John. Georgia Facts: A Comprehensive Look At Georgia Today County by County. Flying the colors Clements Research. Dallas, Texas, 1989.

Georgia on My Mind Georgia Travel Publications, Inc. Georgia Department of Industry Trade and Tourism and the Georgia Hospitality and Travel Associates. Atlanta, GA. 1992.

Ploski, Harry and William, James. The Negro Almanac Reference Gale Research, Inc. Detroit. 1989.

McCray, W.A. The Black Presence in the Bible Seminar Manual Black Light Fellowship Press, Chicago. 1989.

Holy Bible, King James Version, Holman Publishers, Nashville, Tennessee 1985.

Parrish, Lydia: "Slave Songs of the Georgia Sea Islands" Folklore Associates, Inc. Hatboro, Pennsylvania, 1966

Brittin, H. The Food and Culture Around the World Handbook, Prentice Hall 2011.

http: Countries of the World.

Georgia Slave Narratives 1936-1938 – Works Progress Administration-United States Printing Company 1938.

Printed in the United States
By Bookmasters